On the Wind and a Prayer

On the Wind and a Prayer

How a fair-weather daysailing couple from the Northeast managed to find their way to the Bahamas and back

Paul Koestner

Copyright © 2008 by Paul Koestner.
Cover design by Audrey Francis Nuhn.

Library of Congress Control Number: 2007910034
ISBN: Hardcover   978-1-4363-1077-2
               Softcover   978-1-4363-1076-5

All rights reserved. No part of this book may be reproduced or transmitted in any form or by any means, electronic or mechanical, including photocopying, recording, or by any information storage and retrieval system, without permission in writing from the copyright owner.

This book is not intended for Navigational purposes. The prudent mariner will ignore any and all advisories contained herein. Reader's discretion is required. Contents may settle during shipment. Suspend disbelief at your own risk. Any port in a storm. A stitch in time saves nine. Any sins of omission or commission perpetrated by the author should be considered a darn shame. The author had no intention of slighting or otherwise insulting any government, private institution, or individual. Well, maybe now and then, in which case, the devil made him do it. So sue me.

This book was printed in the United States of America.

To order additional copies of this book, contact:
Xlibris Corporation
1-888-795-4274
www.Xlibris.com
Orders@Xlibris.com
42934

Contents

Introduction 15
Wherein I shamelessly pitch the book with the tenacity of a coked-up televangelist. Or am I being redundant?

Prologue 19
Where I make you responsible for the success of our voyage. See, we hadn't even begun the trip when initial writing began. Were I so inclined, I would have bet good money back then against our ever leaving the dock.

SECTION I: THE PLAN

Chapter 1: Water Child 23
My early years, from bathing in the kitchen sink to fishing with worms.

Chapter 2: Water Boy 30
The acquisition of my first real girlfriend, and boat.

Chapter 3: Student of the Sea 36
A college semester on the Irish Coast, where I acquire the two critical sailorly skills of drinking and daydreaming.

Chapter 4: Enter the Siren 40
Meeting my wife-to-be, and sealing the deal.

Chapter 5: Enter the Demons 43
Acquiring the boat, the itch, and a more-than-healthy dose of incipient fear.

SECTION II: THE TRIP

Chapter 6: The Prep 53
The planning stages leading up to the trip.

Chapter 7: The Leap of Faith 64
Leaving hearth and home, transiting New Jersey, and poised at the headwaters of the Chesapeake.

Chapter 8: The Chesapeake 78
Our Chesapeake, at any rate.

Chapter 9: The Ditch 89
Norfolk, Virginia, to Stuart, Florida.

Chapter 10: The Holidays 125
The joys of landlubbing with family in Florida during that special time of year.

Chapter 11: The Stream 136
Crossing over from Florida to the islands of the Abacos.

Chapter 12: Mecca 146
Our extended visit to Hope Town, Elbow Cay.

Chapter 13: The Road to Return 160
Back home via the wrong way, i.e. south to Eleuthera, then to Nassau, and finally Bimini.

Chapter 14: Lubbers Redux 173
Another stay with Deb's family's southern contingent.

Chapter 15: Enter the Dragons 177
Heading north; on nature's diverse plagues, and the monotony that is Georgia's stretch of the Intracoastal Waterway. Oh am I gonna catch it from the Peach State.

Chapter 16: Onward and Upward 182
The return of scenery, the honing of acquired skills, and time on one's hands to think about stupid stuff.

Chapter 17: The Final Push 196
Smelling home, and having to sail the wrong way again to get there.

Epilogue: The Journey is the Thing 203
Thoughts on it being over, with not a dry eye in the house.

SECTION III: APPENDICES

Appendix I: Our Ports of Call (places we stopped) 211

Appendix II: Boat Cards (business cards for boaters) 215

Appendix III: Books We Read to Prepare (but didn't take with us) 219

Appendix IV: Onboard Reference Materials (books we did take) 220

Appendix V: On the Web 222

Postscript: The Leak, Explained 223

Chapter the Last: Paradise Regained 227

For Deb, whom I will follow to the ends of the earth.

In loving memory . . .

Of my parents, who, in a shared act of supreme sacrifice, allowed their children to chase their own muses, however suspect may have been our methods and motives.

Acknowledgments

Sooner or later an author must confess to the fact that he would be nothing without the inspiration, encouragement, and self-invited editorial intrusion of his personal guardian angels. Here then is my opportunity to pay homage to the following key individuals:

Captain Bob, who taught me that life is a far grander experience than the mere assembled components of a human existence.

Captain Lew, who I trust will continue to bitch-slap Captain Bob's message into my meager consciousness as long as he has breath in him.

Captain Art Ross. Folks, if by the end of this book you don't get it about Captain Art, then die an untimely, painful, senseless death.

Captain Flex Clare, a man of top quality, who provided us with knowledge, charts, entertainment, and a contractor's discount at West Marine.

George Martin, manager at Manhasset Bay Marina, a man of sprightly spirit and infinite patience, for everything he tried to teach us before we left. We're sorry, George. But we made it anyway!

David James, of The Rigging Locker, for making sure our *Laura Lynn* stood up faithfully to the formidable forces of our ignorance.

Bret Connors, prized friend of the family, for discovering the Abacos and sharing the secret with us.

David Morehead, harbormaster of St. Augustine, for reasons that will become apparent as you read on.

Doug Underdahl, always an inspiration, for his role in financing the trip by off-loading my gear on eBay.

My friend Carl, who introduced me to *his* friend Ben, who showed me how to get this book to you without the intercession of a "real" publisher. Rest in peace, Ben.

A tip of our Nor'easters to those author-adventurers who blazed the trail ahead of us and made the path an easier one by their inspiration.

To the many generous boating souls mentioned herein who selflessly offered their knowledge, time, and spare widgets, so that we might live and prosper aboard our humble ship, fair winds, all.

And to those countless friends we made along the way, though you may have gone unmentioned here, know that the memories we shared with you will be forever scrimshawed into our hearts.

And in celebration of . . .

My big sister Mimi, the lifeguard of my early chapters.

My younger brother John, who, having outgrown me in many ways, has become a treasured friend.

My little sister Cathy, whose heart could contain the seven seas.

Our sister Laura, whose inspiration far surpasses the mere donation of a name to a transom.

Deb, with the original Laura Lynn

Introduction

Wherein I entice the reader into an arrangement beneficial to all

I tell you what, I'm going to save you some time right here at the top and assure you you're going to buy this book. You don't need it, but you're going to get it. Just drop it in the basket and get on to the serious business of selecting a book that'll teach you something *useful,* like how to jury-rig a rudder out of some live bait and your wife's thong.

Me, I can barely tie a reef knot. Okay, I can do a reef knot (a disreputable knot designed to kill you, by the way), but probably not a rolling hitch. Not on the first try anyway, and certainly not if my life *depended* on it. I couldn't do anything if my life depended on it. I'm quite sure of that. I freeze up, very much the way my home harbor is right now, when the shit hits the prop. And, my friend, shit and worse does indeed hit the prop on a regular basis.

On land, where I'm safe and sound as long as the Ides of April are not upon us, I once stood helplessly by as my toilet overflowed on to my shoes. I remember hearing myself chant out loud to no one present (there is no audience in that last bastion of solitude) "I don't know what to do. I don't know what to do." The flooding after a time stopped on its own. Only then did I know what it was I had to do, and I commenced doing it.

I've since determined that boats do not work on the same principle, which is to say wait for the crisis to abate, and clean up the mess afterwards. The mess on a boat just keeps growing until you're nothing but a hushed story reported at the local watering hole that ends with a round of inhaled whistles.

Up until now my life in its questionable entirety has depended upon nothing other than the obligation to look both ways before I cross the street. Nearing my first half century on the planet, most of that now on concrete, I feel the potent temptation to do *something on which my life truly depends*. And for good measure, I'm dragging my wife into it with me. That ought to ratchet up the fear factor, because you know payback can be a bitch. Women talk about what we've done to them.

My proudest maritime claim to date has been that I haven't fallen off my own boat, yet. I did once take a healthy stab at sinking my father-in-law's boat, on a lovely day, on our own "home waters." Isn't that a comfy-cozy term, "home waters"? Doesn't it conjure up thoughts of no problems whatsoever?

Let me explain something. "Local knowledge" means that in a place where you should know better, you've run into just about every obstruction there is to run into, so you sort of know where they all are now, more or less.

My wife's first instinct upon hearing that her father's boat was most probably taking on water (I wasn't really sure; how much water *should* be down there?), and figuring we might have to swim home, was to pack her shoes (*Canola Poblanos*, I think she said) into a cooler, figuring they'd float safely to shore, if we didn't. How's that for a crack crew?

Oh yeah, you want this book. How do I know? Because I know you. You can't get enough moral support. You're amazed at how that leaking sieve bobbing at its mooring, languishing on its cradle, or peering from its ad at the local bait shop (just kidding; you'll never spot a sailboat ad at a bait shop) could have gotten so under your skin. The sounds of halyards flogging masts are wind chimes to you. You have countless questions about what to do with these feelings, and in lieu of the proper answers you'll settle for the questionable company of misery. Well, my friend, I am the father of misery.

Here's your personal profile. You have bodysurfed at the beach of your youth. You found it most probably what sex would be like if you ever had the opportunity to have sex. When you die, you would like your designated Supreme Being to show you what your favorite body of water looks like completely drained, just for a minute.

You'll stop at a garage sale in the middle of Nebraska (what were you doing in Nebraska?) on the off chance there might be some widget with a vaguely nautical purpose. And you'd put off the next significant phase of your life until you've accumulated all the possible pertinent data available to modern man on the pursuit of personal happiness afloat. Not before. Gotta be prepared. Don't want to be surprised.

Or possibly you're one of those handful of sailors who actually *know* what they're doing on a boat, and you're looking for some suitable diversion while the forty-seventh coat of spar varnish dries on your new hand-hewn mizzenmast. The trunk was harvested from the homegrown teak forest out back of the boat shed that used to house your wife's car till the Taurus *had to make way.* You say teak isn't the appropriate material for masts? Thanks for sharing, Ahab. Time for another coat.

Anyway I couldn't care less if *you* buy the book. There are what, maybe twelve of you out there who actually know what you're doing on a sailboat? You were given birth to in the cockpit, shinnied up masts before you could crawl, would rather polish brass than your pecker, and have prepared ever so hopefully for self-amputation at sea. You prefer the company of barnacles to mankind, and you write all the really useful books on sailing. Who the hell needs you anyway? Don't you have a planet you need to go circumscribe?

This book is for the rest of us, and we are legion.

Prologue

Wherein "The Plan" is alluded to

"*Well, you don't know what we can find
Why not come with me little girl on a magic carpet ride*"
"*Magic Carpet Ride*"—lyrics by John Kay and Rushton Moreve

This is about a journey. In some ways the journey began the day I was born, and in some ways it's one I have yet to begin. Now you just want to slap me silly, don't you? Yet it is that way with all great literary works; the *Big Picture* set elegantly off by some metaphorical gem. Like an oyster's festering pearl. Yeah, like that.

What's it got to do with you and me? My plan, see, is you're going to be the one to see to it that Deb and I accomplish our journey so that you may profit from insights gained during the odyssey. I'm like the manta ray, and you're the remora. You ever see

19

one of those pictures of that unearthly creature effortlessly towing one or more slimy sucking things gripping its belly? It's a symbiotic thing, where everybody wins.

I spent the first half of my life as a child and student in the Midwest, the second half as an adult (more or less) and professional in New York City. It's now time to rework the math, think in terms of thirds, and decide how to flesh out my final chapter, because a perusal of my family's medical history suggests chapter four isn't going to happen. In fact if you're thinking this is my midlife crisis, I missed that ride a decade ago. This is the pre-mortem, maties.

Chapter Three, if you have any say in the matter, begins at sea. The phrase "at sea" is here employed as a literary convention. Mostly I expect Deb and I will be at anchor. We are hoping we'll find ourselves more commonly "at peace" than I have felt in some time. Hopefully we'll avoid the often-documented situation of being "at odds" with each other and our situation, which can happen when humans contain themselves in a space even smaller than the apartment I inhabited for *fifteen frigging years in the "greatest city in the world" oh pleeeeze!*

See, this is what happens when you accept the comfortably mundane over the wildly unpractical. You vacillate, procrastinate, stagnate, petrify, and then snap like a rotten spar. That's called "punctuated equilibrium," a glorious term coined by one of my gods. How far more illustrative than the pedestrian sobriquet "going postal." Basically things have been simmering, shifting, but essentially adhering to the status quo for too long. Something's got to give, and soon.

That's what I'm trying to convince myself of, that's where I need some help, and that's where you come in. Deb can only do so much. Overcoming inertia requires stamina, fortitude, and the resolve of many, many witnesses.

It's like marriage. Tell enough people you're going to do the thing and it's impossible to overcome the surge, the collective force of will, as you sense yourself very possibly chickening out. Listen, lover boy, home equity loans have been taken out for painful shoes and dresses of questionable taste that will be worn but once. Human identities are being risked online for something as petty as a lemon zester. You have a better chance of stopping an avalanche with a soupspoon.

Deb and I are heading to the Bahamas. That's what I said. I have a fair idea of where they are, and we're leaving jobs, home, family and friends, and setting off on the next phase of our lives. And you're going to make sure I don't chicken out. Here we go then. Strap on your harness. This is going to be a wet ride.

Section 1
Wherein the plan is, after a fashion, hatched

What in the world is she thinking?

Chapter 1

Water Child

The author with his mother, sister, fish, and somebody else's pole

   From whence springs this passion in man to take to sea? In which liquid-bathed recess of the brain is harbored that atavistic desire to cast off one's earthly tethers and test one's aquatic mettle?
   More to the point, what in the world prompted Deb and me to decide to trade in the estimable comforts of modern life for the accommodations of a boat old enough

23

to have delivered Noah from the floodwaters? It goes way back, I suppose. I can't say as I remember the moment, but I have proof of the moment's existence.

I see myself in comfortable surroundings, in the company of those I've learned to trust. I have become self-aware. While I'm now familiar to the point of having become blasé about such things as the satisfaction derived from the ingestion of a heaping spoonful of carrot puree, or the inevitable expulsion of the reprocessed portion thereof, here is something new and remarkable. It is a radical form of nature, an altered state of reality, an optical illusion. It's tubby-time in the kitchen sink.

My lower appendages are immersed. They are all there, I know, for I can feel them. Yes, there they are. Yes indeed. But they are veiled in this comfy ether. I can move it. The ether resists, yields, reconstitutes. Miraculous! It is invisible, yet I can see it.

I must be a wizard! My earthly mother is there, a celluloid handmaiden. She smiles deferentially, as she understands the power I wield. I splash playfully to remind her of that power, and how a more capricious wizard might be someone to fear. She acknowledges my beneficence with averted gaze.

What would happen if a wizard descended into this magical realm, if for a moment he were to . . . *Can't breathe! Can't breathe! Heaving coughing stinging eyes burning* **TERROR!**

Ah, but hovering on the surface, that is magic.

There isn't much wiggle room required for a man to locate his pleasure center, and I don't begrudge any man his own passion, though for the life of me I don't know how golfers do it. Ice fishing I guess I sort of get, especially if there's friction at home. A boat though, you don't need to explain a thing. It's just obvious, like a *Victoria's Secret* catalog.

My first one was a beauty. She was sleek, powerful, and intimidating, with twin torpedoes molded onto her deck. She had a modest LOA (length overall, Aunt Emilie) of about a foot and a half, which was plenty for me at the time. You have no doubt heard of her: PT-109.

Waddling in the lake till my feet and hands were pink prunes, I piloted my patrol boat in circles about me, providing the requisite noises for propulsion, barking orders at my crew, attacking invented enemies (not unlike the present Commander-in-Chief), dying and resurrecting myself on a loose schedule. I can still simulate an impressive-looking depth charge.

I was fascinated then, as I still am, at the wake a boat, or duck, for that matter, makes as it scoops through water. That shape is unmistakable through its many iterations: deep, delicate, idling, whizzing by. Its beauty defies scientific description, though I now know which user group to e-mail if I desire one.

Science class for a boy has already begun before he's bussed off to a formal education. Basic anatomy is held in the middle of the road upon which a squirrel has zigged when he should have zagged. Thermochemistry is conducted using whatever solvents are on hand in the garage while dad is at work. I studied the laws of hydrodynamics in the pools, ponds, and lakes that perforate my home state of Michigan. *Water Winter Wonderland* used to adorn license plates of Michiganders, until someone must have pointed out we all leave in winter for more suitable playgrounds. The motto has since been amended to the more realistic *Great Lakes State*. It fits better than *We'll see you back here when the ice packs recede.*

The first boat I remember being able to commandeer from the inside was an aluminum skiff, a common sight on inland lakes, easily rowed, but more often powered by a small outboard. Each usually contains a solitary angler, or a pair, hunched over expectant poles, seeking a free meal or just quiet time, wives willing. Now and then one might be captained by a brace of undersized types in bright orange flack jackets, out to see what the old Evinrude can do.

It amazes me now to think how my parents would let my brother John and me take such an eminently sinkable object powered by a flick of the wrist across an expanse of water, given our propensity for ignoring the forces of nature. Their privately acknowledged oversight doubtlessly played a role in the early demise of the both of them.

I remember the initial wave of expectation as John and I prepared the engine for the series of tugs that would hopefully bring the engine to life. I remember squeezing fuel bulbs, fidgeting with chokes, pumping throttle handles, opening cowlings for a look around, praying to, jeez, who's the patron saint of two-cycle engines?

Then the yanking and yanking until I wept in frustration. I had no clue what I was doing with those controls. I was merely following male tradition. My brother, on the other hand, though infinitely younger (almost two years), would one day grow up to be an engineer. When he twiddled with something even back then, he knew what he was doing and why.

I remember the spitting, smoking, first gasps of combustion, and the sweet aroma of that blended elixir when the engine finally caught. I remember the lift of the bow in response to the effortless wrist rotation, and the rising pitch of the engine, a sound that announced we were young and free and flying like the wind. I remember John and me as rare friends at times like those. I remember, as if it were yesterday. There are occasions now when I wish it were.

The way I see it, this regimenting of sailors, power boaters, fishermen and so on into hostile camps, well I know how we tend to stare at each other in suspicion and disdain from time to time. But when I'm feeling generous with the world, I like to think of us all as splashers. I've had fun running the length of a dock to the challenge of landing on an inner tube, a patch-job from my uncle's trucking business. I've scared myself silly chartering in the Caribbean. I've sat bug-tooth happy on the doghouse of a classic Chris Craft racing to no place in particular. There is no more luscious a sound than that engine right before it blows an oil line.

I've water-skied countless circles around glass-smooth lakes and can now predict the coming rain with my knee. I've shoved a canoe over the skin of an iced-in lake, and I'll be sure never to visit Canada that early in spring again. I've white-water rafted the Hudson, too early in the season, once again. They just don't make neoprene thick enough for that time of year. But it's all good. I'm with Rodney King. Couldn't we all just get along?

Fishing though. Is there anything more thrilling than sitting on a dock, staring down over the surface of a still lake, marveling at how cool your new high-top *Red Ball Jets* are, when out of the corner of your eye you notice your bobber twitch? Then you definitely see it twitch. Then it does nothing for a little while, and you wait now like you'll wait years from now for sex.

Then it twitches hard. And then it heads for the bottom like that drum did in *Jaws*. Adrenaline floods the body like horny housewives at a Target half-off sale. You jerk your cane pole, or maybe its some fancy glass/fiber combo rig, or these days I don't know, some syntho-tech-mylar-spiderdick hybrid, who cares, peace out, and you launch a muffin-sized bluegill over your head, screaming like you just conquered a continent.

Actually, about the rod, I did care. In a photo album somewhere, there is a picture of me sitting on a cottage kitchen counter with some fiber-thing. Mom is next to me holding up a Bigmouth Bass the size of a Shetland pony (this *is* a fish story after all). She is smiling at me, and I'm just staring back kind of wistfully. *Wistfully.* I know exactly what I am thinking while Dad is taking the picture. I am thinking, *This isn't my pole. I didn't catch my fish with this thing. Where is my pole?*

Dad has written in black wax marker, his favorite medium for photo details, **Paul's first fish.** For the record, it was *not* my first fish. I'd been fishing for, I don't know, at least a couple weeks. It was my biggest fish to date, and would be for years to come (it was one nice bass, buddy boy), but I had caught many fish prior to this one. None of them, mind you, with the pole that had been placed in my hand for dramatic effect.

I loved my father dearly. He taught me so much, and the memory of the time we shared soothes and guides me today, so I forgive him for this minor inaccuracy. But not for his switching out the poles for a bogus photo op.

As fascinating as fishing is, it doesn't hold a candle to the act of collecting the bait to go fishing. Not the way we did it anyway. Night crawlers, for those of you so unfortunate as never to have baited a hook, are worms on steroids. I have read that they, along with their lesser brethren, are pretty much responsible for all life on earth.

In their constant, tireless foraging for worm treats, worms reconstitute and enrich the planet's surface soil so efficiently as to make it possible for all plant life to live and thrive, or something to that effect. Darwin himself wrote an entire scientific treatise on worms, if I'm not mistaken. If I am, then write in and tell me otherwise, Captain Dweeb. Now you know where we'd be without worms, and I say bravo, squirmy dudes, but a man's got to fish, so he needs bait.

To get at some night crawlers, you start by giving your mom's flower garden a good soaking. If your mom doesn't have a flower garden, you're just screwed, what can I tell you?

Next, you *wait until dark*. Now if that doesn't light up a child's imagination, we might as well just cancel Halloween and go to bed early. But it gets even better. After night falls, you head with great stealth out to that well-doused garden, carrying a flashlight and an empty coffee tin. It has to be a coffee tin, or you're cheating, and God will punish you in ways he hasn't even invented yet.

You must tread lightly, because the night crawler has an acute sense of something or other, and will rifle back into his hole in half a heartbeat if he thinks he's being stalked. He's a cagey creature, the night crawler. He didn't make it this far up evolution's ladder by being a slacker.

Scanning that same rich loam the worm has provided for your mother's roses, you shine your light across its surface, searching for the distinct shimmer that distinguishes this vital, glistening organism from, say, a wet twig, or a rampant imagination. What's he doing out there on the surface late at night? A worm's life is full of mystery, but I'll say this much, he has his reasons for being there. A worm's got to do what a worm's got to do. And what goes bump in the night can occasionally reward the avid crawler hunter with that coveted trophy, the "double." Now back to the hunt.

You've spotted your shimmering quarry. Slowly, painstakingly, you crouch to within striking distance. Now is not the time for flinching, stumbling, or second-guessing one's right to play God in the scheme of a worm's things.

What takes place next requires robinlike reflexes, and nerves rarely commanded by the squeamish. A pause to center one's self, and a lightning-thrust. There, pinned in your grasp if you've been swift and precise, is a thrashing night crawler.

But the battle is not over, for your semiviscous adversary has never completely left his lair. You must now exercise super-human restraint, waiting out the series of contractions the worm uses to confound, intimidate, and skeeve out his assailant. This is no pansy-ass hognose snake rolling over and playing dead. This worm has backup mojo in the rumpus room. Furthermore, pull too hard, and you end up with half a crawler, and no one wants to see that happen. Not right away anyhow.

It's easy then to see why fishing might be considered an anticlimactic affair. I prefer to see it as the denouement, and I'll feel more strongly about that assertion as soon as I look the word up.

One weekend, my brother and I got ourselves into a "mess" of perch, which is a good thing if you're fishing for them. We were hauling them in as if we knew what to do with them.

We'd been taught that a reliable way to keep fish alive and fresh was to use a stringer. Threaded through the gills, the fish stay in the lake, which is like their TV room, until you call it a day. It's better than keeping forty fish swimming in the sun in a mop bucket tainted with Mr. Clean, I guarantee you. We already tried that once or twice.

The problem is, we must have figured the fish would just swim along behind us as we motored back to the cottage, or more likely we didn't think anything at all, until we went to show off our catch back at the dock. Denouement indeed. With the approach of my fiftieth birthday, I still have nightmares.

One doesn't always get what one is after when fishing. It's hard to forget the image of a baited hook embedded in my brother's face, on an otherwise pleasant lake day.

John had gotten too close to my cousin's back cast on the dock and ended up wearing a writhing red worm on his chin. Luckily the angler responded to my brother's cry of alarm, or you can just imagine, as Mom would say. Fortuitously we weren't using night crawlers for bait, or this one surely would have beaten the shit out of John in a justifiable rage.

Dad, a GP during that period of our country's medical history when things were taken care of rather than tested for, handled it as he handled the countless crises inspiring all families with children. Pandora, the physician's equivalent of a tackle box, made another appearance, and John was back at being a nuisance before lunch. Try removing a fishhook today without the activation of several specialists, the wasting of a geological epoch, the rape of a rainforest for the forms, and the filing of an environmental impact statement for the DNR. Plus we would have had to serve my cousin with a wrongful fishing suit. How times have changed.

The author getting along with his brother. Your eyes were no doubt drawn to that honey between us. That's my older cousin's Chris-Craft. Sweet!

Chapter 2

Water Boy

When in doubt, take the plunge.

The first real girlfriend I ever had—if you don't count Pat Hennessy, who in first grade would kick me in the shins if I wasn't vigilant—was another Irish girl, also named Pat. I met her my freshman year of high school, having apparently stolen her from my cousin Pete, since he told me so in the parking lot around the time of our first football homecoming. Pete is a good guy and we were buddies, so I wasn't afraid when he accosted me. "You stole my girl!" he told me with a raised voice and a pained half-smile. I knew he was hurting, and I knew he was right, kind of. But I also know you can't steal a woman who doesn't want to be stolen, and my heart was full of larceny. Anyway, Pete seemed to find the heart to forgive me, since he's got, I don't know, fourteen kids or something now. Okay, four.

Pat and I had a good long haul, and while there are plenty of things I regret, particularly those shortcomings in my nature Pat was forced to endure (and won't women endure a ton of it without batting a single lovely eyelash?) I see our time together as one of life's enduring gifts to me. I can only hope she found it something near as positive for her.

Pat's parents had a little cottage on a channel off Gun Lake, a good-sized lake shaped like a pair of lungs joined at the sternum by a shallow aneurysm. It was half an hour's drive north from our hometown, the thriving metropolis of Kalamazoo. Yes, our pathetic motto insists, *There Really Is a Kalamazoo!* We're not just that trombonist's goofy song from the forties. We're a vital community of productive Midwesterners, so go pork yourself. Something to that effect, anyway.

As is so common with ownership and the concomitant responsibilities of adulthood, Pat's parents often found themselves too busy to enjoy their investment. It was then as if we two had our own Shangri-la, complete with a sixteen-foot Starcraft runabout and pontoon boat. Two kids in high school, left alone to a lakeside chalet, in desperate love. Who needs cable?

I'll state right now with no shame, were I to retire to the shore of an inland lake, and given the choice of only one vessel, I believe it might be a pontoon boat.

You think I'm high, don't you, Bubba? Listen, there are plenty of things a pontoon boat isn't, but one thing it is, is a highly motivated tub of fun. If you're not in a hurry, and you really ought not to be unless you're in high school, you'll find fun on a float boat. It loves company. You can sun on it, fish from it, grill on it, dance the *merengue*, catch the annual fireworks, and these day's probably watch a movie on a plasma screen, all comfortably from one of the shaded couches lining the thing. It's a floating aboveground basement. Strap a keg on and load the troops.

On still evenings I remember being enthralled by the work of spiders as they spun dinner plates on the framework that gave us a roof. Let's give it up for spiders, lapping up those mosquitoes. Get over the hairy legs, girls. Spiders are the good guys.

We happened to see a pontoon boat during a recent sail on the Long Island Sound. Most everybody onboard our boat commented on the interesting craft passing by. I was stunned, since one might just as likely have seen someone attempting to float a camel there. Big choppy water is not the preferred medium of the float-boat.

Secretly, I gave it up for the guy at the wheel, who repeatedly avoided capsizing in the wakes of everything out there, carrying on in a body of water he had no business traveling on.

I was as far from retirement back in high school as I suspect I am now. Back then though I had some energy in me, buddy boy, and it needed siphoning.

Try as I might, I couldn't do it with a forty horsepower outboard. So when I saw a **For Sale** sign tacked to a futuristic cherry red tunnel-hull with a skyscraper of a Mercury clamped to its ass, I proceeded to do the most audacious thing I had ever done to date. I asked the father of my girlfriend if I could sell his crappy Starcraft, with the aforementioned anemic engine, and pool the proceeds with money I'd earned on a smoked sausage assembly line at the local meatpacking plant. I further proposed to purchase this sweet boat I'd discovered, and register it in his name. I only wished occasional access to it. He may have figured other proposals would eventually ensue, and so gave his consent.

We sold the old Starcraft at a yard sale, along with stuff like a fondue set and a *Pong* game, all priceless commodities today. I then set up an appointment with the owner of the water rocket, a spooky guy with a disreputable haircut. When I met him I got a little queasy, but he had the key and started the engine up right there on the trailer. It made hideous noises, but I suppose you could say it was turning over, which seemed like a positive attribute. He shut it down and warned that running the engine dry for long wasn't a good idea. I figured he ought to know.

I'm the Indian with a scratchy wool blanket to show for Manhattan of hagglers. Deb will confess to this without shame. I'm her worst deal, which she'll deny, like the disciplined negotiator she is. Please don't buy our boat from me. Buy it from her, if she wants to sell. She does all the dealing in this family.

Anything of value Deb and I own has been due to her wrangling, but our meeting was decades away, and the Mercury on this boat was taller than any building standing in my hometown. I was woozy with desire. I paid the asking price. I needed to find somebody with a trailer hitch.

I waited an entire summer for the parts to repair an engine that had been out of production since the previous world war. They sure didn't make 'em like that anymore. By then, of course, they'd come up with far better ways to make them, as they continue to do, the bastards.

I tried to call the previous owner to, I don't know, complain or something, but his number had become unlisted. Wow, that meant that the phone company knew precisely where he lived, and that probably I was mad because I was one of the many folks he'd screwed in some way, and they still wouldn't confess to his whereabouts. Company policy. That lesson taught me I'd better look out for myself in the future, because we know who big business is looking out for, don't we, Tonto?

When the repair work was nearing completion the following summer, I found I had to buy a new battery to replace the old new battery that had sat unattended for a year and a half. That's a lot of ground meat to smoke.

I hate boatyards. They can smell abject ignorance diluted to one part per trillion. As I waited for the final damage report on my girl's dad's water rocket, I manufactured smoked sausage. Lots of smoked sausage.

As a political aside, whenever you buy anything in the future, anything ever again as long as you live, ponder for a moment that countless souls have been employed in a series of mind-numbing, body-mincing tasks so that this thing you *must have* or you'll pitch a hissy fit can be next-day delivered to you for chump change. Indentured souls have toiled like you never will in your life (aside from the time you tried to convince that cow-eyed freshman to stick around through your finals ordeal at the college your father paid for), at wage levels for which you'd rather duplicate the stunts in *Jackass* than accept. All this so you can imagine one or more of the following: your skin is softer, your butt more pert, your wanker stiffer, your hair thicker, you've never looked younger, the world adores you, and sexuality oozes out of you like butterscotch pudding from a toddler's piehole.

When we finally got the dreamboat in the water, it didn't sink, I'll give it that. Soon thereafter though, I learned the strong suit of the tunnel hull design. It liked going fast in a straight line, which is terrific if you live on a body of water called the Great Big Unwavering Arrow River. On a lake of modest acreage, where frequent course alteration is required to avoid a confrontation with one of the many cottages lining its shore, not so good.

My girlfriend's father's skyscraper Mercury bogged down trying to alter the course of its squat, heavy, water-laden host. There was no trim control, no button to push to alter the engine's angle of attack, thus no "hole shot," a guy term meaning, "Hold on tight, mama, we're leaving in a hurry." All passengers were required to lean out over the windshield on initial acceleration to keep the bow from becoming the stern. With a skier in tow it might take up a good deal of the morning, most of the skier's energy reserve, and half our fuel supply to get to the point where somebody was having fun. In the end, and it came mercifully soon, the cost of fuel to come on plane put our fun out of business. But not before I bungled my knee trying to learn to water-ski.

I started thinking it might be nice to have a boat that would cost little to own and operate, and still qualify as fun from an adventurer's perspective.

On small lakes around the country, there is nothing so ubiquitous as the *Sunfish*. There must be, I reasoned, a good reason for this. Look at these goofballs. On a windy day, they're practically falling out of their boats, they seem to believe they're going fast, they're giggling like schoolgirls, and when they tip over they laugh even harder. That kind of behavior tends to pique one's interest.

But I wasn't quite so naive anymore. I found something even better. A rival manufacturer of AMF had the cojones to copy the *Sunfish* in every detail, substituting inferior hardware wherever possible, and substantially undercutting the competition's purchase price. They even went so far as to duplicate the logo and call it the *Funfish*. What can you say to that but, "Balls out, dudes!"

Which is not what AMF's lawyers had to say. Jesus, do lawyers have *any fun?* Maybe after they've bagged up all our money they've earned by billing for thirty-two hours of work a day, and then bought the islands we wished we could visit.

By the time I bought one of the knockoffs, the chubby bluegill logo had been replaced by the headgear you often see on fulsome operatic divas, and it had been renamed the Viking. Which in a way was even cooler. I'd saved a wad, and was now the proud owner of an outlaw boat. There it was then. My first boat, somehow a sailboat. All I needed to do was learn how to sail.

I had previously sailed once in my life, around the age of eight, on another cousin's boat. As it turns out, "Uncle" Paulie (our age separation made that misnomer a convenient way to address him and a cadre of other elder cousins) was quite the sailor, though you would have been hard-pressed to convince me of that at the time. During a crowded Gull Lake sailboat race (Gull Lake is not to be confused with Gun Lake, being more of a kidney shape in design), my cousin seemed sadly incapable of keeping his boat upright. Further, despite his rapid progress through the water with nothing more than a group of juveniles onboard, he threatened repeatedly to sink other contenders who came near him. Still, he remained calm, and we did whatever he told us to do. We came in maybe seventh out of a one-class fleet of about twenty, despite his inability to set a spinnaker, some piece of gear that never managed to find its way on deck.

Essentially we kids had been live ballast, and of limited value in that capacity. My cousin seemed pleased for us all, though seventh place didn't sound so hot to me. Had he asked us to leave bicycle skid marks on his driveway, I think we could've shown him something to get worked up over.

My brother, quite the racer himself, has crewed with Paulie on more serious occasions. John speaks of races where Paulie's strategies have garnered applause from competing sailors as he's passed them by.

Paul also seems to know when acceptance is the better part of valor. When the wind had chosen to fail all contestants on a particular race, he'd disappeared below, later to appear with a serving tray of hors d'oeuvres, and the query, "Anyone for pimento loaf?" There's a guy who knows how to roll with the punches.

Boy do I wish I'd had more time on the water with my cousin Paulie.

So now I was a sailor, having purchased a sailboat. It came with all the documentation necessary for one to assemble it on a cottage lawn, and then admire one's work on a windless day. It said nothing about what to do if one were audacious enough to put it in the water when there was a breeze about. We did it anyway.

Those may be the days I abused my old girlfriend the most, cursing everything in sight, and many things invisible. I cursed the lack of wind. I cursed the fickleness of the wind, and the distance I had to paddle to get to a place where we could safely make use of what wind there was. I railed on the distance I had to paddle to get home when the wind had failed us, and the ignorance my girlfriend displayed in not understanding why I had to curse so frequently and vehemently. In retrospect, I was displaying those attributes most often associated with accomplished sailors. Had I known it, I should have been pleased as punch.

~~~

Chapter 3

Student of the Sea

Somewhere, Ireland

  The small college I attended in Michigan had a program that sent willing sophomores to study in the Irish coastal village of Tully Cross. Two volunteer professors would escort the students for a semester, often with their own families in tow. It made for an intriguing group dynamic, students and teachers living within a rural community, everyone learning from each other.

  I found myself in an environment where I could finally let my hair down, figuratively and literally, until a side trip to Northern Ireland showed me the curse of the literal. Looking fairly seditious from experimental hair growth, I was moments away from a checkpoint cavity search when I was saved by the highly ameliorative presence of my friend and temporary traveling companion, Mary Mitchell. Slainte, Mary!

The Ireland trip introduced me to the sea. I had till then only briefly flirted with the ocean, on family trips to Florida and California, where our family would unwittingly bake ourselves on some beachhead, poking tentatively at *Man-o-Wars* when they'd invaded the shore and made the ocean unsuitable for swimming. On occasions when it was safe for "bathing," I remember that first startling taste of brine on the lips, which must have come an instant before that shock of the stinging eyes. *Gads, we drove how long for this?*

Seeking succor, we'd retreat to our hotel pool, hopping into that turquoise balm to discover *Criminee, the pool is saltwater too! We're doomed!*

~~~

If you ever find yourself vacationing waist deep off some pearlescent shore, and take your eyes off the ocean for a moment, choosing instead to scrutinize, let's say, current trends in beach attire, your water mistress will respond with a perfectly formed curl, nothing special from her repertoire. Something timed *just so.*

The moment you choose to turn your attentions back to her, your date will slap you silly, the shock knocking the wind out of your sails and sending a hint of eternity down the wrong pipe. There you'll be, bug-eyed and gagging, searching for evidence of the assassin, with nothing to gaze at but a string of colorful umbrellas and a sliver of foam underscoring it all.

I once hosted a visit from my sister Cathy to a Cape Cod retreat my great friend Scott (who will briefly shine in Chapter 4) and I had been regularly renting during early autumns. I thought it would be fun to treat her first hand to the "power and majesty" of the sea I'd discovered. It being late in the season, we rented wet suits and proceeded to a place I'd seen surfers having some fun. I believe I've alluded to my love of bodysurfing.

Our wetsuits were emblazoned with the word "Rental" on our chests, an ignominious detail with which I was not thrilled. In retrospect, I wish they'd read "Call 911 NOW."

We got into the surf, and were almost immediately buried by a significant wave that hammered us under and grated us like blocks of Pecorino Romano against the seafloor. When I could finally surface, I saw my sister was still alive, so I put on my best game face and let out a whoop of faux joy, much like a parent singsonging a musical "Whoopsie!" when attempting to fend off a child's hysteria after a pratfall. Cathy's face was ashen. She wasn't looking so much at me, as over my shoulder. I had time to deduce and swivel in time to be greeted by another wall of aqua vitae.

When we again miraculously found each other alive, heaving for air at the surface, no further communication was required. We waddled, hacking and sputtering, as fast as we could to shore before another wave might catch us. Game over.

~~~

For a semester, I found myself in close proximity to the power and majesty. There's just no more apt way to put it. On its serene days, if you have what some might call a soul, the sea will stare you down and send shivers through you.

In Ireland, I didn't have a boat, or a convenient beach to lounge on. What I had was a semester with my thoughts, and an incredible rocky mix of tidal pools and seaweed beds.

Forsaking much of the socializing that was going on at the pubs (I did eventually over-discover the charms of Jameson's whiskey with the aid of 7-Up chasers), I spent great heaps of time at the shore, watching the tides cycle, and examining the pools that remained for stranded life. It existed in droves, and of the strangest forms. One needn't send a deep submersible to the remotest regions of the sea to find bizarre life-forms, and I'm not talking about Irish pubs. Easily within grasp were writhing brittle stars, viscous fanged worms, and intensely colored, startlingly aggressive crabs.

If you give it half a thought, all crabs are intensely odd. Look at those things walking around like that, never taking their eyes off you, willing to take on all comers even when outweighed a thousand to one. Any damn crab will put a Jack Russell to shame any damn day. Watch that dog yip and yap around a little crab fending him off with a pincer the size of eyebrow tweezers. Hey, Jacko. Woof, woof. *Loser.*

I was one day, like many others, investigating low tide by turning over rocks. Entire universes thrive beneath them at low tide. On a seemingly barren shore, a single flip will set loose a diaspora racing for the cover of the next unturned stone. What must the collective blood pressure be of all these creatures, constantly foraging, incessantly hunted?

There I was, playing God again, looking this time at a fairly blank field of sand. I continued to stare in disbelief at the absence of life (I pride myself in being able to read promising condos) just long enough for the desired effect of one huge velvet fiddler crab. He burst from complete immersion in sand to full fighting stance, his red eyes glaring, pincers locked and loaded. I may have done a complete 360 degree roll backward. The scream that erupted from me kept me hoarse for a week. I, a healthy male at the height of my what-have-you, put on my ass by a crab the size of a woman's cosmetic case.

~~~

The most tragic lesson I learned in Ireland came as official news. While the students from our college were inhabiting a series of thatched cottages along the coast, another contingent from the University of Kansas had what seemed the even better fortune of convening on the island of Inishboffin, a mile or so off the coast. I confess I was somewhat envious of those Jayhawks, since I figured only an island could be a neater place on which to "conduct one's studies."

I did find our choice of curricula enviable, as it featured areas of study sympathetic with our surroundings. Our humanities professor was overseeing our Irish Literature studies, as well as monitoring mini-electives on castles and towers, the Northern Ireland conflict, heraldry and genealogy, and a cursory study of Gaelic. Our science professor took us on field trips during our Irish natural history course, and monitored science electives. Keeping tabs on the weather was part of my meteorology course.

The Kansas students, we'd heard, were following a more traditional study path. They were being fed, among other coursework, horror of horrors, Latin.

We'd been invited to their island for a neighborly dinner once, and I remember thinking *here they are in this marvelous place and they seem not to be dialed into its unique nature*. If it was merely my self-inflated sense of superiority that led me to this finding, what happened a short time later did nothing to diminish the pretension.

Word came to us on the mainland that two Kansas students had been lost at sea. It was a shocking report. They'd been part of a foursome that had taken a hike to a set of rock outcroppings that at low tide were connected by a natural causeway to the island, and at high tide separated by a shallow but turbulent tidal basin. The four had gotten on the *Stags*, as they're called, and were exploring the rocks, oblivious to the rising tide. By the time they saw what was happening, two decided to brave the surge, successfully making land to set out for help. When they returned in the evening, with whom as support and with what plan I never learned, the two who'd chosen to stay had now vanished.

It was assumed that the two who had remained, with the sun going down, the tide rising, and the sea crashing around them, had panicked and attempted to make shore. The *Stags* were an impressive sight when the sea was up.

Remarkably, after several days, the bodies of those two Kansas students washed up very near the place they'd been lost. Many of the local population, conversant with the sea's capabilities, and indoctrinated into a nationally inculcated belief system, viewed it a miracle.

A spiritualist might say the ocean, having made her very compelling point, had been satisfied with her lesson and given back the victims for burial. I myself find it yet another of the endless parade of quirks of a perfectly uncaring universe.

The most painful aspect of the human tragedy, from my point of view, was that the two students would have been fine if they'd stayed put. I wondered if, during their time on the island, they'd been taught something of their surroundings. I wondered if they'd studied the cycles of the tides, if they'd ever felt the pull of a rip current.

I wondered if, in the face of our darkest fears, the most crucial of life's lessons become impotent. In the worst of storms, the *Stags* were never completely awash. The two students from Kansas, had they stayed put, would have been cold, but alive.

Chapter 4

Enter the Siren

My wife and I were set up back in the mid-nineties, when each of us was in the process of self-extraction from an unsatisfactory relationship. As an interesting aside, I'd already slept with Deb's first husband before I decided to give her a try.

It happened at one of Tim and Audrey's parties. The Nuhns are NYC expats who continue to import culturally minded decadence to the backwaters of upstate New York. It isn't an easy job, and I was of little help that evening, spent as I was from the loosely organized merrymaking. I am, in the parlance of partygoers, a lightweight.

Tim and Audrey have a sizable couch, and it so happened that Deb's first husband had chosen to sleep off his revelries at the end opposite where I was taking my own improvised nap. The women involved, being freethinkers, had decided to let it slide, since technically there'd been a cat between us.

Months later, as dust was settling over our respective separations, Audrey would suggest to Deb, while my friend Scott was working the male side of the equation, that Deb and I would make a more suitable couple. It now goes without saying that Audrey and Scott have the estimable benefit of lifetime immunity with us.

Deb's first husband was built for speed. He did everything fast, so when Deb ejected him (*shoom* is the sound Deb makes when telling her own story), I found myself accepted into the fold of a stinkpotter. Deb was, by virtue of her previous hubby's interests, the owner of a zippy little runabout called *Temporary Sanity*. How's that for a dowry? It seems to me that if boaters are at all predisposed to judge one another, it starts with the names we've chosen to paste on our transoms.

I myself am built for something else altogether. While in my younger days I was occasionally known to whoop it up a little, pounding chop while wasting fossil fuel no longer holds an attraction for me. *Temporary Sanity* succeeded only in further displacing my already-unstable vertebrae.

Once Deb's father decided I was suitable material for his daughter, which required a sea trial to determine if I was a fit crewman for his twenty-five-foot sloop, the switch was on. In short order, Deb and I had disencumbered ourselves of the stinkpot and become the owners of his *Bobalew*, while he set about painting the same name onto a twenty-eight footer. We'd become a family of ragpackers.

~~~

Love carries along with her much romantic baggage, and mine will survive the details of harmless deceit. I almost proposed to Deb on a sheen of still water one morning long before my normal rising time.

Most guys finding themselves in love struggle with plans for a suitable proscenium for the ritual dropping of the knee. I myself once thought it would be neat to get the host of *The Prairie Home Companion* to declare my intent on live radio. I have no idea why.

Life, though, is a play often beset with muddled stage directions and lousy lighting. Deb's and my magic moment started out rather poorly. She'd had to rise early to ready herself for a business flight to LA. With both of us still officially single (these days she throws a pillow over my head so she can dress without waking her *manimal*), I'd found it tempting to rise with her at what that morning might have been around four thirty, to make for a convivial send-off. With plenty of time to spare, and the prospects of a morning sunrise shaping up nicely, we decided to take a walk down to the water.

Along the way, Deb brought up a question regarding her then present apartment, the lease for which would be expiring in a few short months. Should she, she wondered out loud, stay where she was, or maybe get a larger living space? We were still living separately—I in my New York City hovel, she in her rental jewel-by-the-sea. Logically considering our living arrangement, I proceeded to pull the pin on my rational hand grenade. I honestly told her, hey, it was her place; she should do whatever would make her happy.

I do not have to tell any woman still reading this wretched confession (most have flung their now-sullied copies across the room at some suitably harmless target) my response did not make Deb happy. To the males reading, I will not explain why. If you do not figure this out for yourselves, you will never entice a woman to go on a trip of any significance with you.

We reached the water, which, on the morning in question, an objective viewer would have found quite lovely. A fecund moon was setting before us, a succulent sun rising behind, and all of nature was rising to the glorious commencement of the day. We were despondent. With still some time to kill, we went for a row in the dinghy.

There on the water something of the realization of the grand messiness of nature began to dawn upon me, and it has been since reported it was then and there that I seized upon the sublime moment to propose. It is an innocuous inaccuracy. The actual words that fled my mouth were, "If I asked you to marry me, would you?"

The question was at least a sincere one, and while I can't remember what Deb's response was, I'm confident they made her at least feel that I was considering the long run, which might possibly have been some comfort to both of us.

A plane had to be caught, so we got back to the dock and took a final look at the harbor. The morning was still exquisite, except for the one nagging detail. My stifled question was haunting me. What in the world would it take to convince a tentative heart the wait was over?

Then, a wave of warmth began to envelop me. The good kind. It could have been one of those singular moments of self-revelation, or maybe just the sun clearing the tree line. Deb smiled when I recounted the cowardly question I'd put to her on the water. I rephrased it for clarification. "*Will* you marry me?"

"Absolutely," was her matter-of-fact response.

~~~

Deb and I have a little game we play from time to time, usually after a satisfying dose of contented silence, but occasionally employed after a bout of frayed relations, in order to speed the healing process. I always seem to have the first line, which I rarely need to finish. It goes, "If I asked you now, would you . . ."

To which her response is always the same, "Absolutely."

Chapter 5

Enter the Demons

*The author, with a souvenir salvaged from
Laura Lynn's prop.*

It *seems to be in my nature to worry*, and high on my list of worries is the making of the fatal mistake, the lazy call, the crucial slipup, the *something* Deb and I will pay dearly for forever afterward.

Another worry is that I am simply too easily demoralized by small problems. One thing one learns about boats is they are problem prone. If everything is operating fine and dandy, one is surely moments away from some sort of catastrophic failure. Most boaters are at least resigned to this fact. Some actually get off on it. I prefer to imagine I'll be the first boater in history with a completely trouble-free year at sea. Somebody please hit me with a squid.

Not long ago, Deb and I set off for a weekend on the water. In truth, we set off from the mooring for the dock thirty or so yards away, where we were going to water up, clean up, and then welcome friends aboard for a pleasant day on the Long Island Sound. As I was tying up, Deb mentioned that there seemed to be smoke coming from the cabin.

I really hate this kind of observation. Announcements like, "There's a lot of water in here," "That thing over there is acting weird," "I can't get the what's-it to work."

Even worse is the innocent question, "Should that cable thing be drooping?" "Should there be black gunk all over here?" "Is this supposed to be like that?"

I confess to my eternal discredit that I particularly dislike when a problem arrives in question form. It's a mate's way of letting you know you're in deep trouble, and nobody nearby is going to be of any help to you, Captain Kirk. Is that shower of sparks an okay thing? Hell no it's not, and thanks for pointing out that I must now risk my life to rescue our worthless tub while the rest of the crew seeks protective cover. And please do not ask if we should call the fire department. Not until I'm a screaming pyre of flames, thank you. Shame always trumps fear.

It's perverse, I know, but sometimes I wish Deb just wouldn't notice these things until it's too late. I could then sit back and stare as our problem sinks from view.

In this case, it wasn't too late for me to see the smoke she was referring to, swear a blue streak, and then head down into the engine compartment to see what kind of hell I was in for.

Any boy over the age of two has a sense memory of bad smells he dials into. It comes from many sources: fooling around a little too casually in Dad's shop when he's not there to chaperone, or watching Dad ruin his own stuff when he lets you observe. You get the Pavlovian picture.

The guys in the white lab coats say the nose is somehow directly wired to the brain in some way our other senses are not. Early on in development, a boy gets a nose for certain kinds of destruction. He can detect the telltale odors of appliance meltdown, liquefying insulation and fried circuitry. He can differentiate, much like a chef does with herbs and spices, between the smells of something good (that purring two-stroke) and something very bad (that two-stroke running on pure gasoline). Coincidentally, is the alternator supposed to be making that sound?

What was happening to our boat smelled very bad. I could also see, from the front access to the engine behind our companionway stairs (which is a view of the engine manufacturer's sticker and little else), that whatever the problem was, it wasn't going to be fixed through this route.

Let me now digress to one of my favorite topics. What in hell was the guy thinking when he decided an engine could fit in this boat in the first place? I know I'm not alone here, since I've commiserated with many other boat owners on this topic. Boat design seems, at its core, man's determination to wedge into spaces that which the Almighty has ordained should not fit in there. In fact, I suspect the Almighty might be thinking, *Okay, I knew you guys would figure out how to fly, but I never intended for you to float. What are you, nuts? Make me proud. Go bungee off a suspension bridge.*

Of course, the designer didn't intend for *this* engine to be in *this* boat. This engine came several owners later, one owner of many owners who each had an idea of new and exciting things to cram into what was originally supposed to be a simple floating device. But don't get me wrong; the original designer was full of hubris too.

So here's this engine down here. I don't know how it got there, and some of its mechanical parts have been slowly wearing away at its electrical parts until *punctuated equilibrium* does its thing.

Punctuated equilibrium. Remember her? It's that observation coined by Stephen Jay Gould, the famous paleontologist and educator, who observed that things tend to change very slowly for vast chunks of time, until something really big changes all at once. It is purported to more accurately describe the process of Evolution than earlier notions of gradual, predictable change. For most of time, things change at such a subtle rate you don't know they are changing, until that moment when, as it applies to boats, all hell breaks loose, and you stand there in wonderment as your investment fills with water, flames, or both.

I got out of the cabin and dove (I don't dive like I used to; I sort of spaz around herky-jerky style when there's trouble about) into the port cockpit locker, where access to the house batteries revealed a cable shorted out by long-term chafing against the transmission linkage. It also revealed melting terminal posts, and if I'd had any capacity to think properly, the imminent possibility of a local explosion.

Diesel fuel ameliorated the crisis somewhat. This is a primary selling point of diesel engines; that their fuel is far less volatile than gasoline, and so less likely to send you into orbit. That being said, I frantically worked to open the circuit to stop the short from finishing its work, whatever that might be.

I don't wish to belabor the process, as technical detail tends to slow down literary exposition. Plus, I don't really know exactly what I did, and if I did remember, I might be proving myself a bigger fool than I take credit for. For all I know, I could have turned the battery switch to save the day, but I removed a cable lead from one of the batteries before it melted, and the arching stopped. No explosion. Soon a group of friends would be arriving for their pleasant trip around the harbor. I'd just had my joyride for the day, and I was spent.

West Marine to the rescue. I'm telling you, I'd rather lose our police force, the post office, my bank's local branch, and Taco Bell than see West Marine leave town. We were back in business within an hour, and when guests arrived, they had no idea I'd recently attempted to commit nautical suicide.

∽∽∽

There is something seriously amiss in a system that requires the physique of some kind of *Close Encounters* alien to service it. My perfect mechanic has telescoping arms and neck, suction-cup fingers, a torque wrench for one forearm, an impact driver for the other, night vision on the end of a three-foot antenna, and the ability to hover inverted for three hours without inducing a stroke. He spits WD40, and he works for minimum wage.

A marina I will never again use (I seem to say that every year, and I'm running out of marinas) placed my boat in the water after winter lay-up without performing the requested repack of the stuffing box. A stuffing box, put over-simply, is a thing that keeps a hole in a boat from sinking the boat. When I confronted the owner of the marina about the oversight, he told me, "Listen, you do not want to pay me what it would take to get a guy to do it." He was right. I do it myself now. The job sucks.

Another marina's mechanic charged me three hours labor to bleed a fuel line, after I'd changed filters and introduced air into the line. Diesel owners know this task must regularly be dealt with, and most know exactly which bolts need to be loosened, and in which order, and then to turn over the engine to purge the air. If there are six steps to the process, I knew five of them, not enough to get the engine running. After that hideous bill, I learned how to do all the steps myself in about ten minutes.

∼∼∼

I enjoy telling people that boats are truly alive, which sounds all cute and mystical until I finish my thought. To remain alive, I continue, they must consume human flesh.

On occasion, boats will kill us quickly, with a well-placed boom to the skull, or a maneuver that pitches us into the sea at night when we're offshore and too lazy to hook in. More often though, it is a slow process, like cancer. It attacks your savings, of course, but it goes after the body as well. I have so many divots in my head, it has taken on the contours of the lunar landscape. Each night, my wife and I peruse each other's bodies, not in preparation for connubial rapture, but to see generally if we're mending properly.

One fine day, as we motored at maybe three knots on a glassy harbor, Deb made an attempt to step from one side of the boat to the other, hopping from the starboard cockpit seat to the port side. She misjudged the gap, and went down in a pile on the cockpit sole. I was steering in close quarters to moored boats, and could do nothing but ask, "Are you okay?"

"I think it's broken," she answered, and she turned out right about one of her fingers. What ended up news to the both of us was a bruise on her upper thigh the shape and size of New York State. There is to this day a notable concavity in her leg she will most probably carry forever, testament to that one false step. If that, on a peaceful day on our home waters, what then in the midst of a storm at night on the Atlantic? *What are we thinking?*

∼∼∼

I'll tell you what I'm thinking, as I read yet another story from the annals of those who have passed before us and written about it to subsidize their madness, *if these poor souls can do this, we sure as hell can.*

At times, I'm outright smug about having learned from others' mistakes, generous as they've been with the details of each and every bungle they've made. Jeez, they're sipping piña coladas in the Caribbean, and they've never been up their mast? I have a bosun's chair, and some strange bruises to prove I've used it. I should be anchored next to these guys, not reading wistfully from a winter's gloom of their maritime gloatings.

I have, for much of my life, been an observer of the living, desiring to learn too much before I join in the festivities. When I search Amazon for my next potential selection, a note comes up, *"People who've purchased this book have also selected, well never mind, you've purchased everything else we'd recommend. Thanks for shopping with Amazon."*

It ought to say that, anyway.

~~~

My biggest worry, bar none, is my attitude. Intellectually, I realize that the great barrier to this trip is the block that rests on top of my shoulders. That's why all these other folks made it and lived to make a profit from their stories. Of all their qualities, they'd had the right frame of mind to make it happen. That is what I must work on daily, from the handling of problems, to the defining of those problems as (wait for it) *opportunities.* My mind-set is what stands in the way of our doing this thing we've said we're going to do.

~~~

There are, I've decided, two types of people in this world: people who do things, and people who make lists of things to do. I'm a list maker. When I have free time, I make a list of things to do as soon as I accumulate additional free time. When that time becomes available, I go over my list of things to do and eliminate items that aren't all that important, and so feel as if I've accomplished something.

From time to time, I actually do something on my *to do* list. Upon erasure from the list that thing I have done, I feel a sense of rapture that is difficult to describe. It may be I've succeeded in purchasing low-friction dental floss, a thing Deb covets. As a result I, husband and provider, am king.

This kind of thinking, I'm quite sure, won't get Deb and me to the Abacos, but it's a start. By the way, did I mention that we're going to the Abacos? Basically, it means we're going to Palm Beach, Florida, hanging a left, and crossing the Gulf Stream.

The Gulf Stream is the great mental chasm, the indigo enigma, that obstacle near the end of the journey mentioned so frequently in cruiser journals that it flavors every day of a journey down the Eastern Coast of America.

We're one day closer to having to face the Stream, the fledgling cruiser thinks, after another priceless day along the trip south.

~~~

Is there anything more soul illuminating than being made aware of the fact that snot is streaming out of your nose onto your rented tux?

I was recently caught with new guests aboard as my Danforth dangled against the hull, the anchor having come unseated by the passing wake of a mammoth power yacht. I had no idea it had been wrenched from its cradle until an over-zealous passing sailor had signaled us to proclaim, "Your anchor's dangling against your hull, numb-nuts! It'll smash a hole in your side, and you'll sink and drown if you don't do something about it soon, you idiot." What he said had that effect anyway, in front of all guests aboard.

Thanks, pal. And you've got four fenders hanging over the side, your boarding ladder is dragging, there's a six-year-old on the bow without a life vest, and you're uglier than me. From this distance anyhow.

Bastard. He was right about the anchor, of course.

~~~

I don't know how I missed the anchor thing. I try to keep stuff shipshape and all. Constantly enthusing to Deb over my upgrades to our shared enterprise, I've learned to read her feigned enthusiasm as she recites, "Wow. That really must be a good thing."

She means, of course, I'm glad you're happy your gizmo now interfaces with your fandangle, but *what would really make my day* would be if you'd contact-paper the shelves in the head.

~~~

There are a number of ways of learning how to paddle one's way through life's gauntlet. "Horse sense," something my dad prized in a man, will only get you so far, at least on the amount I was given, which would shame your typical horse.

There are organized schools to take up the slack in a non-self-starter's curriculum. Aside from the occasional adult seminar, I have always sought out the services of the *guru*—the one who has attained the seat of knowledge you desire; the one who will stand over your shoulder to say at the appropriate moment, "I wouldn't do that, if I were you. Here's what'll probably happen. You might want to try it this other way instead, grasshopper."

Gurus are often busy meditating someplace other than where you need them right this moment, and so most often my lessons come in a more convenient form, which is to say, one calamity after the other. Then it's sink-or-swim time.

~~~

What is it about the challenge of an old boat? There should be a name for this fetish, this nautical equivalent of shooting one's self in the foot before setting off on a marathon race. It isn't just about saving money. The fact is, money is very frequently not saved at all, particularly if one factors in the time-as-money algorithm. By the time Joshua Slocum had rebuilt the salvaged wreck that was *Spray*, the only thing left of the original boat might have been the smell of wood rot in the air. The man was obviously nuts.

No, this has a lot more to do with the thrill of making do with less than what is considered reasonable. My life is full of those kinds of thrills. After squandering ten dollars on a frou-frou drink at the local watering hole, I'll labor into the night, hacking away at an ingot of zinc to make my own sacrificial anode for my sea strainer, rather than buy one custom made for the purpose. Saved a buck! What time is it? One AM. Cuckoo!

～～～

Jeez, I'm rambling. So what chapter are we on now? I haven't been paying attention. Anyway that's not important anymore. What's important is I have some really exciting news.

You *did* it! You got us to take the trip. I'm totally serious. It's over and done. We've been away for nine months. It was incredible, and we're back home. I'll tell you all about it, but this calls for a whole new section.

～～～

Section 2
Wherein the trip is taken

Paradise-seeker tip:
It is unwise to linger under a coconut palm without protective headgear

As you may recall, the book was proposed to you as a device, a means of preparing myself, the way an elite skier visualizes a slalom run down some groomed piste before plummeting through those spring-loaded gates. See the trip in the mind's eye, write about the trip as if it were a done deal, and let her rip, with your fans doing their "who let the dogs out" chant at the dock.

At some point along my rambling narrative, the trip gained critical mass and took off on its own. In a whirlwind of events, Deb and I pulled together the various threads of commitment we needed to make the trip happen. The narrative became superfluous. What was required was action.

As many who have preceded us like to say, it all seems like a dream now. Like a movie that talks about itself. Like a freak date with the prom queen. What had ever possessed the golden girl to say yes? Had she also suffered from the ravages of acne during some delicate stage in her development?

The day before her new job began, Deb got all weepy at the thought that it was over. We'd gone and done it, done what we'd set out to do, despite our own doubts, and the doubts of the reasonably concerned. I understood her response. I related, as only a guy celebrating the newly returned gift of alternating current can. I held her close.

But not long ago, as with all expectant journeys, we both could only imagine what might lie over the horizon.

Why cruising books suck. Extract the hues, scents and sounds from an idyllic seascape. Paste a mottled-white sky to a speckle-gray sea with a patch of black, and voila: Paradise, sort of.

Chapter 6

The Prep

*Hear her roar; treat her like a lady.
The Yanmar 3GMF diesel powerplant,
or, if you're a girl, the motor.*

The year leading up to the trip was a list-saturated one. I'd gone out and bought all the books I could find by folks who were like me, save for the fact that they'd gone and done what we were planning to go and do. Actually, it was hard to imagine

I was anything like these people, though they kept on insisting it. Some clearly had worlds of experience since their early first days as cruisers. They spoke matter-of-factly of situations foreign and frightening to me. I was reminded of something I'd read long ago in a humor magazine—the perfectly serious, step-by-step procedure for taking out one's own appendix, using whatever utensils are normally found around the house, and a bottle of Scotch whiskey.

There was a notable exception to the well-versed cruiser, and that was a couple who were so arrogantly inexperienced, and who put together such a shoddy book, it made me livid. Everything about their work was slipshod, including the binding. Pictures were smudges of blue-black ink flung alongside tortured grammar. Aside from wanting my money back, I was now goaded by the insult into action. By the stars above, if these aquatic derelicts could survive a trip to Paradise, so could we. Today I thank them, though not personally in print. They just might possibly have been the straw that whipped this camel into action.

~~~

My primary concerns about the boat included an obvious one. I'm no mechanic, and I had a mysterious Japanese engine hiding somewhere that put out around twenty horsepower, about a quarter the amount that had coaxed around my old motorcycle, another machine that used to give me fits. About a week after we bought the boat for fifteen grand, an amount we considered a bargain, the engine refused to turn over. The problem turned out to be a fried starter, though my nose was of no help in the diagnosis. Professional help was needed almost from the get go.

It turns out starters on Japanese boat engines don't cost the same as the ones on Chevy pickups. Nor do the alternators, oil filters, or any other damn part on the sons o' bitches. You can begin to appreciate the price differential by getting into the habit of calling boat parts *components*. That'll help prepare you for the invoice.

Diesel parts (do as I say, not as I do) are exotic items, like those tubs and tubes of butt cream and whatnot women must own, or die trying to acquire. You know the stuff, there amongst all the other stuff that crams every shelf of the medicine cabinet, causing your deodorant to fall into the toilet when you open the door. Not *that* tube. That's not butt cream. That's eyelid douche.

Take my advice, if you haven't lost a limb already. Don't touch any of that stuff in there. You might exfoliate a crucial guy component.

On a boat, you'll notice a bit of role reversal going on. I wanted all of the space for myself, and Deb had to fight my principled stand for every square inch of storage. Contrast that with our situation now, back on land. Was it the vindictive side of her that banished all my clothes to the guestroom? After nine months managing in a floating shoebox, she took all the closet space back at home. Feminine requirements notwithstanding, that's just mean-spirited.

To properly administer to your auxiliary (there's irony for you, as the real auxiliary power source on a sailboat cruising the ICW is your jib), you must have the service manual. And since the service manual has been translated from Japanese into English by a Swede, it will be of next to no use to you. Stare at the pictures if you like. Exploded views of things are kind of nifty.

Next, because the manual is worthless in your hands, you go out and buy Nigel Calder, because every good boater needs his bible. Nigel is Yahweh, Vishnu, Odin, and Emeril, all rolled into one. Like any deity, he will be at times praised, feared, worshipped, and cursed. You will curse Nigel for knowing what your problem is, for calmly explaining what your problem is, for patiently elucidating that the reason the problem arose in the first place was most probably due to poor maintenance on your part, for commiserating in a fatherly way from afar (which is to say, the other side of the cash register), and for leaving you alone to face the personal failure that will most surely accompany your repair attempt. In the end, Nigel will forgive you for cursing him.

I cursed Nigel for making it all seem so logical and orderly on paper. I knew when I knelt down in front of my engine (sailors are fundamentally supplicants) with a ratchet in my hand, all the orderliness of language would be gutted by the anarchy that rules in the engine compartment. I knew that one of the seven steps required to access Widget A would be impossible, either because of inaccessibility, intractability, a missing tool, or a missing step in the process. For who among us does not own a manual without an addendum that manages not to get addended?

Mostly I cursed Nigel for his most maddening assertion about the efficacy of your basic diesel power plant. He states, without any hint of intended irony, that the diesel engine is a miraculous piece of workmanship, robust and reliable, just so long as not the teeniest, tiniest speck of anything foreign whatsoever is introduced into the pristine combustion chamber. As reliable, I'll wager, as any robust male of our species, on an everything-paid-for bender at an Asian strip club.

The engine scared me a lot, so I signed up for a series of classes at a prominent local distributor who, seeing an opportunity to make some easy money off a batch of rightfully paranoid sailors, continues to offer seminars that include hands-on tinkering. This is crucial, because everybody knows working on somebody else's investment is a whole lot less stressful than working on your own. We were going to be able to get our greedy green hands on an engine very much like the ones hiding in our own boats. In my case it was an engine very similar to my Yanmar 3GMF, not to be confused with the 2GMF, or the 3GMD. I got to play with the 3GM30. It was the same color as mine, anyway.

But we didn't get to play with our Yanmars until our instructor had humored himself by psychologically abusing us for our presumed torture of his beloved engines. In fact, his abuse never abated, and naturally (this kind of thing has been documented) his pupils grew to love him as only prison inmates can of their sadistic-yet-vulnerable warden. I suspect that the real reason for the courses was that they were prescribed therapy for a man who'd spent much of his professional career attempting to wedge his formidable frame into the greasy dark recesses of boats owned by people too stupid to diagnose battery post corrosion.

I spent three days traveling to and from Union, New Jersey, a commute nearly as tedious as sailing is in the first place. If one were to tally the time, a full day of the three was spent listening to Larry tell us why engines designed to last for two millennia if properly maintained, would inevitably last only two seasons while in the care of a well-meaning sailor. He'd drone on about what we ought to be doing to protect our investment, but *nooo*, we were too busy having fun with the engine off. We wrote it all down, but were we ever going to heed his advice? *Nooo*. Dead in the water, we'd be calling him on his weekend, wailing about our broken engines while his complimentary binder of compiled wisdom grew moldy in our bilge.

When he wasn't berating us, he managed to relay some valuable knowledge about the machine that would be transporting us to dreamland. We learned how the engines were intended to work. We learned why they might stop working. We learned how to get them working again. We learned how to minimize the risk of them not working. He then sent us off feeling like confident, prepared boaters. But not before each of us offloaded another grand or so at his parts department. Nice operation.

If Larry hears about this, I hope he knows how much I appreciate what I learned from him. My only real gripe with the class, and I told him so, was that my test engine was presented to me in a brightly lit, spacious, climate-controlled shop, on a pedestal that put everything at eye level. Each part we toyed with had been removed, lubricated and replaced on a frequent schedule, and as a result, graciously obliged us when we wished to remove it ourselves. Try removing something on any engine on the water—work we avoid precisely because it has been avoided for so long in the past.

It has been reported that certain huge valves on New York's ancient water-delivery system are never tested, for fear they'll fail catastrophically during a test. That's how most of us approach engine maintenance. By not approaching it, as it were.

To do the seminars right, the engines should have been enclosed in such a way as to prohibit convenient access to any crucial component. The lights and air conditioning should have been turned off, the sprinkler system activated at random intervals, all of this taking place on a floor poured with a list, and Larry leaning over our shoulders, asking, "Are you almost finished? There's a freighter bearing down on us."

~~~

Another area of concern, if concern can be said to cause cold sweats at three in the morning, was the electrical system. Your basic DC system is supposed to be a simple beast, but staring at the nether regions of our electrical setup was like sneaking a peek at Medusa's coiffeur.

What happens to an old boat is what has happened to an old man. He starts out more or less well manufactured in a simpler time, with simple requirements. As time wears on, things start to complicate. He is sent off to war and gets wounded. Shipped home, he recuperates, is decommissioned, and takes a stateside job. He changes jobs, and with each new job comes a new boss, with different demands. He tries to keep up, hobbling along with feigned enthusiasm. He learns new skills and carries around new technology he tries to understand. The effort to keep stride with the youngsters takes a physical toll.

The tinkerers are summoned. Knees are rebuilt, stents installed, a pacemaker strategically embedded. The old guy keeps chugging along, but signs of potential catastrophic failure deflect the scope on the ECG machine.

The tinkerer in me looked around our boat, and some of what I saw made sense, and some didn't. Some wires were providing a service. Some wires once had a purpose and didn't seem to be bothering any presently useful wires. Some stuff just looked scary-ugly. Switches had been retrofitted, buttons shoehorned, toggles wedged. An old transducer had been abandoned and a through-hull drilled for a new one, the screen for the new one being the size of a grade-school wall clock. I was concerned.

I got introduced to a versatile boat-systems guy whom I ended up feeling comfortable with. You know how you first look at someone who could be in a position to ream you but good if he wanted to? Fellows who make wads of money by informing you you'll need a whole new engine, boiler, dental plate, kidney, whizbang? I hate those consultations.

To prepare yourself for the ordeal, you put on your best game face, the one with the deer-in-the-headlight gaze. You take a good hard look at this guy who's standing there with "Specialist" stitched into his lab coat/jump suit/baseball cap. Then you try to summon something from deep down inside you that hopefully the baboons left behind, some primal sense that will alert you as to whether this animal is a friend or fraud. You've practiced the names of things you figure he'll talk about, you've studied Nigel's Cliff Notes, you've promise yourself you won't babble uncontrollably, and possibly utter some phrase that fingers you as a patsy. Two twenty, two twenty-one; whatever it takes.

This rarely works out well, but Pete seemed like an okay guy. I went over some of the things I wanted for the boat, things I was concerned about. I tried to let him know I wasn't one of those just-send-me-the-bill guys, but I wasn't about to compromise my honey pie's safety, or anything like that. More than one way to skin a cat, know what I mean? I probably just babbled for a while. Oh, let's face it, I squawked like a slit chicken. Gimme some of that there two-twenty-one action. He listened, and then babbled back sociably with me, which was a nice gesture. I could tell he liked boats, he seemed to like his work, and he took the time to explain different ways of going about the task at hand.

Pete ended up doing okay by me, but I think I had that coming. The boat needed the work, and I couldn't do it myself, not safely and swiftly at any rate. One day he set off a bunch of sparks, and you know I kept my mouth shut about it.

I think Pete actually spilled a lot of blood on the job. I asked if I could help, at the very least prep for him so he wouldn't have to spend lots of quality time, if you catch my drift, doing stupid work, and he tolerated me as best he could. I spilled some blood myself. I tell you this right now: I won't believe you've been on your boat today if you don't have a wound to prove it.

∼∼∼

I'm pretty convinced that to have a long happy life with a boat, you have to like crawling into dark, little spaces lined with serrated edges, and you have to be pagan enough to feel secretly proud of how filthy you get in the process. After the job is done, you might choose not to immediately wash your hands. They might just hang there on display, in simian fashion, while you explain to your beloved how you just retorqued the head bolts.

Blood, too, is still the red badge of courage. It announces that, even though your wife may have a more lucrative, satisfying, "life-affirming" career (and I for one salute this cultural advance), by thunder, you've spared her a certain agony, and we now have a working courtesy light at the base of the companionway. At your service, my lady.

Our engine was ready, refurbished to a degree, with spare parts labeled and stored. Our electrical system was sufficiently modernized. I'd installed a new compressor for our icebox, the cavernous interior of which I'd feebly attempted to insulate. I had no idea how it would work down in *Paradise*, but the evaporator, I think you call it, frosted over when we turned it on.

New batteries all around. I'd added a sump pump to our shower system so the "gray water" was pumped overboard instead of funneled directly into the bilge, where presumably it would have mated with other aqueous substances and created new life-forms with distinctively unpleasant odors. Believe, you, me, Deb's sniffer is no stock model. Somebody wearing too much perfume on the subway will send her to the emergency room in a clinical swoon.

My proudest accomplishment though, was one that in the end proved to be an utter waste of time. I'd been reading with interest anything concerning communications on the high seas, and had been intrigued by the possibility of free e-mail, made so by the use of an SSB (single side band, aka: expensive radio) and a special service provided to those who'd earned a HAM (geek) license. My interest was aroused. I proceeded in incremental fashion to acquire this service for our use.

Incrementally, it turns out, is not the way to approach certain tasks. I proceeded first to acquire a HAM radio license. Deb's grandfather is a HAM, with a wall of electronics that choke what could otherwise be a useful den, but not a radio conversation exchanged in decades. All his fellow HAMs, he explained, have passed away. He didn't even remember how to turn on all the tubular technology that made his den look like Buck Rogers's cockpit.

My first task was to acquire the entry level Technician's license, and I studied quite a bit about wave propagation, on-air etiquette, safety issues, yadda yadda. I passed. Ta da.

Then I discovered that to use the frequencies required for the free e-mail transmissions, the next higher license, called a General License, was required. Well hell, if you want to play that game, bring it, Sammy.

Then I discovered that the General exam was a two-step process. There was a written portion—a more thorough version of the test I'd just passed—and, get this, a Morse code requirement.

Now the secret handshake organizers in this elite club will say you don't have to know the Code but at five words per minute, which is no big deal for anybody who never leaves the techno-den except to drain the weasel and assemble another Spamwich. Frankly though, it's like telling somebody with a life that to get a driver's license, you have to show you can hover an inch off the ground for two seconds. That's not so high, and it's not for that long.

I will not get into the absurd political ramifications of the Morse code requirement in our good old U.S. of A. The rest of the developed world sees it as silly, the FCC will probably have dropped it by the time you read this, and with regard to the elite members who practice this ancient art of exclusion between games of tiddlywinks, I wish them all dit . . . dah . . . well.

By the way, I passed the test.

~~~

I finally discovered that the requisite equipment and installation costs would double our investment in the boat. Alright, not quite, but in any event it was now out of the question, so Deb and I went with a VHS radio, already installed, a cell phone already owned, and an old laptop with a Wi-Fi card, double ditto. The moral here is to get the whole story before you tackle phase one of any project.

~~~

One last thing about the code, in an attempt to stave off potential criticism from the secret hand-shaker sect. I don't mean to dismiss what must be endlessly fruitful conversations bounced between continents on the relative merits of the yagi antenna. I only wish to point out that there are travelers out there whose chief reason for securing long distance communication is to keep from dying prematurely. Times change, or they ought to, occasionally.

~~~

There was progress on the home front. We let folks know we were leaving on the trip by way of a custom card made by my sister, who's collection of line drawings will one day make her famous. We commissioned a card with a couple on the bow of a boat leaving New York Harbor. The copy inside read:

Ahoy!

Now hear this. We're casting off our landlubber jobs, hoisting anchor and setting sail for the sunny Caribbean.

The Vitals:
Who: Deb and Paul
What: One year seabatical
When: This autumn, after hurricane winds (hopefully) die down, and before winter gears up
How: On our 34' Morgan, Laura Lynn, via the Intracoastal Waterway
Why: Life is short, we're still mobile and we like each other a lot

We'll keep you up-to-date via wireless technology, regaling you regularly with tales from the high seas, though hopefully not too high. So send us your e-mail address at dpkoestner@yahoo.com. This offer includes one Christmas photo, so be there or be square

Fair winds,
US

We sent off close to two hundred of these to family, friends, business associates, and venders who'd helped us prepare the *Laura Lynn*. We kept in touch as promised, with a sizeable e-mail list that grew as we traveled along.

~~~

On all snowbirds' minds during the autumn of 2005 was what the coming hurricane season might offer. Advances in long-term, large-scale weather prediction had provided some unsettling data. At the time of our trip, the Eastern Seaboard was seen to be at the apex of a general twenty-year cycle, with predictions by NOAA (National Oceanographic and Atmospheric Administration) of an above-average number of storms. Along with a predicted increase in number was an associated increase in severity.

Scientists and politicians were bickering over whether global warming was exacerbating the issue, and the planet's general health continues to be a political lightning rod. There appear to be those who still question whether there is such a thing as ozone, which I find immensely ironic, when one considers these same souls tend to believe fervently in the existence of angels. Whatever one's political bent (I bend in the direction of those who can properly pronounce the word "nuclear"), boaters heading south in 2005 had some interesting meteorological grist upon which to chew.

It continues to be a thorny decision for the southbound traveler to pick the right time to leave home for bluer pastures. Fundamentally, one wishes to head south soon enough to avoid freezing one's patootie off up north (and miss most of the Nor'easters that begin to plague our neck of the woods) but not so soon as to put one in the path of a late-season hurricane. The problem is that tropical storms have begun to exhibit the disturbing propensity to continue their visits deeper into the year.

Thus, no matter when you decide to leave, you're in a crapshoot. And there is nothing that will save even the most well-found, prepared, and staked-out boat from a direct hit by Mother Nature's finest. There are things one can do to maximize survivability, but if you're dealt the cyclone card, make sure you're north or south of the latitudes prescribed in your paid-in-full insurance policy.

Deb and I mulled over our projected sail-away date, revising it every time the local salts, hearing of our intended departure, would massage their grizzled chins, inspect the cloud cover, and spill out half the thought, "Welllllll, I don't knowww . . ."

We didn't know either. Nobody quite does. But as the salty sage says, you pays your money, you takes your chances. We decided on October 2, come hell or high water. On second thought, if it turned out a reasonably nice day.

~~~

October 2 was a Sunday, which meant most working folks, if they cared to, could come on down to see us off. We'd arranged a corporate rental for our co-op in New York City, the conditions of the sublet being agreeable to both parties, quite a relief to us. We hope Perry felt the same.

Deb's sister would oversee our Port Washington apartment. Our hope was to have found a roommate for Jackie to further defray our expenses, but such was not to be the case. Ill-guided attempts to find someone of suitable temperament and accompanying qualifications fell through. To those interested, she's twenty-eight at the time of this writing, lovely, a talented and dedicated teacher, and available. At the time of the trip, we at least had Jackie there to hold the fort, occasionally start the car, and dispose of enough junk mail to effectively denude a Brazilian rain forest.

The boat was rigged, and approaching a state of readiness I was prepared to accept. We were a few months from takeoff.

~~~~

The news of the event that rocked our foundations, and whose tremors reverberate to this day, arrived by cell phone while we were visiting friends in California. It was Deb's father, but it wasn't Deb's father's voice. Always animated, always a wiseacre, in Bob's throat was caught the recognizable sound of bad news. After having submitted to a battery of tests prompted by health issues, he was telling us it looked like he might have pancreatic cancer.

How often must people now hasten to the Internet for answers to the obfuscations posed by our healthcare professionals. Being ever so human in an ever-so-litigious age, they hedge their bets in medical jargon and relentless testing. It must be a terrible burden, having to say what no one wants to hear. One can get good at not quite saying it, so that others can believe they did not quite hear it.

There ensued the requisite dismal passage of time, the waiting on the inevitable, the horror of the foregone conclusion. This man, who'd been more the child to his own children, this jokester, who had taught me, if anything, not how to sail well, but to have fun half-trying, who had always taken pleasure in the denial of adulthood, now showed us too soon the journey we would all one day take on our own.

Deb's father died a few short months after the phone call. His kids, grandchildren, and sailing partner Lew took his ashes aboard the *Bobalew*, the O'Day Bob had acquired after having successfully foisted his previous boat on Deb and me. Bob's son David slipped his dad's ashes over the stern in the bay where Bob and Lew had so often been seen having a grand old time.

As a comedy team, Bob and Lew had rivaled the great duo acts of their generation. Now going solo, Lew found the right timing to stave off the collective surge of melancholy aboard. "I don't wish to cast aspersions," he ruminated, "but I think we just created a new shoal back there."

Rest in peace, Captain.

~~~

Robert Austin
Skipper of the Bobalew

Chapter 7

The Leap of Faith

Pardon me, but is this the way to the Bahamas?

On a pleasant October 2 morning, we shoved off, with a small group of family and friends looking on. Nothing newsworthy, as apparently Ms. Hilton was still in bed with the pooch. There were some awkward hugs, the floating dock being one of those puzzle-lock affairs that handles like a waterbed. There might have been something more to the awkwardness. These were people we were used to seeing on a regular basis. It was exciting. It was sad. What kind of hug is called for on such occasions?

The thing on my mind as we snailed away from home and family, which I'd been fretting over for months, was the hope that we could get through this first day, and maybe another one, without a problem. I don't mean a little boat issue. I mean a *problem.* Please, Poseidon, if you have a surprise for us, let me get a couple days down the road so I'll head for the closest marina, not turn tail and paddle home. Maybe I should've lit a votive.

We made it through Hell Gate, past Manhattan, and under the Verrazano Narrows Bridge. With the ocean opening up before us, we wanted to behave like sailors while we could. We had ample time to make our projected anchorage in Sandy Hook, New Jersey, so we hoisted sail and turned off the engine.

As it turned out, there would be precious few opportunities like this the entire trip, where all considerations for time and travel would take a backseat to pure sailing for the fun of it. We were heading south on the wind, and it felt glorious. The feeling was short-lived.

With Deb at the helm, I went below to check the position of our centerboard. Our boat, a Morgan 34, built in 1970 by the infamous Charlie Morgan, is a classic example of the CCA (Cruising Club of America) design that favored sizeable overhangs. While not in pristine condition, *Laura Lynn* was and is in good working order, and if you're partial to this era's look, she's quite easy on the eyes. She has a proud, upturned nose and a raised tush, a stern referred to as a "counter transom," a detail Deb never hesitates to point out to the uninitiated.

Charlie designed the boat at his St. Petersburg facility with a design draft of thirty-nine inches, to take advantage of the shallow cruising grounds of the Florida Keys and Bahamas. But to improve upwind performance, he added a retractable centerboard, a Rube Goldbergian device that can be lowered and raised to suit the conditions at hand. Heading upwind with the board down, the boat should in theory point higher, and so make better time. Downwind, the board would be retracted to minimize the boat's wetted surface, to make better time. Are you following this jargon fest? Generations of boat designers have invested immense amounts of thought toward an increase in the potential top end of these wind-driven wonders. Thanks to such initiative, our boat has a fighting chance of keeping up with a tricycle powered by a kid with ADHD.

Devices like retractable centerboards continue to be built into modern boats. The design on our own has gone through changes, and we authorized an alteration ourselves, swapping out a cable in order to hopefully acquire a longer service life. We lack what originally appears to be a whimsical, though at one time certainly useful marker system, a beadlike device traveling along a piece of heavy monofilament that would have given the sailor a sense of the board's relative level of adjustment. A clever helmsman, we are told, might adjust the board only partially, to balance the helm more effectively.

There are those who also suggest the board makes for a last-ditch depth finder, since when it is fully lowered, one might feel a shallow bottom as it begins to push the board back up into its slot.

Finally, there are those who think the whole contraption is at best a waste of time, at worst a costly nuisance, and they've gone and glassed the whole thing in.

While I'm not a good enough sailor to accurately weigh its benefits, and while it has given me headaches maintaining it, the kid in me wants to keep the thing functioning. It's like, wacky, man. It gives kids something to play with, thus delaying somewhat the inevitable onset of boredom, and the accompanying wail, "When are we going *baaaaaaack*?"

Without a functioning indicator bead for the board, we can still count the rotations we make of the handle that operates it, or we can do a visual check by raising the sole cover in the saloon (please don't ask me why the interior living/eating space in a boat is called a saloon; we have no cowpokes onboard). Removing this chunk of a trap door reveals the lifting rod that travels back and forth in the bilge, which, by the way, adds another hole in the boat, joy of joys. It also reveals something else.

Making a visual check of the rod, I discovered a bilge completely flooded with seawater. Or was it our entire supply of freshwater? Holy Jesus, where was all this water coming from? Oh, of course: Shit Creek.

I must have yelped, or squeaked, or groaned, or all of the above. Deb deduced that something was up. I probably did one of my special run-on sentences, such as, "Oh holy mother of god the freaking boat has a ton of water in it I haven't the slightest idea why just keep steering I gotta bail!"

So Deb sailed, and I bailed, for longer than I cared to. She tacked a few times, and then we got the sails down because this was no time for funning around. After a while, things seemed to simmer down. The level of the bilge water lowered, anyway, if not my blood pressure.

Even with our unplanned extracurricular activities, we still made it to our chosen anchorage, found plenty of room, got the anchor to hold, and we didn't seem to be sinking anymore. It was little consolation to me. I was physically worn, emotionally shaken, bewildered, and forlorn. Deb, as always, though of little help from a diagnostic perspective, was a pillar of confidence. All was well now, the sun was setting suitably, if not magnificently, and we weren't turning around. Let me say right now before I get too far along in the narrative: Deb is *It*, man. She *rocks*. She's *the Bomb*.

~~~

The bilge was still empty the next day, and we seemed to have freshwater in what we were pretty sure was a sixty-gallon tank. Listen, boats have options too, many of which are hidden from view. The freshwater tank is glassed in under the V-berth. Our moldy owner's manual didn't specify its volume, there is no gauge, and I never did a milk jug test. The fuel tank? We poke a stick down the fill pipe to see how we're doing on diesel. Now just leave me alone. I'm telling a story.

We set out for New Jersey's Manasquan Inlet, by way of the open ocean. Jersey is one of those stretches of the coast that most sailors need to traverse from offshore, as the Intracoastal Waterway, the intricate amalgam of mostly-navigable water channels that spans virtually the entire Eastern Seaboard, is most problematic in terms of water depth and bridge-clearance issues. We skirted the coast a few miles out, close enough to spot the boardwalk an old flame used to drag me to on summer weekends. Ah, memories.

This is what I remember of the Jersey Shore back then. I would have to get up too early on a weekend morning in order to join the funeral procession of cars down the Jersey Turnpike, all of us heading far enough south to reach a beach our respective females had deemed suitable for personable display. The male would drive, searching suburban neighborhoods for a parking spot that would lessen the hike to the beachhead with the requisite military load of gear, while the female applied enough make-up to attend a formal wedding, were we to be diverted by invitation.

Straggling to a boardwalk patrolled by privateers, we were banded like migratory birds after we'd paid for the privilege of broiling ourselves on someone else's property. Reconnoitering the sandy terrain, we'd stake out a patch of silica and dig in. Throughout the remains of the day, a Jimmy Buffet impersonator would drone incessantly, amid the odor of deep fried clam strips.

I love to be in the water, but my girlfriend didn't. She liked to lounge, saving her energy, I suppose, for the trek back to the car. Yet I was the odd bird there at the water's edge. The ritualistic behavior was designed for sightseeing. The only women to enter the ocean went in kicking and screaming, and came out swearing blue streaks while rearranging what little they wore to their original positions.

At some point, the obligatory stroll was taken along the shore, wetting the female to the ankles, thus proving she was indeed wearing a bathing suit, not just traipsing around in public in her underwear. Right about the time I'd worked a comfortable groove the shape of my ass into the hard-packed sand, we'd leave, in an attempt to beat the rest of the troops home, which always failed. The migration home was distinguished by the vain attempt to remain comfortable, despite first degree burns adhering to vinyl upholstery, and fingers of sandcrete forming in the sweat of one's butt crack.

I had tried on several occasions to promote the idea of stopping at Sandy Hook, to me a reasonable option that would have saved us time, money, sleep, and possibly extended, though certainly not salvaged, the relationship. Let's just say the sand wasn't quite the right texture.

The time-honored tradition of hitting the beach is a magnificent way to waste a summer. Yet having confessed to all the above in no way diminishes the impact of Bruce Springsteen, whose *Tunnel of Love* album is among the greatest works of art ever bestowed upon mankind.

~~~

This kind of sailing, along the coast, was generally the best we would learn to expect, for while folks referred to us as being "off sailing," it was a rare moment on the move when our engine wasn't running. I expected this to be the case for anyone not taking the fast and occasionally furious offshore route to destinations south. The inland ICW path simply requires a lot of motoring, if not for the frequent narrowness of the route, which occasionally resembles a wet two lane, then for the need to get some reliable miles in before the sun gives up on you. It's a daytime game show where the penalty for not making it through the maze with visibility is, in all probability, a night with little sleep, in a less-than-desirable anchorage, and the possibility of an early and expensive ticket home.

Listen, I know there are some militants scoffing at me. We met a handful of folks, usually whacked out on principle, who insisted on sailing whenever it was remotely feasible. Occasionally, I privately questioned the veracity of their claims. Regardless, I was thankful our engine held up, and that her virtually constant *thwackada thwackada* didn't drive me crazy, another of my pet fears. My Yanmar, let me tell you something, Bud. Right after Deb, she's my girl.

The challenge of Manasquan, and of each place we would visit for some time to come, was learning how to make our way into a completely new and unfamiliar place, in a mode of transportation we were still familiarizing ourselves with. Once there, we applied ourselves to finding a safe and secure anchor spot for the night, and staying out of trouble. There would be no pulling into a Holiday Inn, sticking her in park, and signing for room 114, down the hall next to the ice machine.

Staying out of trouble seems simple enough if you're still trapped in a schoolchild's mind. It meant get out of bed when Mom said so the third time, put on your uniform, don't forget the lunch she packed for you, do what the teacher says, and get on the right bus for home.

None of these rules are of much aid to a boater. On a boat, much of the trouble is invisible, like a bully in the bushes. When you meet up with it, each event is marked with an emotional seizure.

At the Manasquan Inlet, once we discovered that the anchorage we'd selected didn't work for us, the trick to staying out of trouble was to find someplace that *would* work. By the time we got to the inlet, there was no time for a vehicle with a maximum speed of seven miles per hour to turn around and head for the next convenient parking lot along the Jersey Shore. The length of the day being what it was in October, there was not often another handy stop *a little bit down the road.*

A recurring theme of the boating guides we used is what I like to call the "nautical caveat." Negative aspects of cruising are rarely volunteered in the boating biz, since they tend to have a negative impact on sales; for instance, any mention of the Christmas Winds, in regard to the Caribbean charter trade. Who in the world wants to find out that the very time frame one wishes to escape reality for the solace of a sailboat holiday puts one at the indifferent mercy of these atmospheric hellions?

There is rarely a place you might want to anchor that doesn't come with an asterisk attached. Some anchorages are too shallow for the boat you bought. Some have an overly soft bottom, nice for groping a woman, but not for gripping an anchor. Some are snag prone, which is to say full of all sorts of unidentified crap on the bottom (tree stumps, Chevy in-line blocks, other people's lost anchors), that confound your attempts to leave when you want to. Some provide little or no protection from wind, which again contributes to anchor drag. Some are filled with annoying boaters, which is in no way a self-indictment. Some are subject to strong shifting currents, which raises all sorts of specters. Some are *almost* big enough for a boat to fit safely and comfortably into. And some, the ones that seem to be too good to be true, will be full of boaters who thought the same thing you did last night, and got up earlier than you this morning to beat you to the spot, the sons of bitches.

My advice to folks fitting out for the ICW trip would be to take that money you were going to spend on a nifty EPIRB and buy as many guides as you can get your hands on. You're not likely to be learning a new language on this trip, unless it's previously undiscovered cuss words. Your evening reading will be about where you'll be trying to safely bed down tomorrow.

The most crucial aspect of having a good time on the ICW, in my opinion, is making sure you have a damn good idea of where you expect to be comfortably positioned before nightfall, and if you don't make it that far, know what you'll do instead. As Captain Art would say, have a backup plan for your backup plan. I know I spent too many beautiful days worrying if I was going to be safe and comfortable later that night. That was because Art hadn't laid into my ass hard enough yet.

∾∾∾

Art was a gift. He was a gift of Deb's work, since it was through an ex-boss of hers, Alex Garfield, that we were introduced to him. Thank you, Alex.

Art had been in Deb's business for years, but he also had a waterborne one, making occasional boat deliveries when he wasn't playing on his Pearson 30 in the Chesapeake. Art became our teacher, our confessor, our supplier, our guardian angel. He kept regular tabs on us, expressed shock and dismay at our meager chart supply, shipped cruiser guides, gave suggestions, checked weather systems, and encouraged us along. We might have made the trip without him, but then again we might not have. Every family should have an Art.

It wasn't Art, though, who came to our rescue in Manasquan, but a woman in a kayak. She must have watched us, as we'd extracted ourselves from a light grounding and then made yet another attempt to paste ourselves safely onto the shoulder of a very busy waterway. The attempt wasn't working. Oh God, day two.

"There's a beautiful anchorage up that little creek if you wait until high tide," she said as she paddled by. "Just watch the markers, because it gets shallow."

Yes it did, and once we snuck up and through Glimmer Glass Creek and under our first, and as it ultimately turned out, trickiest bridge opening, we were in Glimmer Glass Cove, every bit the fairytale spot it sounds.

Then we grounded ourselves but good. The bridge tender, after guiding us through a fit that'd make a Beyoncé ensemble look baggy, directed us on the safest path to where we could drop an anchor. For not the last time in this trip, I got my points of the compass confused, and buried our keel in seapoxy.

But Nigel Calder had taught me what to do in cases like this, so I took book knowledge and applied it to the real world. I got into our dinghy, and with anchor in tow, we executed a successful kedging maneuver, getting ourselves out of the jam I'd put us in.

Life was starting to look good. We were communicating properly on our radio (I don't think I'll ever get over being respectfully addressed as "Captain" on the VHF by somebody who actually belongs on the water), we were getting farther from home, I hadn't openly wept yet, and we were in a lovely harbor, with the anchor holding once again.

The next day, rather than leave our newfound safe haven, we did something that would become for us a common ritual. We went ashore in the role of cruisers. And though we were only three days divorced from a land we had always inhabited, we shared a palpable sense that something about us was now very different. We felt out of place among these land dwellers. Here we were, grownups with backpacks full of garbage, laundry (having yet to learn the art of fresh-clothing conservation) and empty water bottles, trying to make our way among these folks, who were, well, they were home already. Were we now homeless? Drifters? Vagabonds? What in fact were we? We had yet to discover our new identities. I looked a bit longingly at these people going about their business, each knowing what his or her purpose was.

Then a special thing happened. We fell into a shop called *Gatherings*. It wasn't hard to fall, what with a model schooner in the window, and among other knickknacks inside, the promise of more things nautical.

After a few minutes of browsing, we naturally spilled our guts to the shop owners about what we were doing with ourselves. The next thing we knew, gifts were being made of the things they'd noticed our eyes lingering over. The caretakers had been taken by our story. They had questions, the answers to some of which we still did not have. They wished to be kept informed. We promised as much, and left as celebrities.

We were to meet the same kind of reception elsewhere. People were taken by the story of a couple chucking it all for some adventure. And while I can now say that, whereas some of the adventure we discovered I'd wished to avoid, we were tickled to provide a glimpse of what was possible to souls willing to stick their necks out. Perhaps we'd stumbled on the essence of our identity. We were windows to the world of possibility, ambassadors of potential, role models for the little guy who wished to seek the special while remaining little. We were still a bit mangy. There was still much to learn.

~~~

On our way to Cape May, we discovered the gravitas of the uncharted hazard. Part way down New Jersey's coast, we started to see white water ahead. It was odd, and disconcerting. I looked at the charts and saw no shoal or other shallow hazard, but there it was, this wall of breakers. Since we were not all that far offshore, we headed farther out. There was plenty of ocean out there, stretching all the way to Europe, if I wasn't mistaken, so getting around posed no logistical challenge. Yet I found myself considerably agitated, if for no other reason than that I didn't understand the nature of the obstacle. Clearly this water, composed of the same material as everything around it, was taking on a disposition that could put a small boat in jeopardy.

In retrospect, the patch of water was easily avoided. Why had I chosen to let it so unnerve me? I suppose I figured, if here, then anywhere; if now, then why not the middle of the night, when we couldn't see it; if uncharted, then who knew what else was out there waiting to do us in?

With all that turmoil in my head, something happened that would repeat itself later down the road. In the midst of my self-constructed hell, a vision came along that, if it didn't entirely diffuse my fear, at least made me consider the perversity of my perspective.

As we skirted the breakers, imagining what would happen to us if we happened to stumble into such a maelstrom, a Jet Skier emerged from the midst of it. She couldn't have been more than sixteen. Were I not immersed in my thoughts of mortality, not to mention being a happily married man, I might have had lascivious thoughts. There was this cute thing waving to us while frolicking amid surf I viewed as deadly.

In some ways, my thinking was anything but perverse. Given the "right" conditions and poor judgment, one person's playground can be another's less-than-happy hunting ground. Still, this sea sprite was having way too much fun on her Jet Ski for my frayed ego.

I remember seeing a series of photographs once of a fellow who'd taken his sailboat through a watery pass near the Golden Gate Bridge. It was one of those *wrong place/wrong time* kinds of scenarios. Funny how a series of silent photos can make your testicles ache, as you watch a boat lifted, pitchpoled, dismasted, and ground up for chum by an indifferent ocean. But the surreal aspect to the photos was the presence of surfers around the event. These guys were in their element, with nothing but a floating plank and a wetsuit for protection. They'd watched a boat get demolished in a matter of moments by something that, to them, was nothing more than a "nice set."

~~~

One must have a fog story when writing about sailing. Ours arrived a few hours before we made the inlet at Cape May. I've heard of fog worse than this, and, in fact, been in some, in a car in the Canadian wilderness at night, on a narrow winding road, where leaving it would have been a very bad idea unless you were a bat. But this was our boat fog experience, and we began to see why people might go out afterward and buy a small fortune in electronic gadgetry.

We had our VHF radio, GPS, an air horn, and our wits. My wits told me not to panic, since the waters in which we were traveling were normally only inhabited by little guys like us, squeaking timidly along. I tried to ignore the voice in my head that said my wits didn't know squat.

There was a lens of visibility that extended out maybe fifty yards around the boat. It seemed as if we were in a globe that traveled with us, with a set of opaque white curtains drawn about the perimeter. Using GPS, we headed for the inlet at Cape May, giving ourselves a buffer so as not to discover its northern seawall the hard way.

By the time Cape May's inlet made itself visible to us, the fog had lifted somewhat, though the weather was still murky and threatening. We found ourselves part of an eerie procession of boats ghosting our way into the harbor via the channel.

You thought I was going to tell you how we missed the Queen Mary by the distance my manhood will never reach again as a result of the trauma, didn't you? Shame on you. I hope you have a safe trip when you give this a try. You might want to skip Maine entirely, though I hear it is lovely when the weather cooperates.

VHF chatter increased, as it always does near inlets, and we acquired a few new communication skills, among them, the security call, which announces a specific need for vigilance, as elucidated by the hailing station. In this case, voyagers were announcing their intent to transit the Cape May Canal, and so were making "any and all concerned traffic" aware of their presence and intent to stay close to the radio at the prescribed channel while conditions remained sketchy.

I thought this was all nifty, so I practiced the speech I heard and then announced our presence as well. I realized days later that I'd been announcing my intent to transit the Cape May Canal, which was not at all where we'd been. In fact we'd entered the Cape May Inlet. Having discovered my mistake, I wondered if there had been boaters out there that day scanning the milky horizon for the whereabouts of the invisible *Laura Lynn*.

Cape May gave us our first taste of cabin fever when the weather went sour on us, and given our distance from a safe dinghy dock, we were forced to endure each other's company in a space equivalent to a TGIF banquette, minus the cheerily suspendered waitperson. We practiced the ancient nautical art of putting to good use the time on our hands. I wrote my first log to the folks back home.

~~~

Log of the Laura Lynn Installment #1
Position :   38 degrees 56 minutes North Latitude, 74 degrees 54 minutes West Longitude
            Cape May, New Jersey

Ahoy all,

And greetings to all our family and friends. It's a rainy Saturday at the southernmost tip of New Jersey, a perfect time for finally checking in. Our apologies for taking this long to communicate. We've discovered that trading in all the complications of a land-based existence for the "simple life" on a thirty-four-foot boat does not inundate one with leisure time.

Our Laura Lynn has kept us busy from day one with all kinds of personal requests, like "I'm hungry for fuel," "This water is too shallow," "I wet myself all over," "I can't see in this fog." The usual little boat complaints. Boats, you know, are living organisms, and they feed on humans.

We chose October 2nd for our sail-away date. On good advice, we were looking for a date not too early in the hurricane season that we'd run into Zelda and not so late that we'd run into the advancing winter icepack. Until last night we've enjoyed exquisite weather, which gave us a chance to get comfortable with our boat and this new lifestyle.

We motored out of Long Island's Manhasset Bay around eight forty-five on Sunday morning to make a favorable passing through Hell Gate in the East River. Smooth sailing through New York Harbor, under the Verrazano, and on to our first anchorage, Horseshoe Cove on New Jersey's Sandy Hook.

October 3 was Sandy Hook to the Manasquan Inlet, where we found a beautiful anchorage in Glimmer Glass Cove. We spent the fourth there as well, organizing and exploring ashore, feeling in a few short days onboard like a couple of aliens visiting a small planet, laundry in tow.

And what friendly natives! Manasquan is a charming town, and if you ever go, please patronize "Gatherings," a nautical-based gift shop where the proprietors gave us a free pumpkin spice candle (my favorite) and offered the use of their car. Hey, Toto, we aren't in NYC anymore! Marylou, Danielle and Nancy, we hope to see you on the way back.

The fifth got us to Atlantic City, where we anchored by the bridge at Harrah's and were treated to the light show on its facade. Never left the boat except to refuel the next day. The only gambling we do is with the weather.

Which, after days of rolling our way, finally went bust here in Cape May, first with fog as we entered the harbor on the sixth, now with twenty-plus knot winds and hard rain. But we're hunkered down, the anchor is holding, and our lives are indeed transforming.

There is so much that happens to you when you make a drastic change in living conditions. Suffice it to say there is a steep learning curve, and you begin to adapt to this new existence. You begin to celebrate simple victories. We found the place we were headed for. Our anchor is holding. This cup of coffee tastes really good. The toilet flushed. We're on the Internet! Oh, no we're not. Oh yes we are. SEND THE MESSAGE NOW!

Of necessity, this e-mail has a general tone. There are so many of you out there we want to keep up-to-date, and you have such diverse backgrounds. As soon as we've caught up, we'll try to get more personal messages out. Deb is much better than me at this. Some of you have heard from her already while I was busy barking my shins and denting my cranium. She's the communications officer; I'm the mechanic. Heaven help us.

This is an amazing journey for us, but wherever we go you folks are close to our hearts. And now, off to the next safe harbor.

Fair winds,
Paul and Deb

Let's just stay here another day

∼∼∼

    This first log began an exercise that kept us emotionally in touch with home, and gave me another sense of mission. While I felt somewhat inadequate as ship's mechanic, I figured I could do a fair-to-middling job of keeping the gang back home informed. What strikes me, as I read back to those first few days, is the somewhat-forced rosy picture I was painting for the home team. Notice I hadn't mentioned the leak that had given me fits. Deb's lecture to me was let's not disappoint everyone with my special brand of bile-laden narrative. These people looked forward to this trip for us. They were investing emotions in it as well. Let's give them a good ride.

    I never did bother to count the number of times the word "vicarious" surfaced in the e-mail we got back. I could have made the argument that painting a realistic picture of the darker aspects of the trip just might content folks with the knowledge that they were making the right decision in keeping their homes and staying put. I may have tried the argument on Deb, but it was hard to escape the sense that this was a shared pleasure, so keeping it pleasurable was a good idea.

∼∼∼

The annual southerly migration of boaters along the Intracoastal Waterway comprises an impressively diverse group of travelers. The ICW certainly sees visitors from the eastern coastal states, but also folks from all across the U.S., many of whom have placed boats at convenient drop-off points for their annual migration. Then there is the very healthy (and may we just say marvelous) contingency of Canadians, who, while rightly proud of their heritage, are at least as keen as your typical Michigander to dodge as many snowflakes as possible. There are retirees, folks like us taking some time off from something (more often than not, midlife), younger and adventurous home-schooled families, and full-time professional live-aboards who make a go of it through investments, house rentals, and so on.

This loosely affiliated group shares the waterways with commercial traffic delivering cargo, tugs pushing, towing and nudging all sorts of non-self-locomotive contraptions, recreational and commercial fishermen in the act of catching, or trying to, anything a man will shove down his gullet and some things he won't. There are workboats, dredgers, day-trippers, and all manner of flotsam and jetsam for which one must keep a watchful eye out.

You will find among cruisers a communal sense I find lacking elsewhere, a virtually instant camaraderie, a shared vision for living life. There are rare exceptions, but there is an assumed bloodline running through cruisers that, while I would never pretend to know what transcends in the recesses of a foxhole under bombardment, I see it as an apt metaphor. We are a band, of sorts. Neither the size of the boat, nor its accompanying cruising kitty, nor the pedigree of the helmsman has a thing to do with the depth of generosity you'll find aboard.

I mentioned exceptions, and the crew of one vessel, lets just call her *Belle*, stands out in my mind. To the deep blue with her crew, and the privileged passengers whose precious pantaloons they wring.

Perhaps I overstate my case. Perhaps a group of musicians working out of a struggling Ford Econoline, having finished their last set at three in the morning in front of a now-comatose nest of revelers, having then peeled their sweat-caked gear from a beer-varnished stage, on preparing to leave the venue, the name of which will go forgotten, for a sum they'll spend as soon as they find a Denny's, before heading back to jobs to which each one day vows never to return, perhaps they share the same camaraderie I speak of, with other musicians. In which case, when they spot another broken-down van on the side of the road, they'll tow that band along with them to Denny's, where they'll share their Hungry Man Specials, before going at the transmission problem, or maybe it's a clutch problem. Is the clutch part of the transmission? Hopefully, though, the crew of the *Belle* won't have kidnapped the waitress, and forced her to serve them exclusively until they've stuffed their gullets up to their uvulas.

~~~

When the weather broke in Cape May, Deb and I had a chance to go ashore and check out an area renowned for its Victorian charm. What we ended up running into was our first meaningful friendship with a boating couple, Pat and Paul, from the vessel *Sea Star*.

Pat and Paul were slipped comfortably in a Cape May marina, and we were looking for a place to tie up our dinghy. Boating friendships begin as effortlessly as a shared glance passed over the rail. I can't be sure who offered up the first greeting in this case, but the formula is always a simple variant of "we're on a boat, you're from a boat, so how are you doing, fellow boater?", and you're off and running.

In our case, we ended up following *Sea Star* to two consecutive anchorages, we the willing stalkers, and in the process, discovering the art of "buddy boating." They appeared at an opportune time for us, as we'd discovered how meager our charting library really was. Paul is a cautious sailor, and their boat, a Nauticat 38, was well prepared. He led us up the Delaware Bay to a safe anchorage near the entrance to the C&D Canal, and then on to Chesapeake City.

It was in that charming town, from which it was a short canal ride to the Chesapeake, that land-based Samaritans took the baton. We were perilously low on diesel, having yet to acquire the very necessary knack for estimating fuel requirements. The only local diesel vender had reneged on a radioed affirmation of an abundant supply. Incomprehensibly to us, they said they were now saving it for their seaside restaurant. They must have a hell of a secret sauce.

I was psyching myself for the task of lugging a five-gallon jerry can of fuel on my head, when a young farmer drove us miles to and from the only station carrying the magic potion.

There was also the guy at the hardware store, who bothered to drive down to the waterfront after hours to deliver the only set of charts of the Chesapeake we could lay our hands on. We were beginning to benefit from the generosity of shore angels who team along the Eastern Seaboard. Was it because we'd become needy for the first time in our privileged lives, or was there something special about these souls who live within striking distance of the ocean's considerable influence? Those with experience tend to be extremely independent. They command a broad range of practical skills, and are generous with them when they discover those of us less well endowed.

Captain Art had read me the riot act over our lack of navigational aids, and was amassing a care package for the day we'd arrive in his area. In the mean time, we could make our way down the Chesapeake with our personally delivered charts.

Fueled and charted, we were able to relax. When boaters start to relax, they tend to collect. Sooner or later they start to make a little noise, usually not too obnoxiously, at least not if their audience is more boaters. We started out as four, and ended up eight or ten maybe, which is a manageable good time. I only bring this up because of one couple, whom I regret to say we never bumped into again, and I can only think that it was because by the time we awoke the next day, they were halfway to the Indian Ocean.

The crew of the *Muskrat* had perhaps the most romantic story of the trip. They were a British couple, having met while he was a helicopter rescue pilot. On a fateful day off a turbulent English Coast, his craft had received a Mayday call from an accomplished crew of a competitive racing vessel that had a critically injured crewman aboard.

When the basket came up, carrying the victim, our pilot described how he'd looked back from his seat at the controls and observed, peeking woozily out from underneath a blood-soaked bandage, *the loveliest pair of eyes.*

The image of those eyes stayed with him, and worked on him in ways that men, when searching for words, usually come up short on. Checking the incident report, he managed to track his passenger down, and armed with a bouquet of flowers and some unsettled notions about life, death and eternity, went to see how she was doing. To make a long story short, he made her the offer of a proper helicopter ride when she felt up to it, she took him up on his offer, and the rest, as they say . . .

Chapter 8

The Chesapeake

Let a smile be your umbrella.

As our trip progressed, Deb and I started to feel like characters in some kind of "pay it forward" movie, longing for the day when we could return the many favors freely offered to us. We hungered for the day when we had either the knowledge or the spare part with which we could bale out some other less fortunate crew. It would take a while.

~~~

10/13/05
Log of the Laura Lynn #2

Position :   39 degrees 9 minutes North Latitude, 76 degrees 15 minutes West Longitude
             Rock Hall, Maryland

Greetings all:

    The anchor line is taught, fighting off a northeast blow, the sky is battleship gray, spitting rain at anyone on deck with a chore to do, like keeping the topping lift (a piece of rope with a fancy name) from rattling against the mast all night long. Me, I'm happy as a clam.

    Why, you might ask, you envious seekers of Paradise? Cuz I'm sitting in a warm cabin that smells like BAKED CHICKEN! That's right, Chef Deb is doing chicken and a meatloaf simultaneously, with enough dexterity left over to make me a peach/berry smoothie. Plus, she's drying my shoes, bath towel, and wool cap with ancillary oven heat. Life is good.

    Now the women are howling. I can hear you all from here. What did I, the e-mail doodler, do to deserve this? What gives me the marbles to sit here and e-ruminate while Deb does everything else?

    How's about save our lives like five times yesterday? Which about breaks me even, when you consider I almost killed us both six times, give or take a fatality.

    Since last I tickled the keyboard, we have exited Cape May in South Jersey and spent a whole day going the wrong way, which is to say up Delaware Bay, away from the Bahamas. But there's a plan in there somewhere. It's a great way to experience some beautiful country and a great deal of nautical history in relatively protected waters.

    From Delaware Bay we transited the Chesapeake and Delaware Canal (C&D to intelligentsia such as ourselves) and started heading down the Chesapeake, reaching our present position in Rock Hall, Maryland. To get here, we've had to endure the most pleasant people you can imagine along the way. Folks who have given us rides for fuel and for groceries, folks who have delivered needed supplies to us, stranded as we are with nothing but feet to get us around on land. Folks who have taken the time to coach a couple of obvious neophytes in the ways of Poseidon. We are filled with gratitude to these people, so perhaps now is a good time to insert a couple of personal notes for all to view.

    Thank you, George (manager at our boatyard), for readying our boat for travel, and selflessly spending your own time teaching us countless lessons you've learned the hard way.

    Thank you, David (of The Rigging Locker), for setting up the Laura Lynn for the rigors of the road. She just took us for a sleigh ride yesterday, where we surfed the Chesapeake downwind, dodging crab pot buoys and wondering where everybody else was.

Oh, that's right, it's October, there's a small craft warning out, and the WEATHER SUCKS. Well rather, it blew, but the Laura Lynn took it in stride while a dismasted vessel was putting out a pan-pan message to the Baltimore Coast Guard.

Thank you, Mike (our surveyor and insurer), for having given Laura Lynn the once-over so we could go surfing with confidence, knowing we were properly insured. Should I have mentioned the surfing thing? Just kidding. We're hanging out in a slip sipping on sundowners. Oh, Cabana Girl? Another maraschino, please.

Thank you to our family members for provisioning our boat for us. You are in our thoughts constantly as we chow on soups, pastas and cookies in the warm glow of our lantern (courtesy of Aunt Janet), while Laura's bungees hold everything together. Honestly, Laura, I'm thinking we might sink without them.

Thank you to the kind-hearted crew of Sea Star, Pat and Paul, from Keane, New Hampshire, for letting us "buddy boat" for a crucial leg of our journey. You epitomize the generosity exhibited by fellow boaters we have met along the way.

And then there's Captain Art. Listen everybody, Captain Art's name is one whispered in awe on this boat. He is our guardian angel. He is the kid two years ahead of you making sure you don't screw up in school, that you know where the cafeteria is, and what food will make you puke. He lets you know which teachers to steer clear of, and makes sure nobody messes with you on the playground. Art, you rule. Thank you also Alex, for among all the other things, having introduced us to Art.

There are so many others out there, and we'll get to you. Thank you for your emotional support, for your e-mails, and the palpable sense that you are here with us. Know that if we could, we'd contact you more often. It's a challenge finding a Wi-Fi hot spot out in these anchorages. Deb is quite a sight, standing out on deck, laptop raised over her head in offering to the e-gods, hoping for a lock-in lasting long enough to get and send our mail. It would be a whole lot easier in a slip, but then we'd be paying upward of three dollars a foot per night for the privilege. Laura Lynn is thirty-four feet long. We anchor for free. We smell a little funky.

I suspect doing what we're doing is a little like having a baby. No matter how many Dr. Spock novels you read, how many parents you interrogate, how many binkies you stockpile in that gaudily appointed room, you're never quite ready for what shows up. Yet you survive, because you must. And you flourish, because, well I don't have that figured out yet.

Deb is looking at me because I'm using up far too much battery reserve, which is to say she fears I'm boring you. So be it. You have a delete button. You're adults. Except for you, Emily! Hi, sweetie-pie! And Tom and Joe! Hi, you guys! Here's my advice to you kids. Buy a boat together. And NEVER GROW UP!

That's all for now.

Fair winds,
Paul and Deb

Tastes like chicken!

~~~

Emily is our niece, and at the time of our trip, she was ten years old. Her mother Laura is our boat's namesake. Emily, who was born prematurely, has always been the cutest little thing. Times may be a changing for her, but at the time of our trip, it seemed appropriate to name our dinghy, an inflatable so small as to turn heads whenever she took us anywhere, after our little niece Em.

The rubber boat looked bigger in the West Marine store. We wanted something small enough to be able to store inflated on the foredeck, and still leave plenty of room for us to work around up there. I'd read that towing a dinghy offshore in rough weather was a bad idea, and while bareboating, we'd seen a few interesting things happen ourselves.

On our BVI charters, we weren't required to remove the outboard from our tender while underway. On one particularly squall-infested day, we once looked back in horror to see our tender going airborne, apparently attempting to disencumber itself of the irritating engine strapped to its back. Things tend to work their way loose on boats.

In the Leewards, where there is considerably more open-water sailing, the charter companies require that you remove the engine to a designated bracket when sailing between islands. It's a wise policy, but a pain in the neck, and elsewhere, a pain I addressed with conspicuous aspirin consumption.

I suspected a lot of work was in store for Deb and me, and I sought to avoid as much as humanly possible, since task avoidance is my strong suit. Life is full of compromise, and I gambled that a small dinghy, while limiting us to a certain style of travel, would pay for itself in ease of deployment and retrieval.

Inflatables aren't cheap, but this one, being small and on sale, was easier on the wallet, until I discovered the engine we presumed we already had for it turned out, at five horses, too large. The awesome powerplant overwhelmed the blowup, threatening to buckle it near the stern when power was applied. Technically, it was one horsepower over the legally prescribed limit of the dinghy's design parameters. I imagined being boarded by "Coasties" eager to make me pay for the extravagance. Hey there, Mr. Hotrod. Looking to smuggle Gummi Bears in from the deep end?

I looked around for a smaller engine, running ads, seeking a trade, but nothing came up. I found myself back at West Marine, purchasing a 3.3 hp, springing for the "deluxe" model, one with a "transmission" that provided neutral as well as forward. Interesting—an engine with no reverse. I tried hard to warm to the concept.

We stopped using neutral altogether, after severing two shear pins in short order. I guess the engineers who designed this little wonder wanted to protect its tender innards, and they did it with shear pins that would have snapped under the load placed on Pam Anderson's bra. New concept: pull the cord and you're off and running. Want to go backwards? Spin it around and point it the wrong way.

It goes to show you (I'll be repeating myself, since it's one of the great lessons of the trip) you can get used to about anything if you have to. I'd like that to be a hopeful thought, not one that fills you with anxiety. Humans are resilient buggers. We're resourceful, even the dumb ones, and can adapt to prevailing conditions as well as any vermin on the planet, given the motivation. If it's important enough, we'll figure it out.

Deb and I needed transportation to and from the mother ship. We needed to be able to store the dinghy, despite a paucity of deck space, an absence of davits (transom-mounted hoisting mechanisms), the accelerated dissolution of my spinal column, and a mate who claims to be muscularly challenged. There's more than one way to skin a cat, and when it comes to tenders, folks have stripped the kitty raw in ways that bring entertainment to the educated eye. Where there's a will to get someplace, there's a way to make it there.

~~~

We'd gotten ourselves a good way down the Chesapeake, and were contemplating the irony of what the guides had to say about our trip thus far. Our transit of Delaware Bay, a shallow body of water said to be fraught with danger under the proper conditions, had been a cakewalk. On the other hand, the Chesapeake is generally hailed as an Eden for boaters—beautiful and beneficent. In our few days upon her, we'd discovered her dark side. There was plenty of wind and rain, nasty chop, and we were further dismayed to find it so full of crab pots as to rival the coast of Maine for floating obstacles.

I began to curse the crabbers, these insatiable sea-meat mongers, who wouldn't even leave the main channels alone. In bad weather it's tough to spot the buoys, often appearing, when you can see them, as dark shapes against a dark sea, popping in and out of the chop. Deb would stand on the one side of the boat, I'd lean out the other, and we'd call out the approaching buoys in clock talk. *I got one at ten thirty. You see it? Got it! You're getting pretty close. I see it, but I got one at one o'clock too. I'm going to split 'em. Okay, here comes another one at eleven . . .*

Frankly I was a bit relieved to leave the open water of the Chesapeake for the narrow, snarling industrial traffic of Norfolk. Dodging freighters seemed for some reason a less threatening proposition. But to thoroughly dismiss the Chesapeake would be a maritime crime, for with any limited visit to a place, one runs the probable risk of misinterpreting its possibilities. Who of us doesn't have a skewed opinion of a person, a place, or some damn thing as the result of a visit of overly short duration? *What was it like in the desert? It was cold and wet, man. Cold and wet. The night I was there, anyway. Yeah, we were interviewing Saddam Hussein. That guy was a hoot.*

The fact is, the Chesapeake is a mammoth, multifaceted creature. I know this because I read about it. Beyond that, I'm unfit to judge other than to describe my very personal and limited experience upon her. Ask Captain Art, a man who has spent countless days investigating her every crevice (a tantalizing-sounding prospect), and his face lights up. Mention a spot you passed over for an alternative recommendation and he'll wax on for as long as you let him about what you missed. Art knows his watershed.

When we made it to Art's neck of the woods, he treated us to some down-home hospitality, driving from his boat in Oxford to take us to dinner. Another reality cruisers must come to grips with is the time-space continuum. It took Art twenty minutes to get to us by car. Had we boated to him, it would have consumed an entire day. You're right, you're right; that's part of the charm, but I'm glad he came to pick us up.

Art coached us in the journey we had ahead, handed over enough books to cure *Laura Lynn* of her port list, and then took us to a restaurant where we had the finest crab cakes I will probably ever experience as long as I live. May the stars allow me to put that assertion to the test countless times in the years to come. I'll take restaurant suggestions if you've got them.

~~~

This book will not be about listing every darn place we hit, and what all you should see and avoid. Many others offer that kind of book. They'll tell you where to stop, where to eat, and seeing as you've been traumatized by head duty, where to take a convenient dump. You should buy those books and read them religiously. You will profit from them in ways I often did not.

Me, I'm here to say that if you do this thing, and you *can* do it if you put your mind to it, you will have the experiences you're aching for. You'll cry at weird times from emotions the journey triggers, and you'll be confident that when you die, you'll do it with a big fat smile on your face. And that's the point of this cosmic trip, isn't it?

Oh all right, the restaurant is called *The Bridge*, and it's on Tilghman Island. The cakes seem kind of pricey, when you figure the crabs were snatched out of their rec rooms about a block away, but Art paid. Get your own angel; Art belongs to us.

Our boat was north of Oxford, in St. Michael's, a place we really enjoyed, particularly its maritime museum, which includes a boat-building shed where you can volunteer. Some places you go to and you just say, "And?" Other places you go to and you say, "Ah!" Why is that? Some places are just designed by man or nature to stroke the senses. Some designs feel right, like a woman's torso.

Of course not everyone's sensibilities are piqued the same way. There are those who thrill to the energy of the streets of New York City, which I personally find incomprehensible. There are those who warm to the chill of a mountainous trail, nice with the right shoes and a fresh bag of *gorp*. Some folks will refuse to leave the mall even if you napalm it.

I remember long ago standing in line with fellow enthusiasts at an extremely popular Michigan ice cream parlor, protectively clutching ticket stub #489 or so, when an industrial compressor blew a gasket, spewing a cloud of refrigerant into the atmosphere. People were bug-eyed and wheezing, but nobody gave his number up on the lengthy cue. Nothing spells bliss like a double dip of pralines and ammonia.

Then there are those who can think of nothing more soul stroking than a stand of palm trees clapping their approval of a tropical sea breeze. Yum. Whatever blows your skirt up, as Deb would say.

∾∾∾

We hadn't made it to the palms yet, but we did get our first sighting of dolphins, and it's hard to imagine ever growing tired of their company. We were pulling into one of those places that have no name but an improvised personal description. Some days you're in the mooring field in Spa Creek in Annapolis, some days you're on the north side of the channel where it widens off that first bend in the Little Wicomico, with a view of the old farmhouse. You don't even know how to pronounce where you are, but it's just lovely. And look over there. If it isn't *Sea Star*!

It happens all the time on the ICW. It may be a big country, but it's a narrow band of a waterway, with treasured stops along the way. The friends you make are usually heading the same direction you are, often with the same final destination. Regardless of the size of the boat, it'll usually be found about forty miles south of here tomorrow, barring engine failure, iffy weather, or the fact that you're having such a fine time right where you are. Often, after a conversation flavored with "sundowners," plans have changed to take advantage of newly forged friendships. We heard it more than once, and then started using the line ourselves; a boater's schedule is written in jello.

I think we might have known Pat and Paul were going to be there. We'd said goodbye at Chesapeake City because we chose to stay an extra day to look around, while they'd chosen to move on, let's say to attend a floral show, though conceivably simply to ditch us. Who could blame them?

Often your ears do the spotting. Most recreational boaters are not required to carry a VHF radio, but if they do and it is turned on, they're supposed to monitor channel 16. While this is generally a regulation more often honored in the breech, cruisers tend to be somewhat religious about it.

These days, there are a lot of electronic gewgaws available to your typical cruiser. You've got your depth finder (dynamite in the Ditch, for sure). You've got your GPS (killer, absolutely), your SSB (vinyl pocket protector optional), radar (pass the Grey Poupon, Tiffany), cell phone (who on the planet doesn't), and laptop with pirated navigational software that somehow interfaces with the aforementioned GPS. Without getting into it here in a major philosophical way, I'd say the VHF radio is still the most important piece of electronics to a cruiser on the ICW. Let me think about it. Yeah.

Aside from the VHF radio's utility, there is the obvious shameless pleasure of eavesdropping on what is essentially a nautical party line. Cruisers listen in to the live drama of Coast Guard rescues, and the aggravated complaints of commercial skippers trying to navigate through fleets of oblivious pleasure craft. We pick up security calls from neighboring boaters, who warn us of hazards ahead. We listen in to the convivial conversations of passing boats, sometimes joining in if we have useful input. Occasionally we rediscover the whereabouts of boaters we've made friends with along the way.

～～～

To "make friends" with someone—isn't that sweet sounding? It gives me goose bumps. The world should try it more often.

～～～

So here were our friends again. We had another chance to hop on over and share a sunset together. Get caught up. See how they were doing. Trade new stories. How often do you do that with your neighbors, whose porch you can hit with a paper airplane?

We always tended to hop Pat and Paul's way because, to put in frankly, their boat was so darn comfy. We were the sprightly ones, "the kids," ready at a moment's notice to toss ourselves into our dink to go hobnob with those who'd traded their stationary homes for floating ones. While I've made the claim that those on board tend to be a uniform lot when it comes to hospitality, the same can not be said for the boats we inhabit. Some of these babies are scrumptious. When it's your primary residence, it's fun to splurge.

Most of us on the water are curious as to how the other guy is pulling it off, and I can remember wanting desperately to see the interior of a Catalina 27 inhabited by a middle-aged couple. Coming from a thirty-four footer, I knew I could manage with forty. You visit the bigger boats to casually gawk. You visit smaller boats out of an aching curiosity.

How did they do it? With ingenious attention to detail. There was a place for everything, and everything was in its place. Furthermore, there was no place for anything else, and anything that had a place had multiple roles. This interesting couple was doing far better than surviving. They were flourishing in a floating phone booth without the phone.

∼∼∼

Log of the Laura Lynn Update #3
Position: 36 degrees, 50 degrees, 67 minutes North, 76 degrees, 18 minutes, 0 seconds West
Hospital Point, Norfolk, VA
Mile Zero of the Intracoastal Waterway

Ahoy all,

Most importantly, we're in a hot spot, so we can say hi again.
Since many of you are vicariously living the good life through these updates, we figure you need some details to color in the dream. Get out your Crayolas . . .
The head (toilet) is backing up. The boat is leaking like a sieve. The water heater is inexplicably delivering cold water. Inexplicably of course means Paul is too stupid to fix it. Paul has struck his head on boat appendages so often his skull has taken on the texture of a driving-range golf ball. He must raise a muck-laden, thirty-five pound anchor, plus twenty feet of chain (weight unknown) by hand each day with a dime-store spine before heading off for the next Shangri-la.
Then there's this hurricane on the way, named Wilma. Who in the world names these godforsaken things anyway? To be done in by a thing named Wilma would be the height of ignominy.
Yet we share the undeniable sense that something wondrous is happening to us. Here's the proof. During Paul's life on land, he was able to tolerate an entire day, and at the end of it have difficulty in recalling what had just happened to him. These days, we are able to recount our entire trip, at present two and a half weeks in, with near photographic recall. The good, bad, and ugly all stand out in vivid detail. We get giddy at dolphin sightings. Dodging crab pots, searching for navigational buoys, getting coldcocked by a Chesapeake wave—all are emblazoned in our memories. Normal routine events become nautical challenges, as when we were children learning to tell time, or tie a shoe. Little victories, like the successful retrieval of Oreos out of a

flooded compartment, are celebrated with high fives. This may change as we settle in, but we're still feeling what a small bird must feel when it finally has the nerve to take that first leap. Look where I am! Look what I'm doing!

There are friends back home who don't want us to rub in this sappy, life-affirming malarkey. So for them, we say picture yourself trying to take a shower in a phone booth with nicely chilled well water while somebody anxious to make a call is shaking the booth. Don't forget to remove the toilet paper or you'll soak it. Did I forget to mention your tub is your toilet, too?

We continue to meet warm and fascinating folks, people generous with their time and knowledge. We guess an obvious reason is we are all in this thing together. Life is admittedly more tenuous when lived on a boat, and you can use as large a support group as you can muster. In effect we become part of a human insurance policy, which isn't meant to sound glib. There is undeniable pleasure in sharing this challenge we've taken on. The saga continues.

Fair winds,
Deb and Paul

PS: Sexy or not sexy? After a long day of wave-bashing, you take an invigorating cold shower, convert the kitchen table into a bed, take all your clothes off, cuddle up, and count to see who has the most bruises. Lacerations count two points. You decide.

PPS/ some personal shout-outs:

- Mimi, St. Chris is doing a great job. Thank you again.
- Victor, there was no room for a guitar. Paul has a kazoo though, and is working on "Proud Mary."
- Cousin Rich, no idea when we'll get to Charleston, but when we do your doorbell will ring.
- Karen G, we'd like to pitch a new show, "Eating Out on $4 a Day."
- SZQ, we did what you suggested. Seven times.
- Mark S, their size hasn't changed. Deb made me do this. I wanted to stay home.
- Alex, I could clean up on the ICW. Think wipe-and-wear apparel for a new line.
- Big John, you are so right. He who owns little is little owned. But we could use a new head. And a bigger boat.
- Art, thanks again, Cap. We're alive because of you. Where's the closest hurricane hole?
- Jessy, we threw some of Deb's shoes out and there's room for you now. Meet us at the mouth of the Dismal Swamp.
- Iza, we found your Trumpy!
- Emmie, there is something special for you in one of the pictures!
- Bosco, it is a big ruse. Answer the door, would you?

*While Pat & Paul's boat was spacious,
they did tend to struggle with draft issues*

~~~

    The Chesapeake, the huge, historic body we'd only taken a peak at, was now behind us. Taking an audit of the stops, we'd hit in order, Georgetown off the Sassafrass, Rock Hall, St. Michael's, the lovely spot on the Little Wicomico, and Solomons.
    We had a considerable list of places we'd been told not to miss. We missed them. People spend lifetimes on the water discovering the Chesapeake. We reminded ourselves we had another shot on the way back. *On the way back.* The thought gave us chills.
    For all the emotional mileage we'd racked up, we were now officially anchored near Mile 1 of the ICW. Huh? Well, that's the way the Army Corps of Engineers sees it. Perhaps it had been agreed upon by the folks who make the maps. You stay off of our turf and we'll stay off of yours. We'll handle the Chesapeake. Okay, we'll take Delaware Bay and the C&D. Somehow folks tend to stay clear of Jersey (too shallow, as the euphemism goes), choosing to gawk at the Ferris wheels from offshore. Yo, what're you lookin' at, pal? State yer bizzness, or move yer fanny on outta here, like pronto.

Chapter 9

The Ditch

I hope they're not just following me.

There was the visceral sense that we'd entered a new phase of the trip. The broad expanse of the bay constricted as we approached Newport News, and the commercial traffic increased in frequency, size, and intent.

In short order we found ourselves hugging the shoulder to let huge container ships and military vessels pass us by. I had my first opportunity to identify the nautical sound of alarm, five short blasts, as a cruising sailboat inexplicably sauntered across the bow of a rapidly approaching container ship. I monitored Channel 13 and 16, waiting for what I figured would be the fuming voice of the big ship's captain, but never caught that show. Distances are hard to estimate on the water, particularly when they involve the big boys, as I'm sure this cruiser discovered. It sure looked close, to me.

Switching now to the books and charts Art had provided, we found a suitable anchorage at Hospital Point in Norfolk. As always, what appears a reasonable stop on the charts will have its challenges upon actual arrival. Regardless of how early you get up, someone will always have preceded you and taken up the choice anchor spot, thus initiating the intrigue.

Now the latecomers to the dance must keep their distance, not only from the anchored boat, but from any other obstruction, based on the swing room defined by the amount of rode the first guy puts out. One takes a look at the terrain, and the chart. There are rotted pilings over here, and there's a private mooring buoy over there, unoccupied now but maybe not later on. If he shows, he'll swing in a whole different pattern, and this is his home. It's too shallow over there, and too deep over here. Often within a few short yards of a preferred depth, the bottom will fall off, requiring considerably more rode (line attached to your anchor), thus creating a prohibitive swing radius. We'd be too close to that day marker when the current shifts, and too close to the channel over there. That spot looks nice, but the guidebook—not that one, this one—says the bottom is too soft, and everyone drags there. But *this* one doesn't say anything about it. Yeah, but *this* one does. Maybe that's why nobody else is there. And maybe we're all just a bunch of blind beggars leading each other to hell in a hand basket.

Our buddy Flex, whom we intended to catch up with down the road a spell, has spent his life on the water, first up where we live, when he was one of the water rats Deb's dad used to serve while bartending at Louie's, when Louie's was a respectable dive. Louie's, what was it, fourth generation of owners, grown weary from years of cracking open chilled oysters, had the good sense, I suppose, to sell out. Mr. Zwierlein, wherever you are, all the best to you. I'm sure you did the right thing for yourself and your family.

The new Louie's is a deplorable affair, a thoroughly rebuttressed (the old place was minutes away from falling into the sea) and redesigned cathedral to conspicuous consumption. The workmen did a marvelous job. The staff are forcibly gracious. It's just—what can one say?—spiffy.

Folks who used to drop by unannounced for dinner will now find themselves cued up for a half hour waiting on a table, only to find that the menu has, uh, changed, along the right-hand column. The bar stretches four times the length of the original. Gone are the hodge-podge of photos and memorabilia tacked like bandaids to the old walls, gone the mounted fish that no studied attention of the taxidermist could save from decay. Gone, I'm quite sure, would be the minipearl I'd found in an oyster, and then lost in a panic, it swept away now by the agents of entrepreneurship. Nothing is familiar. Waitpersons introduce themselves, but I do not know them. In short, Louie's no longer exists for me. It's said you can never go home again. While I may have a few hopeful oysters and a beer from time to time, I'll never find my way back to Louie's.

Places like the old Louie's are dropping like flies, succumbing to the pressures of waterside real estate values. Deb tells a story of a mother of an old friend from her business, before good old Doris herself passed on. As Doris's mom picked through an old photo album, an arched finger jabbed away at faces frozen in time, "Dead, dead, dead . . ."

That is the fate of many a fine dive. The last one I was aware of here, after we'd been displaced at Louie's, was a place we called "Bills" because we could never remember its actual name. It too is gone, despite the fact that plenty of folks showed up for, lets be generous and call it "the ambience," pronounced with a cynical trucker's drawl.

There's the rub, I suppose. In place of these shrines to my preferred way of life arise, well you can guess. Depending on the zoning, what pops up are private estates, condo developments, and where a restaurant endures, the implied theme is, "Bring your money, and we mean all of it!" The new Louie's, as a result, caters to a different clientele, one of gilt transportation, garish attire, and urgent hormonal issues.

Hey, where did Flex go? Well he made his way to Wrightsville Beach, South Carolina, where he spends a lot of time inside very large custom-designed boats, outfitting them with fanciful electronic innards. Erstwhile, he moves the floating estates back and forth for people too busy making money to pay for those innards, or too frightened to make the trip themselves. He's spent some time living on boats as well. Flex is a salty sweetheart of a guy, and I've finally come to my point. When the subject of dropping the hook comes up in conversation, he shudders. As regards the art of anchoring, Flex proclaims, "I hate it!"

~~~

In Norfolk we were again with old friends Pat and Paul. We finally bummed a ride with them on their tender, and "dinghy lust" was born. They had space, they had horsepower, they had range, and they had a high-and-dry ride. Think it over, and when you go, get as big an inflatable as you can reasonably accommodate.

A swell time was had in Norfolk. Now came the fork all cruisers are faced with, two intriguing choices from which to select one path. There was the well-scoured industrial route, the Virginia Cut, or alternatively the shallow, iffy route with, to our sensibilities, the far more enticing name: the Great Dismal Swamp Canal.

Because of their deeper draft, *Sea Star's* crew had selected the Virginia Cut. Because of Charlie Morgan's shallow mindedness, and the waterway's charming moniker, we were headed for the Dismal Swamp. This meant our paths would diverge, and given the vagaries of cruising, we might not see them, well, ever again.

~~~

The Great Dismal Swamp has a history far more dismal than the view. Slaves were largely "employed" to dig this trench for patriots like George Washington, who, among other national luminaries apparently, had a financial stake in its construction. It was doubtlessly a dismal job in the making, and striking off the now well-beaten path would have been equally unpleasant. That is precisely what more than a few slaves had done, forming communities within this swampy wilderness that our forefathers, concerning themselves with their own notions of freedom, cared less about scouring for lost labor.

One young singlehander, seemingly well versed in history and more than willing to share it with any captured audience, told us something to watch out for along the swamp route (you will run into the occasional cruiser who comes off as just a bit too congenial. When you do, run for it if you are short on free time. More on this topic later). The fellow claimed that escaped slaves, in creating reliable hidden pathways to their enclaves, had placed notches in trees to guide knowing travelers to safety. The trees that had survived till the present have grown some, so we were advised to look high up to discover those very way signs placed so many years ago. Now I've not been able to verify this, and my brother, one of my gurus, has informed me that a notch cut into a tree will stay right where it is, heightwise, no matter how tall that tree grows. What then to make of our chatty singlehander's story, do you suppose?

Let us know if you take that route and find any notches somewhere up there. If you are interested, hurry. The nation's oldest hand-dug canal, annually threatened with financial ruin, may not be long for this world. I'm guessing it could be saved for the price of the ordinance hanging from a single wing of any of the ubiquitous fighters that frequent the skies along the ICW. A nation's got to have priorities though. You will see quite the air show from time to time—Teenagers protecting our freedom over routes that slaves dug for patriots.

~~~

The Dismal Swamp Canal provided the first opportunity for Deb and me to try our hand at a set of locks. Upstaters, Canadians, and Great Circle Routers face them in New York, and locks are encountered elsewhere, including the Virginia Cut, but I must say it's a gentle carnival ride. Read of the procedure ahead of time, follow the directions of the locktenders, and enjoy your liquid elevator ride.

A lot of the anxiety of boat handling can be assuaged ahead of time through a little practice, as suggested by one of our mentors, George Martin. Our shipyard manager advised us to go out and practice maneuvering our boat around a channel marker or buoy of some sort. He advised us to just keep practicing pulling up to it, in forward, in reverse, putting it on the starboard side, on the port side, with wind and currents coming from different directions. He was showing us how to become familiar with the way our boat handled under motor, which is how one is very frequently getting around, despite all the nicely furled canvas onboard. It is a great idea. Never seeming to possess the spare time, we opted instead for the anxiety.

The northern lock of the Dismal Swamp, Deep Creek Lock owns the distinction of having as its regular tender Mr. Robert Peek, a charming, entertaining young man, and generous with his knowledge of the area. I will save a Robert story for later. Keep it on Channel 16.

After Deep Creek Lock, it's a couple of straightaways to the Dismal Swamp Visitor Center in North Carolina. Here was our first honest-to-goodness raft-up. We were three deep, in about three columns. I've been told the center has hosted boats five deep, which would make it virtually impossible for another boat to pass by, but then why would one want to? It's *Animal House* for the boating crowd.

Having earlier in the day paid our fond farewells to the crew of *Sea Star*, we were now faced with an orgy of new friends. On average, every two boatloads of crew will yield at least one party planner aboard, and that evening there was a smorgasbord onshore of impressive scope. Deb and I, still new to the game, took copious notes. There was information on food storage, storm avoidance, stops one mustn't miss, and when I mentioned our leak, it was a matter of minutes before four self-made mechanics were on their hands and knees, flashlights in hand, poking around in our bilge. In retrospect, one of them had had the solution. I simply was unable to believe the symptoms pointed to the disease he'd suggested. Harley and Betty, how are you guys? Well, we hope. Jeez, we miss you.

Most all of us headed off the next day, first negotiating the South Lock, a breeze since we'd passed Mr. Peek's class the day before, and then on to the famed complimentary slips of Elizabeth City, North Carolina.

~~~

Log of the Laura Lynn Update #4
Latitude: 38 degrees 17.91 minutes N
Longitude: 76 degrees 13.11 minutes W
Elizabeth City, North Carolina
The Welcome Dock

Ahoy!

Here we are in one of boating's friendliest communities, made so to a large extent by the efforts of one man, in memory of his beloved wife. Fred Fearing has been welcoming cruisers since the early eighties, and with the aid of his "Rose Buddies" has created a seaside area with free dockage for transient boaters in a charming community. While the traditional roses he used to hand-deliver to visiting female crew members have gone the way of the economy, he and his group still see to it that boats make easy entries and exits at the complimentary slips provided. Fred and Rose Buddies, we heartily salute you!

Some foul weather here has given us the opportunity to contemplate the great irony of the trip so far, as well as ameliorate its many symptoms. It turns out that our attempt to escape the rat race has far from delivered us from the compulsion to race. In fact, we find ourselves racing incessantly. We race the sun, as we attempt to reach a safe anchorage each day before dark. We race local and large-scale weather systems. We race river and tidal currents, and bridge and lock schedules. We race the approach of winter, and our desire to be comfortably anchored instead of pounding waves in the cockpit. We even occasionally race our fellow boaters. We pretend we're admiring the fine lines of their vessels (lovely, certainly), but we are in fact checking our progress against theirs. We wave merrily at each other, fellow travelers, inspecting each other's sail trim as we do. Oh yeah, it's a race. The Laura Lynn doesn't fare too badly, all in all.

When a little bad weather comes along, we relish the opportunity to stay put for a while, and attend to the many projects that have lain dormant. Those persistent leaks, that unpleasant odor, this e-mail to you all.

Fair winds,
Paul and Deb

Here's a new feature: What's Hot/What's Not

What's Hot:
- Squeezable condiments
- Discovering the many food products that do not need refrigeration
- Advice from boaters far more experienced than you
- An anchor that doesn't drag
- Dolphins surfing your bow wave
- Finding the source of the leak (please, God!)
- GPS
- The kindnesses of strangers
- Wi-Fi connections
- Canadians
- Colombians
- Oreos

What's Not:
- Laundromats at which the soap dispensers do not work
- Finding things floating INSIDE the boat
- Cold showers
- Five feet, nine inches of headroom (here and there), Munchkins excluded
- Humidity

Personal Shout-Outs:

~ Father Bob! You are in our thoughts each day. Stay off those skates for a while, okay? We'll send you some pix of the Locks in the Great Dismal Swamp. Brings back memories of you and Perk.
~ Kara, my one and only goddaughter, I hope you get this. I love you.

- Mike L. and Mike P., our computer gurus. How do we make these jpegs smaller in Windows 2000??? Some folks are groaning at the huge downloads. Also, how about keyboard access to the degree sign for my lats and longs?
- Sharon, the pillows are fantastic. Give Sasha an ear-scratch for us.
- Doug, thanks for liquidating the business for us. You're financing our trip with those eBay transactions.
- To the fine staff at the North Carolina Welcome Center, thank you for everything. Good luck to you all.
- Henry, you are THE MAN!
- Andrea and Lisa, a canoe ride on a still pond is sounding real good to us right now.

~~~

Deb with Fred Fearing. I've got an eye on you, Fred.

~~~

We were starting to get enthusiastic feedback from our logs. In particular, the *What's Hot/What's Not* section was resonating, not all that surprising when one thinks about it. Don't you often grade your day as it nears its end? *How'd it go today, honey? Well, I got a hint that I might get a raise, I got stopped for speeding but was issued a warning, and I stepped in some dog crap. I give it a solid B.*

It was also my opportunity to say hi to important individuals, because I sort of clam up when I realize how many people I should be saying hi to, and how few I've gotten to so far. I often succumb to "task saturation," a great phrase I learned from *The Perfect Storm*, one of those books you should save till your trip is over.

This bulk e-mail thing was kind of cheating, like using the power of the computer to solicit business:

> Hi, dear friends **Paul and Debbie Koestner!**
> It's been a while since we've contacted you to ask how you are, and whether you feel all your insurance needs are being met . . .

I'm including our logs as they originally appeared on everyone's computer at home, minus the typos, which have been pointed out by the more anal recipients, and the photos, which are cost prohibitive. Then what self-respecting author manqué wouldn't want to take advantage of the opportunity to do a little fine-tuning from a cool remove? After all, the logs were written under some form of duress. If cold showers aren't torture, I don't know what is.

Doug Underdahl, a.k.a. Long Valley Equipment, deserves his own book, and he'll write it himself when he has time. I met him after I'd graduated with an MFA in film and television from NYU, and he was an undergraduate there. Frankly, he was the teacher then, and still is today. He is self-nicknamed "Underbudget," but I call him "Can Do Doug," so he's got quite the handle in my PDA.

Doug took the viable hardware of my forsaken film career and sold the components off on eBay. Online auctions require skills I have yet to master. It's a shame, my wife feels, looking at all the miserable crap I've accumulated. She's since opened a PayPal account, so I suppose "learn to eBay" should go on my "to do" list. In any event, Doug took a reasonable commission, and Deb and I went sailing for a year.

Doug is the kind of guy who, when you tell him you have to go to the hospital for brain surgery, goes, "Oh man, you don't need to waste your money on those guys. We can do it ourselves," and he'll put together a list of tools to rent at Home Depot.

Invariably, Doug has been proven right, so the weirdest irony about this trip is that I took it, not him. All I can think is that he's probably waiting to do it in an innertube, family in tow, his leak a self-inflicted one just to make it interesting.

We did not burden our loved ones with the details of Hurricane Wilma. In fact I will not now succumb to the dramatic tyranny of inflating any personal experience we might have had with any hurricane that had an impact on the United States in 2005. If you are deeply disappointed you're not finding stories here where life and limb are regularly threatened, google the 2005 hurricane season and read to your heart's content, sicko.

To those of you with a healthy aversion to catastrophe, I welcome you back. Chicken Little.

Hurricane Wilma was to be the closest tropical storm system we had to contend with. We thought we were safely tucked into Elizabeth City, at one of those complimentary slips.

The problem with a slip is that it pretty much insists on presenting you to the weather the way the slip is oriented, regardless of the direction from which the weather is actually approaching. Many seasoned cruisers prefer lying to an anchor in foul weather. Connect yourself properly to a well-placed, well-scoped anchor, and you can ride out a storm much more comfortably than when staked to a slip using two bowlines, two stern lines, four spring lines, and enough fenders to cushion the shock of continents colliding.

We found that out in Elizabeth City with Hurricane Wilma. We happened to be caught in a poor angle in the slip, with too much fetch, which is the distance the wind has to work on an open body of water. The greater the fetch, the larger the waves are allowed to build. Wilma's winds were coming off our starboard quarter, or right hip, at about thirty-five knots. Had fate not been kind to us, it could have been worse.

What's to be done, though, when your boat is bucking like a horny stallion anxious to mount the seawall, and you've insufficient line to prevent it from doing so?

You stare in wonderment and gratitude when total strangers, seeing your predicament, hop aboard without asking permission, carrying spare lines and fenders, and proceed to secure your vessel against harm. They work like fiends, sculpting knots quicker than you can name them. Then they leave with a kind word or a quick nod, oblivious to the tears of relief hidden by the rain, on to take care of the next boater in line for triage. This is the kind of treatment that humbles one to the depth of one's humbleability within the boater community.

Our bow pulpit had gotten popped off its perch, but that was the worst of it. Before the night was over, the winds had died down, and we had weathered Wilma. There is a special sense of oneness with nature after having survived a quarrel with her. The world is a lovely, benign place to inhabit once the squall has petered out. Hard-learned lessons will be reviewed with a confidence they will not be forgotten. The day after Wilma, everyone was taking in deeper breaths, relishing longer views of the scenery, spreading wider grins. We tracked down our Good Samaritans and thanked them profusely. New lesson learned. You can never have enough properly sized line onboard.

The kindnesses of strangers would not abate. In Oriental, North Carolina, Ken, aboard *Second Wind* donated a day to the plumbing problem that had prevented us from having hot water. What was supposed to be an ingenious use of the heat generated by our running engine to provide hot water had till this point been a painfully broken promise.

~~~

Log of the Laura Lynn Update #5
October 31st
Latitude: 34° 43.5' North
Longitude: 76° 40' West
Town Creek
Beaufort, NC

Two words. Two words that instill in every cruiser a craven lust that will not abate until it has been appeased. Two words, uttered like the confession of a wanton criminal setting his conscience free at the gallows. Two words to make a grown man giddy as a schoolgirl doused by Usher's sweat glands. Hot showers.

And now we got 'em, thanks once again to the immense generosity of another water-born Samaritan. Thank you, Ken, out there somewhere with Donna aboard **Second Wind**, for reading our service manual cover to cover, discovering a plumbing mistake, correcting it, and in the course of giving us our humanity back, making me a better boater. As the saying goes, "Give a man a fish, and he eats today. Teach a man to fish, and he eats until he gets sick of eating fish." Thank you, Ken, stunt pilot, mechanical wizard, Good Samaritan, teacher.

So here we are, smelling like a rose, working our way down the Carolina coasts. What have you missed? There was that primal anchorage before the Alligator-Pungo River Canal, where we could easily imagine we'd entered a prehistoric time warp. What are those flying above us? Pterodactyls, perhaps? No, judging by their cry, wing shape, and air speed, those would be FA-18s conducting mock dogfights. Yowza.

We watched, bemused, as twenty-year-old pilots practiced maneuvers into the evening. Our tax dollars at play. I'm no mathematician, but I'm guessing that about every four seconds those kids burned enough fuel to get Deb and me to and from the Bahamas. Bill Wander probably knows the stat, but I know what he'd say. Classified info. If he told me, he'd have to kill me.

Here's one of my favorite sayings Bill taught me, from his days hobnobbing with Navy pilots, one Ken might get a kick out of: flare to land, squat to pee. That's an insider for the flyboys out there.

Here's another we just heard in Oriental, a town named after the nameplate pulled off a sunken ship. The saying goes, "If I were doing any better, I'd need a twin." That's just how we feel. The trip is exceeding our every expectation. There is something about these seaside communities. They sense the simple urgency of a boater's life. It's an ethereal existence, living on a surface that never stops moving, one that conspires to ruin your sleep if you aren't meticulous about your every chore, or ruin it anyway with the aid of Mother Nature's many minions. Each time we see a beached boat, there's an eerie feeling not unlike that which accompanies the discovery of a dead animal along a scenic hiking trail. Always there are lurking the darker realities.

Ooh, spooky-scary. But then it's Halloween! Whatever will we do if we get trick-or-treaters? Oreos and a dinghy ride to shore, I suppose. No, Deb says she has some Reese's Pieces, just in case. Now that is sweating the details.

What's Hot/What's Not

HOT:
> Crab cakes
> Nora Jones
> Those pigtail holders with the little balls on the ends
> Cream of Wheat
> iPods
> Peanut butter and jelly
> Compatibility
> Bungees

NOT:
> Catastrophic bungee failure
> Sticking to the plan when the plan sucks
> The suction cups on any kind of caddy gizmo. Just bolt it on!

> And automated answering services of businesses:

> "Thank you for calling the company that double-billed you for services never rendered. Please take note of changes to our menu options. If you'd like to listen in Sri Lanken, press one. If you'd like to listen in Pig Latin, press ootay. If you'd like to continue in English . . . That is not a valid option . . . If you'd like to . . . That is not a valid option. If you'd like to continue in English, press five. If you'd like to speak to an actual person, you can just forget about it right now. Push all the buttons you want, we're not answering. Operators are standing by, eating Krispy Kremes and listening to you on speaker-phone whimper like a child. We're taking bets on how long you'll stay on the line before you slam the phone against the wall in a homicidal rage. You're up to forty-seven button pushes now. It looks like Larry stands to win fifty bucks. Now here's some Sade to further push you toward the brink of insanity . . ."

> Observation of the day:
> It takes water to live. It takes coffee (very light for Deb, light and very sweet for Paul) to live large.

Shout-Outs:

~ Too Too! How are you? Where is your town? Can we sail there?
~ Geoff, is the part of the deck I helped with still standing?
~ Perry, not only did we wave, we hugged and kissed it for you too.
~ Lisa, Deb hasn't had a pedicure since we left! They're no longer feet, they're paws.
~ Thank you Michael P, cyber guru. Now our pictures are smaller and we can send more!
~ Karen P, congratulations on your engagement to Mike! Think honeymoon in the islands.

~ Jennifer "Scuba Bud," we haven't been seasick yet, but we've done precious little in the way of severe weather sailing, our path being a generally protected one. We're told it's only a matter of time. Claustrophobia is a different matter. While it hasn't reached critical mass, we often find ourselves repeating the common cruiser's lament, "Oh for a couple more feet of boat."
~ Hola, Miamians Jana and Larry! Are you in one piece?

~~~

A temporary village is assembled At the North Carolina Visitor Center

~~~

At Oriental, a significant mood shift occurred. We'd solved two of the three nagging technical issues dogging us. We now had hot water, which primarily meant hot showers. Not to overstate the issue, but we Americans can really become ensconced in our creature comforts. There are other ways of warming water on a boat, but it was great to simply turn on the engine, roll down the river, and turn on the spigot. We had a solar shower, an inflatable bladder that would prove itself in the Abacos, but it was now November, and we weren't far enough south for it to become trustworthy just yet.

You know what it's like to get up on a chilly, gray November morning, with a layer of condensed water vapor, your last night's living act of defiance, coating everything?

Your greasy mat of a head has assumed the appearance of unidentified roadkill, and the rest of you isn't about to point fingers. A cold shower, if you're living at home, is unacceptable. On a boat, under these conditions, it is morale obliterating.

We'd also been dogged with a head problem. Our toilet was becoming more and more reluctant to flush. I'd finally worked up the nerve to undertake a rebuild of this simple, hand-operated mechanism. I didn't have to proceed far when I discovered the problem, a deformed joker valve.

There are few items on a boat that seem so perfectly named as the joker valve. It is a duckbilled affair that, when it ceases to do its job, takes on the personality of the insidious malcontent who plagued Batman. Modern plumbing is another blessing of the gods that receives too few prayers of thanks from land-dwellers. The toilet at home, aside from the occasional need for a handle-jiggle, just about always works. When it doesn't, we are in the mood to order human heads to roll, and a new pair of shoes.

On a boat, you thank the heavens every time the head works. You praise Allah for conveniently spaced pump-out facilities, and the heavenly hosts when the service is free. You tempt the Devil offshore as often for the opportunity to pump overboard what inshore you must by law and good conscience store in that pathetically small holding tank. That tank, try as it might, never quite comes up smelling like a rose.

Fixing the joker valve, while simple, is not a joke. It is, like all head duty, an unpleasant task. Get used to the notion of unpleasantness. I had to replace the valve on the trip twice. Each time the job was over, I was more relieved than the day we heard Hurricane Wilma was heading out to sea.

All that was left was the mystery leak. Were that to be solved, I could die in peace.

~~~

As previously mentioned, when you spend only a day or two someplace new, all it might take is a great meal, a chance meeting, or a lost filling to seal its fate in your memory. As I look back at the trip, my taste for Georgetown was tainted by the hours wasted there attempting to recover money that had been consumed by an ATM machine.

I once went on a vacation with an old girlfriend (the one from the Jersey Shore) to Cancun, where, after consuming a colorful drink, she proceeded to vomit for five days straight. I haven't seen her in decades, but I doubt she's ever returned to that vacation hot spot.

In the case of St. Augustine, a town that has left many with pleasant memories, I was left only with the desire to leave. But that's a story for later.

The trip was, like a life, a series of emotional stops, where always there is the temptation to imagine ahead. While we occasionally convince ourselves that we may pass this way again, in truth, time is the terrain we are traveling over. Northbound, next season, tomorrow, everything will be different.

~~~

Log of the Laura Lynn Update #6
November 6th
Latitude: 33° 08.942' North
Longitude: 79° 19.209' West

    The parade continues. That's what it is on the ICW. Some days we start alone on a secluded river, sometimes rafted up with a gaggle of snowbirds. Sooner or later we're all in line taking in the scenery at the breathtaking pace of about seven miles per hour, give or take a knot. A knot is equivalent to, oh just look it up. Most of you could keep up with us on shore with proper track shoes and a chain saw.
    This is precisely what the doctor ordered. We pass communities along the way, peaceful, laid-back, with citizens sporting unfurrowed brows. We see families on docks, couples in skiffs, buddies on bass boats, fathers, sons, wives, and daughters, sharing unhurried time. All are enjoying the outdoors. Okay, maybe not the shrimpers. That there looks like real work.
    We pass on through, this parade of Northerners from Toronto, Sandusky, Elmira, Port Washington. The locals watch and wave, and we wave back. Or we initiate the wave, and it is returned, sometimes a big double-armed one, occasionally the windshield wiper, or a papal "screw-in-the-lightbulb," sometimes just a raised hand and nod of the baseball cap. It is rare that you get the vacant stare, likely a remnant of the Civil War. We did after all just see our first Confederate flag yesterday. We are in The South now.
    Forgive me if I effuse over the wave. I really dig it. Welcome to the pleasant planet earth.
    When I was young, I attempted to overcome powerfully nerdy tendencies with the acquisition of a motorcycle, hard-won from summers spent wrapping smoke sausage on my arm at the meat factory. I remained a nerd, but enjoyed the exhilarating feeling on the bike, not unlike the feeling one gets while sailing.
    An ancillary pleasure of cycle riding was the privilege of sharing the biker wave, an understated raising of the left hand at passing fellow bikers, as if to say, "Yes, we are brothers, members of a rare breed, flying by the seat of our pants. Ride like the wind, dude." None could tell that beneath the Darth Vader helmet there lurked the soul of a nerd. Except the Harley riders. Those ugly-by-design road villains (I make the obvious exceptions of my brother John, neighbor Dan, and cousin Tom) recognized me for what I was, a geek pansy on a rice-burning scooter. They had my number.
    The Harley rider's equivalent on the water is dressed head to toe in camouflage; his boat is camo, his girl and bird dog are in camo. He's still angry he was born too late to fight for the Rebs, but he can get even some by staring at your arm as if it were some kind of sissy-boy way of surrendering too late. He's got some fish to fry, Bud.
    Most folks, though, honor the fine maritime tradition of waving at every passing watercraft that offers the congenial salute. It generally comes with a nice smile too, and I'm glad to say that the tradition appears to be getting dutifully passed on to the next generation. Encountering a small boat with a father at the helm and two preschoolers cute as buttons next to him, we offered our special kiddy wave (it is different from an adult wave. Try it. See?). "Wave back, girls," the father gently commanded, and they did, though I'm not sure they understood its import at their tender age. I suspect, as with shoes and boys, they'll come around in time.

We move on, the faster passing the slower (we always seem to end up the caboose) after polite radio exchanges, making our way toward whatever next anchorage we've chosen for A) anchor holding quality, B) protection from wind, C) current and D) scenic potential.

Along the way we see remarkable things, among them, the frequent dolphin sightings. I swear they come to our boat more than others, and I have a theory as to why. It's because of Deb's squeals of delight. I believe she has unwittingly fallen on precisely the same frequency they use to communicate. Further, that sound that so terrifies me when caught unawares (three times now, one shy of a heart attack) and convinces me we're about to strike a bridge, is at the same time announcing in Flippereze, "It's party time, and there's an open bar!"

A fellow boater swears dolphins like to listen to music. I asked what kind they might prefer, and he said anything with a beat. When pressed, he suggested Dean Martin. I have one Deano song on the iPod, so we've been listening to a lot of "Dream a Little Dream For Me."

Folks Want to Know:

Bill Wander has this to say:

So, I bet you don't get lost on your boat like you did on the Stennis (author's note: We did a job together on that aircraft carrier). How much time are you spending under sail, and how much time under motor? Do you miss turning the water on and just letting it run? Getting your grog ration? How are the limes holding up?

No Bill, I haven't gotten lost on the boat, though we've been lost in the boat more times than I care to remember. Following this ICW trail can get tricky, believe it or not. And I've lost just about everything I put on the boat, at one time or another.

We motor most of the time, motor-sail whenever possible, and were able to sail exclusively much of the Jersey Shore and the Chesapeake, when conditions were favorable.

Regarding water consumption, as Jimmy Buffett says, "It's all about the water, H2O" (from "Don't Stop the Carnival") We knew this would be a challenge. Sixty gallons of freshwater will go fast if you're not extremely careful.

Deb is making sure we are properly nourished and I'm suitably lubricated but still fit for duty.

What's Hot/What's Not

Hot:
    Free weekend cell service
    Spooning
    Keeping up with personal hygiene
    Global knives

Not:
    Crows relieving themselves from the spreaders

Shout-Outs:

- Pierrick, welcome home! Glad you made it back with the same size head.
- Aunt Emilie, If we had a tub of your peanut butter pieces, this trip would be PERFECT.
- Nora, don't know if the reason our ribs are aching is from bouncing off bulkheads or reading your jokes. Keep 'em coming
- Vin, we'll take 10lbs of elk packed in dry ice
- MB, isn't mental telepathy spooky? Really, you don't say. Tell 'em we said hi. Oh you did.
- Mom, only 386 miles to go!

The Boater Wave

Deb's mom was anxiously awaiting our arrival in Jensen Beach, Florida, several hundred miles down the road. I was confident we'd make it for Christmas, but Thanksgiving? Please, not another reason to hurry.

We'd established a rhythm to our days. Our routines became fairly polished, our chores delineated. On a trip where every day or so we'd be someplace new, there is a certain comfort in knowing just what needs to be done, and who is going to do it.

On those days where we were staying put, there was an air of decadence about us. No reason to rush anything, no beating of the Joneses to the anchor, no factoring of mileage, no comparison of suitable anchorages. The singular thought was *are we ready for coffee?*

Little things matter a lot. The boat is staying put, batteries are charged, toilet is working, with ample holding tank capacity, coffee smells great, night decor has been swapped for day.

There was nothing fancy about it, but our commitment to sleeping in the saloon was an important one. It freed up the V-berth for storage (I'm willing to bet storage is an issue on the Queen Mary), and once we came up with the simple conversion method for creating a queen-size bed out of the kitchen table, we were living large.

Sleeping well cannot be overstated. I'm a particularly antsy sleeper, and had been anxious about how I might fare on the trip. Would I constantly worry about a dragging anchor? Would I be a raging bag of restless bones?

A successful string of safe anchorages goes a long way toward encouraging a good night's sleep. As you gain experience, you grow to trust your ground tackle and techniques. We were getting the hang of picking our spots, and learning to cope with the situation when we were wrong, and had to move. Too often for my taste, a wind or tidal shift put us too close to somebody who only hours earlier was a safe distance away from us. People were generally congenial about close quarters, but I found myself a whole lot more comfortable putting my head on the pillow when I knew we could swing like salsa dancers and not end up in our neighbor's cockpit.

All this good karma goes away in the blink of an eye when things go haywire. I remember a certain side channel we sought refuge in, off the main thoroughfare. We'd been pushing into a heavy current, with no immediate relief in sight. We realized we could plow away for several more hours, burn lots of fuel and maybe get to a good anchorage, or stop right there and make the best of it. The spot was listed by Skipper Bob, a popular provider of waterway guides, as a viable anchorage, albeit with a heavy shifting current (damn!) and a questionable substrate, with potential for snagging (double damn!).

We'd recently switched to using a 33lb Bruce anchor to save me a modicum of agony over the 35lb CQR. The Bruce had been working admirably, and so he went over the side with an anchor buoy attached. There was one other boat nearby, a single-hander who seemed to be sticking. We set up shop, and I began to monitor our position.

Usually you can tell pretty soon if you're going anywhere or not, but for the life of me, I sat there thinking, *if we're dragging, we're doing it awwwwwfully slowly.* Boy did I want to believe we were holding. You either are or you aren't, simple as that, right? I kept picking out combinations of ranges, a pole here and a power line there, a sign here and a tree there. Wait and watch. Much as it pained me to admit it, we were heading downstream at a snail's pace. So we reset, something I never love doing, mostly because we have no windlass. I prefer anchor hauling to be a once-a-day affair.

After resetting, we ended up with the same result. Damn. It was time to reintroduce the CQR, so as Deb maneuvered to keep us within striking range, I swapped out anchors, and we tried again. This time we stuck. How do *you* spell relief?

That evening we'd been the live entertainment. Boaters do that for each other. We provide a free show, often attached with a cautionary lesson. Another boater may have seen my anchor buoy getting hammered by the current and decided against its use, thinking it detrimental to the holding power of the anchor. What to do, what to do?

The other fellow, he must have felt for us, though most assuredly he was happy we were the ones with the problem. I wouldn't have blamed him. He was not only without a power windless, but also without any crew to help him. We got a chance to meet him again down the road and learn a lot more about this fellow traveling the world all on his own.

~~~

If I may digress for a moment, much is written about the lousy sailor. He provides grist for cautionary articles in boating magazines, and fuels derisive e-mail among Internet user groups. I think it's time to take a fresh, unjaundiced look at this misunderstood and mostly unappreciated creature. Of the countless benefits the lousy sailor provides, I have observed the following:

The lousy sailor . . .

Keeps our beloved mechanics, marinas, chandleries, and waterside bars solvent. He does so with amazing efficiency, by buying the wrong equipment and vainly refusing to return it, going through expendables like there is no tomorrow, destroying equipment long before its service life is over, losing things overboard at an alarming rate, and failing to maintain various onboard systems, which must as a result undergo untimely overhauls. Being generally incompetent at repair work, he thus requires the hire of skilled labor for the most basic of services, among them the repair of attempted repairs he has botched himself. Seeking solace from his ineptitude, he hastens to the local watering hole to enact his penance. *Mea culpa, mea culpa,* may I buy another round?

Provides the boating community at large with countless hours of entertainment while attempting to maneuver his vessel, comprehend the laws of physics, flout nature, remain onboard, return to his mooring, and preserve his marriage.

Provides free on-the-water clinics on how not to conduct one's self on a waterborne vehicle.

Tests the Coast Guard's response system.

Keeps other boaters alert.

Invents new knots for which one day there may be found valuable purposes.

Gives racers a dynamic obstacle with which to test their tactical skills.

Puts fellow boaters in good stead with the Almighty by offering them frequent opportunities to perform as Good Samaritans.

Fills said boaters with smug satisfaction over their own nautical prowess.

Finally, the lousy sailor helps beautify your harbor with the scenic addition of his pride and joy, regardless of his inability to commandeer her properly.

And she's a sight to behold, let me tell you.

Do you remember where we parked?

11/13/05
Log of the Laura Lynn Installment #7
Position: 32°25.753' North Latitude, 80°40.807' West Longitude
Beaufort, South Carolina

Ahoy, all,

    Those of you who recall our attempts to summon dolphins for a close-up, well Dean Martin just isn't cutting it anymore. And creamy as his voice is, it's starting to grate on us. It's not Dean's fault, when you consider we only have one of his songs onboard. Oh for a little Mel Torme.
    We've had promising moments with Bruce Hornsby, and a section of a Don Henley song just begged to be answered by our cetacean friends, but no go. We have sightings off in the distance, disturbingly close to other boats, which suggests my theory—that Deb is channeling dolphin-speak—is just another of my countless half-baked ideas formed in an effort to convince myself I'm a master of my domain. More and more, it becomes apparent I'm simply delusional.
    Then it dawned on me: we have our Dolphin Green burgee! Why hadn't we thought of it before? Surely dolphins would recognize their own image and be compelled to accompany us. So after a fretful night, in a quiet anchorage to which Deb seemed allergic, we unraveled our little flag, a white dolphin leaping on a field of green, and gave it a go with Sarah McLachlan. Nothing. Then some compelling Bonnie Raitt. Zippo. I find myself for now spent of harebrained schemes. Needless to say, Deb is inconsolable.
    On a brighter front, Deb is now convinced she can hear the sounds of shrimp feeding on microorganisms adhering to the bottom of our boat. Don't scoff, for there is science behind this claim, or at least a sailor or two claim it is so. I might have heard the "clicking" sounds last night, but I'm always hearing things now. I had my hearing checked before we left (Deb wanted to make sure I wasn't just ignoring her), and indeed I've lost certain frequencies in my left ear. They are, however, being replaced by the intermittent sounds of an electric motor with brush problems off in the distance near a lighthouse running its foghorn over the breaking waves at its base. That's kind of what it sounds like, if you add the noise you make when you reach the end of your milk shake and keep sucking on the straw.
    The possibility of shrimp cleaning the bottom of our boat nightly does not sit well with us for the simple reason that we love to eat them so much. A few nights ago, in the still very active shrimping town of Southport, South Carolina, we were treated to an exquisite appetizer of a pile of steamed shrimp slathered with cocktail sauce. The shrimp had just come in off the boat. Friends, it just doesn't get any better than this. Our hosts Pat and Paul of Sea Star then moved us to the dinner table where spaghetti and meatballs were served, also fantastic. Pat's a maestro in the galley, but I could have just stayed with the shrimp till I grew my own set of antennae. And now to think that the little guys are constantly pulling all-nighters to keep our boat clean, I'm really torn. Almost.
    We are now here in Beaufort, South Carolina. If you're experiencing a sense of déjà vu, it's because we have in the past reported from Beaufort, North Carolina. The one to the north, pronounced "BO-furt," was lovely, as I'm sure we'll discover today of its southern counterpart, pronounced "BYEW-fert" by the locals. We've been admonished not to get the pronunciation wrong if it comes up in conversation. Should you wish to form your own town with the same spelling, you'll be required to pronounce it something like "BOW-fahrt," or perhaps "bee-YAY-fort." Just so you know, you've been warned.

The larger towns we visit remind me Paradise is getting crowded, and we're late to the party. Nearing each anchorage, the anxiety builds over whether we'll find a suitable patch of water in which to safely drop our anchor. The competing influences of wind, tidal range, currents, boat design, and anchor line length and configuration (chain, nylon or a combination thereof) conspire to create a scenario that reminds me of a square dance on water. For those of you who have never attended a square dance, here's what happens: you show up with your date, and then the fiddler gets started and the guy with the mic starts barking orders. The next thing you know, you're mixing it up with a bunch of total strangers for the rest of the night. I never liked square dances. I could never keep up with that guy. And the catamaran that seemed a comfortable distance away an hour ago is starting to get awfully cozy with my Laura Lynn.

I suppose we could always opt for one of the more secluded anchorages, but we'd have no Internet connection, and where would you be then? Which reminds me, thank you all for your wonderful words that inspire us onward. It helps get us through some of the tough times, knowing you'll be there on the other end if we can anchor close enough to a Wi-Fi source.

Our last large town was Charleston, SC, a city of abundant resources and historical importance. Its importance to me lay in the fact that I got to visit my cousin Rich and his family. It is the common lament that there is never enough time at these meetings to adequately catch up, but I'm thankful for the time Rich, Kate, Sarah Jane, and Charlie gave us from their schedules to take in a couple of wayward drifters. A little time with family is far better than no time at all. Thanks, you guys. Remember, if you're ever in NYC . . . And Sarah Jane and Charlie, keep flapping those wings, and you will indeed fly.

We'd like to mention someone whom we can't even reach through this medium. Though he's told us to stop thanking him, we want to speak about an old friend of Deb's father. Paul "Flex" Clare has been there for us as promised, 24/7 from his home base in Wrightsville, North Carolina, for anything we might need. We get great advice on the phone, and while visiting Wrightsville we were treated royally to a tour of the area, tales of the sea (Jimmy Buffett once exclaimed to his old boat neighbor after a long separation, "My God! You're still alive?"), chauffeur service to West Marine and other ports of call, charts of waters yet untraveled, and much more. Flex, I hope someone else lets you know, since you're sick of hearing it from us, you're a gentleman and a scholar, and now a true friend. If only Bob were still here to share this trip with us, comfortable in the knowledge that we were well cared for.

So now it seems we have two earthly captains to guide us: Captain Art and Captain Flex, with Captain Bob in the fly bridge. I'd say we've got our shoulders covered.

What's Hot:
    Fresh, and we mean FRESH, shrimp. Lawd amighty!
    Morning stretches
    Pumpkin pie, fresh out of the oven
    Bleach

What's Not:
    Mold
    Chafe
    Frost warnings

Shout Outs:

- Dr. Dave, I had a dream last night that you were giving me your e-mail address for this trip. Sure enough, you weren't on our list when I checked this morning. Shame on me, doctor, and be advised we'll get you up-to-date with passed installments. Give Wheezer a squeeze for me.
- Michael Harvey, my nephew, welcome aboard. What an unnerving full address you have. When I think "weapons of mass destruction," I picture a case of Cheez Whiz.
- Bosco, stop being funnier than me, you sumbitch.
- Mary Epstein, our love, first press "Time of Day," next enter the time of day, then press "Time of Day." We miss you too.
- Kay, any plans to visit the other coast soon? We'll need details.
- Aud, the sciences give us a means to live; the arts give us reason to live. Rock on, painter girl.
- Big John, we've traveled over half the Eastern Seaboard and haven't seen anything lovelier than that trout stream. Can we make it there with a three-and-a-half-foot draft?
- Jackie: So, Sis, did you trip the light fantastic, or what? Call soon. Deb is turning pink holding her breath.
- Cathy and Geoff, are you expecting a barbarian siege? That's not a house; that's a fortress.

Byewfert: One rockin' town!

Beaufort, North Carolina was the Big Mistake anchorage. We opted for the anchorage that was reported to be less problematic with regard to currents. As a result, we were again an extremely inconvenient walking distance from a charming town that, when we finally got there, seemed to sit in front of a perfectly viable anchorage. Wait till you hear what happened to us on the way back. Suffice it to say we didn't find it anywhere near as charming and viable on the return trip.

Beaufort, South Carolina, was the Big Walk. We started from the dinghy dock, through the town proper, over the swing bridge, and way too far into the practical part of town, meaning where the hardware store was. The old town is cute and mostly useless. See what I mean? What a callus thing to say of a perfectly nice place. But it didn't have a widget store, and I needed a widget. Wait till you hear what happened to us on the way back. Suffice it to say we didn't bother with the Big Walk.

~~~

Time is a narrow, one-way road, often unpaved. Do not listen to Steven Hawking. Listen to me. It only seems to change speed, at a rate commensurate with the present state of your personal comfort. What you discover in the end is that it has always been racing along at a break-neck pace. You can never go home again, since the passage of time denies you that privilege. You can only go someplace else in time, someplace that may remind you of where you've been before, but maybe not. If you're lucky, there's at least an inkling of a memory there that provides a signpost for the direction of your destiny.

~~~

I don't believe in destiny, but I believe that any day may provide the opportunity for you to do something so bone-headed, future generations will pass on stories about you as if you were fated to suffer for your monstrous ignorance. Does that make me a fatalist? I think not, but I do think it tends to make me flatulent.

Deb's cooking, however, is beyond reproach. There she was, down there amid the sounds and smells and sloggings of a small boat, rising to the challenge of providing square meals out of boxes and tins and jars and packets and tubs and tubes of dehydrated, deoxygenated, salted, frozen and hyper-heated supplies. Let us bow our heads in deference to the titans of the industrial revolution, for coming up with all this stuff.

We took to calling one of our dry holding areas the Horror Hole because it was a vast repository of space so poorly situated as to initiate civil strife if either one of us were to suggest that the other should fetch something from its bowels. I'd rather keep watch through the entire night, in a sleet storm, wearing an undersized Speedo, than have to pull the lid on that demon den to go scavenge some Triscuits.

Astern of the stove, an antique, three-burner alcohol job with an oven that might give salmonella a limp when cranked up full, the Horror Hole was strategically designed to crack three ribs going in, and give you three stitches on the back of the head coming out. If there was any seaway up, the prudent mariner would go in with full body armor and an EPIRB strapped to his ass.

~~~

Our boat stove reminds me of the nightmares conjured when America was young and virile, and families would pack the trunk with one or more of everything Coleman manufactured, in an attempt to squander an otherwise perfectly good weekend at the nearest KOA. At the campground, the family would assemble a tent constructed of leftover WWII inventory, the purpose of which was to provide a suitably moldy environment for the care and feeding of the local mosquito population.

The best part of camping was watching the Alpha member of the group reduced to tears at his inability to keep his clan alive in the woods for two consecutive days without the aid of Sarah Lee. At some point, the campsite would be abandoned for the nearest drive-in theatre or ice cream parlor, or whatever was open and heated at that hour.

Sleeping could be delayed, but not put off entirely, so a few token hours were put in before the frost sounded its alarm and camp was struck by those not involved with the maiming of the pancakes on the Coleman pressure stove. We've come a long way since we crawled out of the cave, have we not?

Our alcohol stove, like each of us, has its quirks. It spits and squawks and flares up and pulsates and blows itself out and singes the eyelashes and requires constant attention and pumping and priming and fussing and fidgeting. I'll say this for it. If we lost any weight, and we did, it shared some of the credit.

Most modern boats have propane systems, so you don't have to worry about all our niggling problems. With propane, when something goes wrong, you're dead just like that, which is a real relief.

~~~

11/14/05
Log of the Laura Lynn #8
Position:
32°25.753' North Latitude
80°40.807' West Longitude
Amelia Island, Florida

I don't know how to put this delicately. We skipped Georgia.

We went right by the state. It was off to starboard. Technically we did see it, a sliver of horizon sandwiched between water and sky. After another lovely sunset, we identified the vague glow of Savannah, followed by the lesser glows of smaller towns along the Georgia Coast.

Which is not meant as a dig on smaller communities. I prefer small towns. Perhaps we'll visit some of them on the way back. But Deb and I have been following the Intracoastal Waterway for over six hundred miles, from Norfolk to Beaufort. Cognoscenti refer to the ICW as "the Ditch" for good reason. As it winds its way down the Eastern Seaboard, it borrows names for itself, such as Pungo Creek, Alligator River, Elliott's Cut, C & D Canal, on and on. As these names suggest, along much of the route you could plant your best friend on the opposite bank and have fun with a Frisbee. This is not the sort of route that conjures up imagery of Yours Trulies as grand explorers. We felt the urge to live up to the hype, and you all needed to stretch your imaginations a little.

For us, it was time for a sea change, and we decided to head "outside" for an overnight experience on the ocean. Here's the word for the ensuing experience: "enchanting."

Now I know this kind of thing is done by your average cruiser all the time, but put yourself back in your own shoes as a kid when you first tied them successfully, or finally deciphered the machinations of the wall clock, or had your first kiss. And I don't mean with Aunt Edna. T'was a deed. Goosebumps, epiphanies and further great expectations. I can tell you this: after only one night at sea, I now know why sailors will blow a month's pay on their first night in port.

We saw whales, falling stars, and tracked the moon from rise to set, so nearly full and luminous that one could spot food particles in the teeth of one's sailing partner. We comfortably motor-sailed for hours until I wished for enough wind so we could turn off the engine and still make good time. I got my wish and then some. First the clouds. Then the wind. Then the rain. Then Deb started barfing.

Did I say barfing? I meant burping. A little gas was all. Might have been the meatballs. Got your attention though, didn't I?

So here we are, against all smart odds, in Florida (Deb's mom is thrilled we're finally in her home state), basking in our overnight success. As an aside, the anchorage here is the ugliest we've ever visited. It appears the local seaside industry is solely concerned with the export of carcinogens. There was no mention of this eye-ear-nose-and-throat-sore in any of the guidebooks, which all mention the most charming town one could imagine. Remember Jaws? Amity means "friendship." I smell a payoff.

Later this evening we'll test my new hypothesis (I'm back in the game!). For now, after thirty-plus mostly consecutively awake hours (we were too pumped to sleep), I'm comfortably sprawled on a cockpit cushion, successfully spent, with my Crocodile Dundee hat tucked strategically low so just a slice of Amelia Island peeks through. I can easily convince myself we've reached nirvana.

As Jethro Bodine might exclaim, "Ponce Dee Lay-on, we is here!"

Things We've Named:

Our boat is named Laura Lynn after Deb's beloved sister.

Our dinghy is named Em after Laura's daughter. Hi Emmy!

Our outboard motor for Em the dinghy is "Freddie." It's a Mercury. Get it? Ask Vinny.

Our diesel engine is named "Jenny," because it seems the sailorly thing to do. The engine is often referred to as the "Iron Genny," a salute to a kind of sail called a "genoa."

Our primary anchor is called a Bruce by its manufacturer, but we call him Bruce Almighty. It's easy for a sailor to become emotionally attached to his anchor.

We built a jury-rigged anchor roller to aid my failing back in raising Bruce Almighty, with the invaluable aid of Flex (remember him?) and some hardware from a boater named Mark, so it's the Flexomatic Mark I.

We also got an ancient autohelm working to steer for us, and it was a lifesaver last night. You can't imagine the punishment of having to steer a boat constantly for twenty-two hours straight. He worked like a champ all night, with only two or three hiccups, probably magnetic anomalies. He's named Artie.

What's Hot:
    Falling stars
    Whale sightings
    Pancakes slathered in butter and syrup
    Triscuits and cheese
    Artie the Autohelm

What's Not:
    Fighting a hard current coming right on your nose
    Running on empty
    Having to fetch something out of the Horror Hole

Shout-Outs:

~ Lynn and Dave, we're really truly sorry about missing you in Savannah. What's it like? How about like, May?
~ Tom and Joe: Wish you guys were here. Then you could lift the anchor for me. Ouch! We need crew!
~ Heather, please send our best to the Ninth Street Gang!
~ Lety, we made a wish on a falling star.
~ Aloha Jackie Chan! Hang loose, dude. Give your Mom and Dad big kisses for us.
~ Welcome to this world, William Walter! You should have one rib—tickling time with the parents you've picked.

The sun setting over Georgia, we think. Come back soon, big guy.

~~~

    An overnighter at sea is one of those things a lot of folks have to get their heads around. When the conditions are favorable, it's as easy as pulling one at home, right? Something exciting is going on. Let's stay up and watch.

    It's different, particularly for a crew of two, to go offshore for an extended period of time. You have to get your act together for that. The long haul requires careful preparation. An overnighter you can get through on adrenaline, with the knowledge that when this stint is over, you can crash in the cockpit, bathing in the glory of the accomplishment.

    Lest I be accused of diminishing the importance of preparation, let me now say this: it is important to prepare. More than that, it is important, I think, to consider whether sailing through the night is for you. We are, after all, creatures of light. Severely curtailing our vision involves risk. Big ships can sneak up on you at night. I'll never forget the photo, seen in a cruising magazine, of the mangled remains of a sailboat's rigging hanging from the anchor of a freighter. The crew of the big ship hadn't known what they'd wrought in the middle of some nameless night till they'd made port. It sent shivers through me, as doubtlessly it did that crew. As to the feelings of the crew of the sailboat, we will never know.

We'd rigged jack lines, safety straps that run the length of the boat on each side. We each had a harness we could snap on to those lines, which allowed us to walk forward and aft along the boat, and, in theory, drag along next to it, had we fallen overboard. We'd also worked out the timing of the trip so that we'd be exiting and entering Class A inlets, during the full light of day. These are large, well-marked waterways that are suitable for all water traffic. Our old autohelm would do the bulk of the night steering, a chore that took a considerable strain off our duties.

It's been mentioned elsewhere, but I'll throw my two cents in here. Most modern boats are now equipped with autohelm. Because of the nature of the ICW, you will of necessity spend a lot of time steering by hand. However, on those occasions where you can pick a course and go, autohelm is a godsend. For extended offshore work, windvane steering is often used, but in any event, spare yourself the agony. You will want some form of self-steering for offshore passages.

My cousin Rich, an ex-military, ex-commercial diver, who now finds stuff underwater with fancy equipment, told me simply, get an EPIRB, a device that will tell the Coast Guard precisely where you are should it be set off by some crisis I prefer not to think about. We did not follow his orders, and I've since apologized to him. We also carried no life raft. We had a small dinghy and a ditch bag ready in case we felt we had to abandon ship.

Insane, you say? In the course of nine months, we spent the sum total of four days traveling through the night offshore. On two of those nights we were members of a small flotilla keeping radio contact with each other, and we were always within VHF range of someone. The days were picked with congenial weather being tantamount to our decision to travel. I was crazier for ever having hopped aboard a motorcycle.

Our boat is poorly set up for reefing of the main. It's an old-fashioned affair, jury-rigged after the original setup had been determined substandard by a previous owner, and disabled. We rarely reef, having been for the bulk of our careers fair-weather sailors. I know mainly in theory what I should do if we encounter heavy weather in our boat. On the ICW, when we knew bad weather was coming, we stayed put. When we were already out and about and saw it coming at us we got our sails in, all of them, and motored through the mess.

We could unquestionably have benefited from more heavy-weather experience, particularly on our own boat. We'd had some against our wishes on previous charters to the Caribbean. Reefing from the cockpit of a modern boat hardly counts as practice, since on our boat we have to get out there and hang on at the mast when faced with similar conditions.

Some risks we don't calculate all that accurately. Every one of us manages to get in a bit too deeply sooner or later, including the disciplined ones. And there is the nagging suspicion, if I wait until I convince myself I'm ready, will it be too late to go have fun? Who of us doesn't have at least some idea of what he ought to be doing instead of watching the Crock Hunter? Now there was a guy with lots of experience, and may he rest in peace.

I knew where and when I was pushing my envelope. If I didn't always have the right postage, I knew enough when to hold on to the mail. Others wouldn't have batted an eyelash in the kind of conditions that get me awfully concerned. Know your limitations.

The weather report for our transit of Georgia's shore was ideal. We had a full moon and predicted moderate steady winds that would put us on a beam reach all night. We were strapped in and the temperature was mild. One of us would take naps while the other kept an eye on our course and the horizon.

Nature chose to remind me that anything can happen, modern weather reporting notwithstanding. A few hours before dawn, a small front came through, just enough to remind me that we were not as prepared as we should be. The wind picked up to the point where we were sailing hard. I sat there thinking, *Please don't pick up any more than this, or I'll have to consider doing things I'd rather not be doing in the middle of the night.* It didn't quite, but it could have.

It's easy to find fault with another's plan, or dismiss the concerns of Nervous Nellies. Watching any of the flock of shows depicting disaster-prone careers prompts one to exclaim, "What are those guys, nuts?" Well no, not quite. I'd never do what they do for that kind of pay. I'm not sure I'd do it for any kind of pay, and yet they've reached a certain comfort level in the risk/reward decisions they've made. Are they ready for anything they'll meet out there in the open ocean? Their history and the graphic footage presented for our edification suggests otherwise. Common sense tells you it's not humanly possible to prepare for everything. But common sense also suggests you get some practice in before you tackle Mother Nature on her home field.

~~~

The moon set, and the sky brightened in the east. With the arrival of the sun came a form of victory. We'd sailed through the night. We hadn't sunk, drowned, or diverted a freighter. The sea vampires that stalk lonely sailors sank back to the ocean floor to rest atop the chests of gold that make for nice mattresses, if you're one of the undead. We welcomed that special transition that marks the Earth's schizophrenic nature. Is the night a head trip, or what?

I have a small handful of friends who come alive at night. I wonder if, as babies, they were mishandled by the stork company and delivered to the wrong planet. Whenever I find myself staying up all night for some reason, usually against my will, it has always been with a primal sense of wonder for me when the sun finally shows. I might otherwise have convinced myself that this inky void was intended to be my last.

The sun now up, we were met with no accompanying ticker tape parade. There was just a quiet warmth that grew, along with our realization that several more hours of nondescript sailing were necessary before the anchor would drop, and we could enjoy some real rest.

It's easy to see that, as with other novelty acts, one could develop a routine on a longer journey that would make overnighters less a Broadway production and more an assembly-line one. I don't see us spoiling the experience anytime soon. Deb and I are, at our core, creatures of the land.

∼∼∼

11/20/05
Log of the Laura Lynn #9
Position:
29° 12.624' North Latitude
81° 00.333' West Longitude
Daytona Beach, Florida

Welll, lets see. Whaaat to talk about. Juuust hanging out here in PARADISE, basking away among the divine palm trees and diving pelicans. Something to grab the reader's interest.

Oh, okay, there was that thing in St. Augustine where the OCEAN TRIED TO DESTROY the LAURA LYNN.

"How so?" one might ask. In the most insidious and despicable way, we reply. The harbor of St. Augustine tried to induce the Laura Lynn to commit suicide.

"Omeegosh, like how?" you further wonder. Well here's how. The Satanic forces of the harbor—a seditious northerly wind, in collusion with those vile, fluctuating tidal currents—twisted our nylon anchor line around our keel's centerboard. While we were blissfully off purchasing supplies for our bright future, that keel was slicing through the line keeping us in place in that wretched harbor we will never again visit, so help me. Ponce de Leon, bite my shorts.

Long story short, chafe (remember that "what's not hot" item in the last update?) slit through our anchor line and set the Laura Lynn adrift in that cursed harbor. Thankfully it happened during the day, and with adequate time for a fellow boater to notify a marina official (bless you, Dave), who then captured our wayward vessel while she was on the run. Otherwise, the Bridge of Lions, kittyless while its statues were being restored, might have been renamed the Bridge of Laura Lynn. Which in a bizarre way would have been way cool, sort of.

The tourist town of St. Augustine is not without merits. It boasts the oldest house in America, the oldest schoolhouse in America, and we'll bet somewhere nearby all this decrepitude is the oldest outhouse, the oldest cathouse, and the oldest House of Pancakes. We were particularly taken by the oldest continually functioning animated mechanical statue, that of Ponce de Leon himself. How it works is, you get to ask the statue one question, and he'll wiggle and whir and answer it. Deb asked Ponce where our anchor, worth about five hundred bucks, might be located, hoping we could salvage it with a grappling hook. I don't know where she learned about grappling hooks, but it kind of turns me on.

Anyway, Ponce thought it over and said, "I believe it is right over there. Then again it might be directly over there. On the other hand, it just may be over there." He then segued into a rusty song and dance send-up of a Scarecrow number called "If You'd Only Used More Chain." I'll send a picture of Deb asking her question.

I ran off and bought eighty feet of 3/8" chain, and attached it to Bruce Almighty, who had only a day earlier been demoted for dragging at the previous anchorage. I swear Bruce looked like he was smiling when I shackled him to the chain. Back on the job! The next morning, we got out of Dodge fast on a screaming flood tide. At some point we'll have to replace the CQR, a considerable monetary setback, one we'll attempt to offset by slashing the budget elsewhere. We are therefore soliciting any and all recipes that utilize Cream of Wheat as the primary ingredient, particularly for the dinner menu.

To be fair to St. Augustine, we came at a bad time weather-wise, what with a full moon and an unusual northerly wind blowing. Maybe we'll consider a visit when different weather conditions prevail. At what time of the year, pray tell, does hell freeze over?

And before I forget, an apology is in order to the fair citizenry of Fernandina Beach, whose town, it turns out, is indeed cute as a batch of newborn puppies. It really is. As we walked its main street one evening, after having dined at Lulu's Bra and Grill (sic), I felt like we were extras in a Walt Disney movie. All that was missing was a cameo by Hillary Duff singing "Tomorrow, tomorrow, we'll luv ya, tomorrow. Oh please do not sailawayyyyyy."

Still, we left.

What's Hot:

St. Christopher

Eau du Coppertone

Dr. Scholl's Odor Destroyer

What's Not:

@#$!!$ CHAFE! Imagine a wad of steel wool in your shorts during the March of Dimes Walkathon.

Spoiled milk

Shout-Outs:

~ Mary Mitchell, our hearts are with you, my fine friend.
~ St. Augustine Harbor Master Dave Morehead, thank you for saving our Laura Lynn.
~ Michael Tineo, you are in our thoughts every day.
~ Nanie, as we write, our cabin is being filled with the tempting aromas emanating from the pressure cooker. Can't wait for dinner.
~ Tinna, it's your curry stew. Fellow boaters are starting to anchor suspiciously close by, all downwind.
~ Jackie DeRosa. Yes you were right. We didn't give Amelia enough of our time. Maybe on the way back. We'll consult you before then.

~~~

The man who saved the Laura Lynn, Harbormaster David Morehead, signing my birthday shirt

~~~

St. Augustine was an emotional depth charge set off at close range. To head back to the boat at the end of a lovely day of playing tourist and find her tied up at the municipal dock was a mindbender, when the plan was to hop into our dinghy and head out to her anchored position in the harbor. Doubtlessly the glass-is-half-full among you will point out it beats seeing four feet of your mast poking above the water line. I'll spot you the observation, bright eyes, but it's a shock, nonetheless.

As we scampered down the gangway and lengthy dock to her new berth, a sizeable scamper made more demanding by the load of stores we'd just bought, there was time to wonder all sorts of things. What had happened? Why is she there? She's floating, but is she okay? Is the rest of the boating community okay, i.e., did our wayward boat sink or damage anybody else? Would we be sued? Arrested? Was our trip over?

I didn't then even have the knowledge to wonder if admiralty law had recently made her the property of some salvager, but as I got to her, I could see that her bow was fastened to the dock by what was left of her nylon anchor rode. There was the eighty-foot marker announcing the depth of the crime, like police cordoning tape. The end looked as if it had been gnawed through by a frustrated pit bull that's been given too little exercise.

There was another clue. The bitter end (believe it or not, that's a technical term, though I think I'm using it incorrectly here) of the line was stained rust red, the color of our bottom paint. We puzzled the evidence together with the harbormaster, who had earlier received the call that a boat had begun to drift through the harbor. As it happens, the call had come from the singlehander who'd gotten the free show from us at an earlier anchorage.

The harbormaster had lassoed our boat after she'd deftly threaded a path through the entire anchorage, striking not a thing along her merry way. We'd lost a prize anchor and a good chunk of rode, but my mind was racing as the sun was setting, racing with notions I'd been entertaining for some time since we'd been watching how the real cruisers were doing things.

I was going to convert us to all-chain rode. At least enough of the stuff that would anchor us with all chain in most of the conditions we'd be in. With our draft and the cruising ground we'd chosen, I figured that a hundred feet would do it. What I didn't know was what size chain I should get, and how much it would weigh.

I was given the name of an outfitter that handled commercial boaters in the St. Augustine area. Don't go to West Marine, I was told. Money could be saved with the outfitters. I grabbed a cab and gave the driver the directions, asking in shallow breaths if he'd be amenable to staying while I made the transaction. Turns out he was, as long as I buttered his bread properly, know what I'm saying, Cap? Cabbies are cabbies the world over.

I'm sure these outfitters handled professional fisherman in a professional manner. With an amateur cruiser suffering from elevated blood pressure and an absence of verbal skills, these guys looked at me like I was speaking Swahili.

I needed help. I needed somebody to decide for me the proper type of chain so I could get back to my boat and regain my composure, safe in the knowledge that we wouldn't be hanging by dental floss anymore.

The pros were not about to decide anything for me. So, looking over my options, I decided 3/8". Then I saw what a hundred feet of 3/8" looked like. So I went with eighty feet, as I wasn't about to compromise on strength.

What the heck did I know? Man, that's a lot of heavy metal. I wonder at all the mistakes that are made by people in a hurry. I wonder it often in the midst of my own frantic escapades. You must occasionally find yourself babbling stuff like, "I really shouldn't be making important decisions right now in the state I'm in. I should slow down, take a couple of deep breaths, look up a few things, make a few calls, maybe sleep on it, and do it right the first time in the morning." Then you plow into a busload of kids, it bursts into flames, and you're sitting there with an airbag in your face going, "I told me so."

My cabbie had hung around for some time as these guys pulled out merchandise for me to muddle over, so I threw money at him when I was back at the marina with a cartload of chain to splice on to what remained of our rode. The dock master looked upon our condition with pity, and allowed us to stay free of charge at the dock. I threw what remaining cash we had at him. We were throwing the greenery around like it was confetti, but then he'd saved our boat from near certain destruction, and technically the boat could have been his. You've gotta be kidding, right?

That evening, Deb and I enjoyed the security of attachment to land as we regrouped. I rerigged our anchor system, which now consisted of a thirty-three-pound Bruce shackled to eighty feet of 3'8" chain, spliced to another maybe hundred and seventy-five feet of nylon. I saved that last bit of the nylon rode, the part that had been sawed away by our centerboard, as another memento of my limitless ignorance.

There's irony for you. We'd dropped our centerboard at the advice of another boater, in an attempt to halt the crazy motion our boat had at anchor. That day boats were all over the place. At one point we'd heard a thud, and when Deb had looked out a portlight, she'd given a yelp. Inches from her nose was a bowsprit, the owners of which were absent from their boat. No damage, so we pushed the boats apart, and watched as they separated, like a couple of preoccupied puppies, to a comfortable distance.

Why did we stay where we were? Where were we to go? St. Augustine was a perfect example of an anchorage that challenged every choice you made of dropping anchor. Too deep here, too close to that guy there. And what seems reasonable right now will not seem so once everyone in the harbor does his one-eighty, which happens for each boat at a different time, four times a day.

So you can head to some safe anchorage too far away to allow you a visit to St. Augustine, thus defeating the purpose of the trip. Or you can stay where you are, right there where you are, on the boat, never leaving it, for fear something will happen while you're away, thus defeating the purpose of the trip. Or you can do your best, learn as you go, get off the boat and visit, which is after all the purpose of the trip, and in so doing, jeopardize the future of the trip.

We left St. Augustine the next morning, resting a little low in the bow. Should've bought lighter chain.

∼∼∼

11/22/05
Log of the Laura Lynn #10
Position:
28° 37.540' North Latitude
80° 48.653' West Longitude
Titusville, Florida

Well it had to happen sooner or later. Those of you who've been keeping up understand the forces of nature at work here. It was just plain inevitable. Deb went and bought a pair of shoes.

In all fairness she got a great deal, and they are ostensibly seaworthy. They're Sperry Topsiders and she got them at the Sailor Swap Store, to which I dragged her in the first place, so I had it coming. But then again they're a bit too barnyard red, and have no backs. No backs! I have no idea what Mr. Sperry was thinking, but Captain Aubrey would be apoplectic.

I don't have a positive count, but I plan on a shoe audit in the near future. We have absolutely no room for anything else onboard, and have had talks about off-loading other noncritical gear. When I reminded Deb of this and suggested we'd have to get rid of something as a result of this acquisition, she was in complete agreement, and immediately jettisoned my foul weather gear and half my underwear supply. This is a take-charge kind of gal.

And here's another thing about her. It could just be me, but it seems like Deb is starting to develop a very sexy way of talking these days. Check out the kind of stuff she's been saying to me lately. Here's a recent conversation I've transcribed from memory:

Deb (at the helm): Paul, outta my way, I can't see the depth here.
Paul (caught standing in front of the depth indicator): Oh, sorry.
Deb: You wanna check the chart for me? I need to know which side of the channel I should favor.
Paul: Okay.
Deb: We're really getting hammered by the current here. If this keeps up, we should look for an anchorage closer than we planned.
Paul: Really?
Deb: Yeah, I'm running thirty-two hundred rpm and we're making three knots over ground.
Paul: Jeez.
Deb: Jeez is right. We're probably burning a gallon an hour and getting nowhere fast. I hope the jerry can is full.
Paul: Uhmmm.
Deb: Oh, mother. Better give me some anchorage options yesterday, big guy.
Paul: I'm on it.
Deb: I'll bet you are. Looks like we'll be hitting the sack early tonight . . .
Paul: I'm with you there!
Deb: . . . so we can get up around five and catch the flood tide to Titusville.
Paul: Righto, Cap!

And now the envelope please:

For the musical artist with the strongest influence in attracting cetaceans to accompany our vessel, the Flippy Award goes to . . .

Whitney Houston! Whitney's inspiring medley of hits from her "I'm Your Baby Tonight" album garnered a ten-minute escort by two dolphins on the Daytona to Titusville run. They particularly seemed to like the song "My Name Is Not Susan," after which tune they peeled off for a nearby ocean inlet. Whitney could not be here to accept our award, a tin of dolphin-safe Bumble Bee Tuna, as she's, well we don't know where she is; probably on a boat bigger than Delaware, getting nasty with Bobby Brown, or something.

What's Hot:
Whitney Houston
New music from Alex!
Manatees. Why can't we buy one of these at the pet store?
Pelicans. I know they've been on the list before, but Elton John has won more than one Grammy too.
Limericks. Here's one my dad taught us kids when we were young (if you never had a dad like this, I pity you):

An amazing bird is the pelican
Whose beak can hold more that his belly can

*He can hold in his beak
Enough food for a week
And I don't know how the hell he can*

What's Not:
*Impromptu Man Overboard Drills (our sun shower went over in a gust)
Hand-raising a 33lb anchor with eighty feet of 3/8" chain attached
Pollution: I'm not swimming in that stuff*

Shout-Outs:

~ *Hey, Ginger! How's married life treating you?*
~ *Too Too, what's a good day to visit in the next couple weeks?*
~ *Jessy Momma! The reason you don't see the flip-flops you gave Deb is because they were the only things she wore for two months. They are nautical history.*

Ready for any occasion that calls for feet

Chapter 10

The Holidays

Only fifty-twelve more bridges before we get to open our presents.

You know what mom says. When you fall off your horse, you have to get right back up on it again. And give it a good, swift kick in the haunches. Our brush with disaster put us in the mood to make time down the Florida coast. Our mindset was, let's push and make it to family by Thanksgiving. That meant get to Jensen Beach, where Deb's mom, Joan, has lived for the last umpteen years with her second husband, Rich. Also living there was one of Deb's sisters, Jennifer. We were looking forward to spending the holidays on land, while our boat was safely and securely attached to the generously offered dock of good friends of the family.

Chris and Lisa are wonderful neighbors, and their home on the water in Jensen Beach was being built at the time. The dock was already there, built by Chris himself, with occasional help from Rich. I would never have doubted its structural integrity.

125

What I began to doubt though, as we wended our way south, was whether there was enough water depth at the dock to handle the *Laura Lynn*. The family was out of the country on an African photo safari. My charts of the area were sketchy. It looked thin. I should have thought more about it. Instead, I did one of those things I do too often, which tends to get me into trouble a lot. I hoped for the best.

It was an exciting day, the day we figured we'd pull up to a Florida dock and see family, who would in turn see us on a boat that was supposed to be in New York. We were going to make it this far, at least. That would be an emotional victory.

We tried to synch up our arrival, but it didn't quite happen. Just as well, perhaps. Tension mounted as we spotted the dock from the waterway. It became evident that, despite docks the lengths of football fields, we might not have sufficient depth to park the boat at Chris and Lisa's. It occurred to me there is a reason they build them so long in the first place. We anchored a little offshore and dinghied in with a marked boat hook to test the depth.

Sure enough, the only place that could handle the length of our boat had two feet of water over the bottom. We had no place we knew of to go. We'd made only one plan, one that had never been put to the efficacy test. As the knot in my stomach drew tight, Rich and Joan showed up. Well that was nice. I sure wasn't feeling like the conquering hero. After receiving the prerequisite warm welcome, we listened in to Rich's thoughts on the matter at hand. The wheels are always turning in Rich's pilothouse.

I wasn't at all feeling lucky when we tried a marina a stone's throw from our present position. What particularly turned me off was the proprietor's air, one that announced that there was no space available, and there hadn't been for some time. The underlying inference I got was, what would make us think we could just show up unannounced in Florida and figure there'd be a place to stay? Perhaps he was just a busy man with a lot of unresolved boat issues.

As I was preparing to sail back to New York in as many consecutive overnighters as it would take, Rich mentioned there was another place past the bridge where he remembered seeing sailboats. Well, there was some daylight left.

Stuart is a wacky little water community, tucked under a new fixed bridge that towers over the old but still operating double bascule, that kisses right up to a very active opening railway bridge. This was the tightest grouping of bridges we ever had to negotiate the entire trip. The openings were narrow, the traffic heavy, and the current strong. Crap, crap, crap.

Southpoint is Stuart's municipal marina. At the time, it was still recovering from hurricane damage from the previous year. Southpoint was Oz, and if Deb didn't have ruby slippers onboard she did have those Sperry Topsiders. Time to tap those absent heels together and make a wish.

In short order, we had a monthly mooring contract for about ten dollars a day. There are times when it all falls together in a split second. That's when you hit the deck in a full-on slide and come up . . . safe!

We got our boat to her mooring, attached a big fat pennant that looked like it could handle a cruise ship, packed a few things, and headed off to become landlubbers again.

∼∼∼

12/6 /05
Log of the Laura Lynn #11
Position: Deb's mom's house
Jensen Beach, Florida

You can do it in a plane in a couple hours. You can do it in a car in a couple days. It took us just shy of a couple months to do it on the Laura Lynn, and we feel like Lewis and Clark.

We have arrived in Jensen Beach after a conscientious push, the catalyst for which was the treatment we received at the hands of St. Augustine. We looked at our close call, looked at our schedule, looked at each other, and said let's get to the welcoming bosom of family by Thanksgiving.

The push was on. We put in the daily miles, enjoyed the scenery along the way, and forewent the earthbound delights of such communities as Daytona Beach and Titusville. Know what? Been to Spring Break, done the Viagra-sponsored cars going fast in a circle thing. I did however miss the opportunity to see if Skeeter's Big Biscuits is still doing as brisk a business as when I visited last millennium while working for MTV at Spring Break. Hey, it was a living.

Our Laura Lynn is now safely attached to a municipal mooring on the St. Lucie River, coordinates unknown, while we reacquire our land legs. Actually, it took a couple minutes for the legs to return. What took a little longer to cope with was the culture shock.

Maybe not so much a shock as a twinge. After all, land has been our medium for all but the last couple months of our lives. Even a few months, however, aboard the insular environment of a small boat can distance one from the America we have become.

A few observations about us Americans:
We are addicted to television. I went from watching no TV at all, to reconstituting myself as a mesmerized, tunnel-visioned zombie in the time it takes to surf four hundred and twelve channels. Still got it where it counts, baby—the opposable thumb.

We are pathological consumers. We must have our stuff. And the stuff we must have, always "on sale" (the phrase that appears to have replaced "for sale") must come packaged in blindingly bold, styro-suffused, hyper-stapled, hermetically sealed uberboxes. In fact, the entire stockroom of a Wal-Mart will fit in your broom closet once it's disencumbered of its packaging. As for the stuff inside the boxes, it's best if a football player recommends it, and it still pays to get the deluxe model.

We have no lower extremities. We need cars to get us anywhere. Remember Sniglets? Here's one I made one up. A "starker" is somebody in a car who follows somebody with a shopping cart to his car, and lurks there while the cart is unloaded so the starker can take that parking place, once the old shopper leaves. While this process may take upwards of fifteen minutes, it will generally spare the starker the brutal extended trek of about twenty yards to Piggly Wiggly's.

Americans are obsessed with cleavage. That's just all I have to say about that.

On a hopeful note, I see we Americans can once again carry scissors onboard a plane, as long as the blades are shorter than four inches. A very concerned airline attendant has gone on record to say she felt her security was once again being compromised. I'm thinking, maybe she ought to switch to baggage handling. As for me, I just want to know when I'm getting my deadly mustache scissors back.

What surprises me about the airline debacle is how the homeland security folks have completely overlooked the threat of a pair of bare hands clutched around the throat. I'm not sure how you screen for that menace, but there ought to be some kind of way to ID anyone who's ever taken a martial arts course. I figure careful screening would ground about 80 percent of the juvenile population, surely a step in the right direction.

Well, this log has a distinctly low-sodium flavor to it, but that's part of the story. We are comfortably into Phase Two, land based for the holidays, with more sea adventures to come. Clearly the want of a boat beneath me does not leave me short of words. If that overstuffs your inbox, I got two more words for you: delete button.

Now I think I'll take a walk around the block.

What's Hot
    A walk around the block
    Dry feet
    Showers that last for days
    Getting one wear out of the naughty bits before they hit the hamper
    The smell of cut grass
    Christmas decorations. Get out the boxes. Join the party.
    Charlie Brown. Still the best Christmas album ever.
    Gardening. Who knew?
    "It's a Wonderful Life"(see if you can spot Alfalfa).
    Floridians. They're just so happy to be alive.

What's Not
    Jessica Simpson. How much is there left to plumb? Great set of pipes. Nice rack. Bats in the belfry. Case closed.
    Traffic. Makes you want to head out to sea in an overly small boat
    Fire ants
    Oprah. Shut up and let someone else talk for a second. Except that putz, Dr. Phil. Somebody put a sock in that piehole too.
    Socks.
    Grits. What am I missing here? Did they once lace this stuff with something the same way Coke did?
    AOL dial-up. Satan's best weapon to date.

Shout-Outs:

- Rich, please ask the Dunkin Donut guys to consider a white frosting-filled chocolate glazed roll. They don't have to call it a Smacker if they don't want to. I'll make it worth their while.
- Remember Skeeters, Harv? Oh for some biscuits and gravy! With some hash browns and corned-beef hash, maybe a couple eggs overeasy, toast, some bacon, a big glass of OJ, and a defibrillator on the side.
- Mark Scholl, am I right or am I right? Tell me those security guys don't run pawnshops in their spare time.
- Alexandra, we could use another green thumb down here.
- Jackie, I'm starting to like Spooky.
- Dolli, do you actually listen to Tin Huey, or just pretend?
- Lisa and Chris, we're so glad you weren't eaten or mauled. Look, we're waving!

~~~

Oh, it's great to be home for the holidays. Note any family resemblance?

~~~

    I'll be honest with you. We were proud of what we'd done. We'd traversed a good deal of the Eastern Seaboard, on a boat we'd slept out of town on for a total of two nights prior to the trip. We were dogged with some vexing problems that contributed to our anxiety and discomfort, and didn't give up. We'd anchored virtually every step of the way. A rare exception was Elizabeth City's free slip, where ironically we'd had one of our toughest times staying in place during foul weather. Then there was St. Augustine. It was a relief to put our boat issues on the back burner for a while.

Make no mistake about it. The boat never leaves the back burner. In the introduction to his marvelous book, *Away All Boats,* John Cole has this to say:

> "Becoming a boat person, even in the most basic level, is becoming a different sort of individual who leads a different sort of life. It's a state of being comparable to the difference between being married and being single, or being a parent and being a child. At the very least, it is a life of concern."[1]

Find the book if you can. In the mean time, know that as long as your boat is in the water, as long as you own her, you'll be wondering if she's okay. Is she taking on water? Are the through-hulls intact? Are the zincs adequate? Is the rigging flaying itself to death? Has she been broken into? Did I attach the mooring lines properly? Is our chafe protection adequate? Are the batteries self-depleting at an advanced rate? Will our water turn poisonous? Will mold overrun the boat? Will bottom growth overwhelm the hull? Will rain make its way into the interior? Is the dinghy okay? Has someone stolen our outboard? What all will rust away or decay while we're off having fun? What am I forgetting?

One suppresses those concerns to a degree, largely because one is sleeping comfortably, taking hot showers, eating wickedly fresh Dunkin Donuts every morning, going to the movies at night, and generally living high off the hog. But they're there, always nagging at you, when the weather gets nasty, or some casual reading sets off a thought, or you allow yourself to daydream about the things that could happen to a boat while it's left unattended. Then you wonder, *Did I close that one seacock or not when we last checked the boat?* You will not quite sleep as well that night. You will wonder if you'll forever rue the day you didn't check that thing you should have checked.

Even so, I was having a grand old time in sunny Florida. I wondered if it was because I had finally arrived where I was intended to be all along. Was I a born Southern suburbanite? I sensed these Floridians were noticeably friendlier than the inhabitants found near New York City. I wondered if I was hallucinating, or if it was the weather, or the fact that there were more retirees, hence there was less stress. I wondered if maybe because the mean age of people with whom I was interfacing was higher meant they were trying that much harder to have a good time with what time they had left. I wondered what the hell made me use the word "interfacing." I wondered if maybe I

---

[1] John Cole, Away All Boats, *A Personal Guide for the Small Boat Owner,* (Henry Holt & Company, 1994, p. xxi)

was overthinking everything. I wondered if I should have another donut and a swim. I went with that wonder.

Deb and I both had lost a nice healthy bit of weight on the way down without thinking about it. It tends to happen on a boat trip. There is no freezer full of fudgesicles, no easy impulse trip to the Dairy Queen. Even the process of making dinner takes up twice the energy to prepare, what with diving into pantries, pumping stove pressure, and struggling to keep upright while tending to regular chores. You are out in the elements for much of the day, and even the cabin is generally cooler than a home up North, so your body is burning energy to stay warm.

Gaining the weight back in Florida was equally effortless. The holidays were upon us. Deb and her mom played off each other's cooking talents, and Rich, a tireless workaholic (who's working hard on that problem now), had taken a side job with Dunkin Donuts, hence my daily breakfast scenario.

I've always been an opportunist when it comes to food. If it becomes available to me, I eat it. The list of things I will not attempt to digest on principle is a very short one, and if I'm on my own, with no way to get to any fast-food franchise, I will eat things most people would throw away on sight. I've only resisted sampling pet food because of the stigma attached to the act of getting caught scarfing a Snausage. I am, in short, a bottom feeder.

This does not prevent me from appreciating a really fine meal. I've had plenty, made particularly appetizing on those occasions when they were on somebody else's dime. From time to time I lay down the big bucks, and I inevitably come to the conclusion that a fat, juicy cheeseburger would have been just as satisfying, if not more so, at a tenth the price.

Deb is an excellent cook. She could run a restaurant, and I mean a successful one, in New York City. Her mother is no slouch either. I suppose it's the Italian thing. What I'm getting at here is there was no way in hell I was going to keep the weight off during my extended layover in South Florida. What would be the point? If it came to it, I'd have a closed casket funeral. Now dish me up some pasta, prego. Mama mia.

I did a little work. The gardening, one of Joan's passions, was surprisingly enjoyable. It would be nice to have a passion, I think. I'm putting that on my list of things to discover before I die of carb overload.

I also did what I'd hoped would be my last lighting job, a holiday number on the family house. I took it seriously, but let me tell you, Radio City Music Hall has got nothing on a Florida suburb during the holidays. These folks mean business. The utility companies must have a hell of a time keeping up with demand, what with air conditioning competing with the umpteen million lights and inflatable nativity scenes running 24/7 down there. I made money lighting things in New York City, and I can't say I was even in the voting in our neighborhood. Let's just say we were presentable.

Part of our commitment to those we left behind was a Christmas e-card to fill in for our annual holiday photo funny, a tradition that extends back to before Deb and I were married. It's an important tradition, and one that creates a certain anxiety each year, since we never seem to come up with the idea till crunch time. This time we took our dinghy and threw it in the pool. Deb was navigating by chart, oblivious to the drama of my being attacked by the automated pool-cleaning device. Please one's self first and foremost, is my motto.

∼∼∼

1/14/06
Log of the Laura Lynn Update #12
Position: couch

We are frauds. We are charlatans. You signed up with us in good faith, hoping to hear tales of the high seas, and we've been shopping Florida malls for two months.

In fact, my mother-in-law has trained me to be a power-returner. I, who once refused to acknowledge any foolhardy purchase, now stand in line to fill out forms and stare down skeptical service associates in order to be reimbursed for shorts "a little tight in the crotch."

In my past life, I would have hung on to virtually anything I was dumb enough to buy, no matter how overpriced, ill-designed, ill-manufactured, ill-fitting, or ill-suited to its task, rather than dig out the receipt and go admit my gullibility to the vender who suckered me in the first place. I've watched Joan travel halfway to the Gulf Coast to return a $1.29 packet of paper doilies that just didn't fit the bill. I'd have saved them for Christmas decorations. They make nice snowflakes.

I think I'm coming around to her thinking though. I've been returning all manner of merchandise, much of it purchased from West Marine, so there may be hope for me as a cruiser yet. A credit applied to my MasterCard almost feels like income. It's the next best thing to dumpster-diving when it comes to frugality, and I'm no slouch in that department. The green streaks on my shins aren't grass stains, baby.

The sad fact, though, is that the only boating I've been doing lately is ferrying goods back and forth to the Laura Lynn via our dinghy. We've been stripping off cold weather clothing and anything that has proven itself of dubious worth so far on the trip. As it turns out, we have to make room for all the food Deb is planning on vacuum packing in the next few days. Lord protect us from Salmahootchie, or whatever those bugs are that make you wish you'd just bought out the canned goods section at Wal-Mart.

And we've been "fixing" things. Fixing things generally means attempting to fix things, in the process breaking them further, then going out to buy new things to replace the old ones and getting the wrong replacements and having to take them back. I do know how to take them back now.

What I'm not so good at is everyday maintenance, the kind that comes at you from every crevice of a boat, at an alarming rate. There are leaks and sparks and growths and sounds that make a haunted house seem like a Buddhist temple of serenity. We've rebuilt the head to combat the odors picked up by Deb's highly acute olfactory system. We've re-plumbed the bilge area to keep us floating and further nice smelling.

Now I'm reinsulating our icebox, in hopes that our food might stay fresh a little longer on the blocks of ice we'll soon be transporting to augment what I fear is an inadequate refrigeration system. Adding insulation involves standing on my head in order to shape, cut, and attach layers of stiff insulation, followed by a layer of this other stuff that looks like the inside of a fridge. Where we once could store a side of beef that would admittedly go bad overnight, we'll soon be able to keep a head of lettuce and a pint of milk safely chilled for a full two days.

Adding insulation also involves bruising my ribs and grazing my scalp against the top edges of the icebox opening. Being upside down also causes sweat to drip onto the optical surface of one's corrective lenses, causing a distinct loss of vision, which causes confusion, frustration and miscalculation. All these things raise the blood pressure around one's brain, assuming one has one, to levels convenient for a stroke. And these catalysts all lead to profuse cussing.

My dad taught me to cuss. Not intentionally, of course. He thought he was removing four layers of skin from his knuckles with a crescent wrench in the privacy of his workshop. I'm glad he taught me though. It's the easiest way to find something you've been looking for, for too long. When you've finally had enough of looking in the same place for some lost widget, you commence to swear a blue streak, looking to the unseen world like an utter fool, and sure enough the thing shows up immediately. It works for a lot of other problems too, as long as there is someone nearby to hear you and wonder what kind of nut job you are. I bet I could balance the federal budget if I swore loud enough in front of the right crowd.

Cussing is also a good gauge of how badly you are in trouble. If a mile long string of high volume profanity does not make you feel better, you might want to consider calling 911, for something is seriously amiss.

So we're going nowhere fast here in sunny Florida, which has prompted me to at least write about it in order to get something accomplished. In service of that goal then, we're jumping on a popular bandwagon and doing our own TEN list. Here then, are . . . .

Ten Lame Reasons Not to Set Sail for the Abacos:

10. What if we can't find them?
9. It might ruin Deb's pedicure.
8. I've forgotten which side is starboard.
7. We're not sure if there is a Cold Stone Creamery in the Abacos.
6. Deb isn't back from Target.
5. There's a pool with a slide where we're staying.
4. It's been kind of chilly for Florida recently.
3. A Jackie Chan movie is playing on HBO.
2. I have a splinter.
1. We forgot where we parked the boat.

What's Hot:
Weather windows
Visits to recently lost friends
Joan's going-away meal.
Jenn and Brian

What's Not:
> Last-minute searches for spare parts
> Losing the edge
> Northerlies in the Gulf Stream
> Canker sores. What is the POINT of these things?
> A cracked cap. Thanks for the bodywork, Dr. Sidor.
> Leaving family behind.

Shout-Outs:

~ Dave and Wheezer, so great to see you kids. Thanks for lunch. We promise not to divulge the location of your secret Paradise. My favorite topping is pepperoni, and Deb's is mushroom.
~ Jana and Larry, wonderful to see you cats too. If you need a PA, I'll be available full time in a couple months. Watch your bottom time.
~ Mike Kurnides, we are honored by your mention of us in Boating World this month. When in doubt, go with the hammer.
~ Aunt Joyce and Uncle Bob, has the gator surfaced yet? Thanks for taking it easy on Paul during "May I."
~ Spooky, I think I'll miss you the most. But you've got to learn to relax, cat.
~ Joan and Rich, for everything, not the least of which is simply tolerating our fishy presence for so long. You have our eternal love and gratitude.

Final thoughts: Our plan is to hop the Gulf Stream on or about January 16, after which time our cell phone will not work, and Internet availability will once again be spotty. Please don't send us large files or goofy forwards unless you feel strongly about the material being sent. We'll try to stay in touch and let you know what our situation is, but Phase III of the trip is a new and unknown challenge. We're taking you along in our hearts, even if you hear from us only sporadically.

~~~

Happy Holidays!

Chapter 11

The Stream

Do not mess with this chick. She's busy.

The Christmas tree was a shadow of its former self. Passing by it in close proximity would cause a shower of needles to tinkle to the floor. It was time for it, and us, to go.

We packed all our gear into the donut truck, transferred everything to the boat, and started to cry. It had been a great stop. I felt a knot in my stomach. I'd found a home away from home in Florida. The cats didn't even make me sneeze. Was this an omen? I'd been away from the boat so long, I wondered if I could continue. To the left is port. To the right is starboard. Left, port. Right, starboard.

No sweat, right? It's just like riding a bike. You just have to get out there, and it all comes back to you in a flash of recognition.

An hour and a half after stepping off land to continue our trip, we were hard aground in the St. Lucie Inlet, with an outgoing tide swirling sand around our hull as if a school of piranha were feasting on us.

We'd committed the foolishly casual mistake of making an impulsive course change, deciding what the heck, let's go outside instead of inside. It's a beautiful day. Let's be sailors. That kind of thinking, sadly, is not very sailorly, and can occasionally reward you with story material.

There in front of us had been the prodigious expanse of the St. Lucie Inlet, a huge runway leading to the wide blue yonder. I barreled right down the middle, toward the ocean, which is not how you make it to the ocean at the St. Lucie Inlet. I was oblivious to the channel markers hugging the southern shore, marking the exit strategy necessitated by the shoaling that plagues this area.

As the water got lighter and the depth meter began to squawk, I asked Deb, who was below, what the computer screen was telling her. She checked. "Go right," she said. I turned to starboard. "More right," she said, a bit more urgently, and too late.

I tried all the tricks in Nigel's book to get us off the sandbar, attempting to kedge, sail, and heel the boat by hanging off the boom. A local fisherman tried to help us off, but succeeded only in nearly removing our steering pedestal from the boat. Somehow his offered towline had gotten looped around our wheel. When I noticed it, I had an instant to throw the loop before he throttled up and popped a U bracket on his transom. Cheese and Chryslers, we needed professional help.

It took insurance and horsepower to get us off. We called Tow Boat US, and three hours later we were tugged to the deep water a few short feet ahead. Subtracting all our earlier futile attempts, the ensuing wait, and the filling out of forms, it took around five seconds.

There are a few lessons here ripe for the picking. I'll settle for one. Own a good pair of binoculars, and use them. I guess that's two.

I was becoming aware of a sign posted mid-channel directly ahead of us, when we ran aground. The fact that it was a post firmly planted in the substrate should have been enough of a clue. The sign said, "Warning, Dangerous Shoaling." I'd almost gotten close enough to read it with unaided vision.

What would have been a lovely, leisurely reintroduction to the pleasures of the ICW now became an urgent dash to our appointed anchorage in Lake Worth. We got through the last bridge as the sun dipped below the horizon, and dropped anchor in the waning light of dusk. Word for the day: *inauspicious*.

～～～

Lake Worth. The Big Wait. The holding tank where slow boaters sit out the parade of low-pressure fronts, waiting for the proverbial weather window that is loosely defined as three days of predicted high pressure with winds having no northerly component.

I'll say again, no northerly component. Why? Because the Gulf Stream flows in a northerly direction. If that current hits winds traveling in the other direction, which is to say from the north, therefore labeled "Northerlies" (Have I *claimed* to be a meteorologist?) Mother Nature does her rendition of *Momma's Got a Squeezebox*.

How hard could it be in sunny Florida to get three days of nice weather in a row? You'd be amazed. Word for the week: *purgatory*.

It was eerie. One, I was still reeling from the grounding, unsure of myself, trying to get a feel for the boat again. Two, the weather was not cooperating. Three, while previously we'd always felt the warm camaraderie of other boaters, this group of waiter-outers seemed an indifferent band of loners. During our forays to shore, conversations seemed curt and formal. Worse, when we shared our plan, nobody seemed to have chosen Lake Worth Inlet for their hop-off point; everyone seemed to wish to head further south. Our research, indicating Lake Worth as a suitable on-ramp, was being contested by these cruisers. What in the world had I been snorting?

It was a pressing desire of ours to become associated with a crossing flotilla of some sort. We had until this point been of the shared opinion that it would be no problem to attach ourselves to just such a parade. Simple as saying howdy, when are you leaving for the Bahamas, and mind if we tag along?

I was now starting to get spooked. When I hooked up with a frightfully gregarious captain, a glimmer of hope was dashed, when he turned out maniacally interested in taking over every aspect of our lives. He'd show us a better way of cleaning off that boat mustache. We'd need a bigger rod to haul in dorado for dinner, and he had some cheap ones onboard. He also had an anchor roller that would work for us, and he'd install it, presumably at a later-to-be-determined fee. We could put in a windlass too! Why not follow them to Fort Lauderdale and cross with them there? He'd call on us when they were headed out. His wife was onboard with him, but she said virtually nothing, as there was virtually no opportunity.

I like friendly people, but overly friendly ones give me the willies. We were, once I'd pealed the man's claws off my dinghy, unattached again.

It was, then, a double-edged sort of solace provided by the visit of Deb's mom, several days after we'd made it to Lake Worth. What had for us been an emotional trip to our present location, followed by a period of being waylaid by weather, and then Captain Congeniality, was for her a thoughtless forty-minute commute. She couldn't help herself, and invited us to return. We'd all had so much fun we gave it a half-serious thought.

We settled instead for lunch together, after which Joan ferried us to a laundromat, and when that was over, there necessitated another round of good-byes. Exhausting work.

~~~

But darn it, we meant business. We continued to watch the weather, and with or without escort, we intended to follow our plan to cross from Lake Worth, Florida, to West End, Bahamas.

Then the window arrived. Holy shit. We got ourselves ready to reanchor a few miles down the road, near Peanut Island, the on-deck circle for a Gulf Stream crossing. This was one of those pivotal moments for a couple who'd never been more than a few miles offshore.

I was taking a solace-inducing shower when I heard Deb talking sociably to someone. By the time I was presentable, the boater had left, but Deb was wearing one of those saucer-eyed smiles of hers that announces life has just gotten a whole lot better.

She'd just finished a pleasant conversation with an experienced sailor who'd asked if we were making the crossing from Lake Worth, and if so, would we like to tag along with them?

Does the Pope wear a goofy chapeau?

Don and Linda, aboard *Epilogue*, had been making the crossing for years, and it had become their amicable custom to invite other cruisers to join them. They'd rounded up two other boats for their flotilla, and we'd make a fourth. Deb was containing such a serious giggle I thought she'd wet herself. I would have voluntarily done in my best shorts to insure just such a development. We had us a convoy.

Oh, what a difference a day makes. Our group prepared to relocate to Peanut Island, but not before one more uncomfortable visit by you-know-who. I suspected he would show and attempt to convince us of his superior plan, and he didn't disappoint. He was rapping on our hull around 7AM. *Well sir, what do you say?* I broke the news that we'd decided to follow in the wake of others.

The captain's face darkened, his head began to wag, and I thought he would rip the stanchion he was holding from its mount. "I wouldn't do it," he warned. "You're opening yourself up to the whole Atlantic Ocean." I'm uh, what?

I hate these kinds of moments. Please, just go away and leave me to my fate. I tried to explain to him, *Well you know, this had always been our plan and, uh, we're going to stick with it and* . . .

"Not a good idea. I wouldn't do it." He kept shaking his head as if I might succumb to a certain prescribed number of noggin-wobbles. I held my ground the way a rabbit does, by not moving, while a wolf looks him over to determine if he's a healthy meal, or a disease-ridden ticket to the runs.

Then he let go of our boat, and headed off to his own. That was the moment I realized we were going to the Bahamas.

∼∼∼

1/24/2006
Log of the Laura Lynn Update #13
Position: You really don't care about coordinates, do you? We're in the Bahamas, Mon!

Eureka! Our ship has come in. Veni, vidi, vici, and whatnot. That's one small step for mankind, one giant leap for Deb and Paul. Thank you, Father Bob, from Earth Base Illinois, and Captain Bob, from the conning tower. As I peck away, we are anchored in Black Sound, Green Turtle Cay, the Abacos. That's the Bahamas, folks. We found 'em.

Okay, we had some help. After an anxious week of waiting on an ever-so-ethereal "weather window," we were invited by a group of fellow travelers (thank you, Don and Linda of Epilogue, for the gracious invite) to play caboose to their choo choo. So on Tuesday, January 21, our caravan arose at 1:30 AM, anchors up at 2:30, and we began our traverse of the Straits of Florida, and with it, a crossing of the legendary Gulf Stream. Seventeen hours later, we'd made our way to the safe harbor of Great Sale Cay, a few hours before the window slammed shut on the wings of an advancing cold front.

Sailors will talk your ears off over the weather. It weighs more heavily on the mind than the Super Bowl point spread. Don't know who's in it this year, and frankly don't care. Need to know where and when the next wind shift is taking place. Your bed always faces the same direction, laid as it is on a solid foundation. I never quite know where I'll wake up. Always with the same chick though, and that's a good thing.

To those as yet uninitiated, the "Gulf Stream" is a wicked misnomer, a mean-spirited term concocted most probably by a cadre of overly grizzled salts (shoveling coal, I now trust, in Davy Jones's Locker) looking to get their jollies from the misfortune of others with the redefining of the term "irony." The "Stream" is the most massive movement of water on the planet, a humongous current pinched through the Florida Straits in a giant Venturi effect, where its northerly "set" can reach four knots in speed. Doesn't seem like much? Try walking at a quick pace into a brick wall. Close your eyes so you don't cheat. Sissy.

Keep in mind our boat weighs about seven tons and doesn't do much better than six knots. So as we're crossing the stream in an effort to make the Bahamas, the current is trying to divert us to Boston. Nice town, but we're not interested in visiting the Green Monster this time of year, thanks. Now factor in the wind. If any component of the wind is from the north (northwest, north-northeast, etc.), it strikes the current that's running the opposite way, folding up the water like an accordion—A giant, violent, liquid accordion. Oh, to stand on a large floating object made miniscule by the magnitude of nature, thus further reducing you on the scale of the infinitesimal, and then have Poseidon turn on the blender. Like I need weirder dreams to haunt me.

So all the wisdom says wait for a favorable window. Be patient, advises the salty sage. It's winter in Florida too. Cold fronts are the norm. You might need to wait for, maybe, a month or so.

Wha?? Like, I've got plans and stuff. People to meet. Fish to spear. Kaliks to quaff. After one week in Lake Worth, a popular waiting depot for like-minded travelers, Deb and I were chewing on our bed sheets. It got so bad, I dug out the sandpaper. We've got lots of stores onboard for all those bogus projects we promised we'd tend to sooner or later. Deb has Spanish tapes. When I heard her conjugating verbs, I headed for the V-berth, got out the 80 grit, and went at some faded teak. Let me tell you something, there is no surer sign of the coming Apocalypse than a sighting of me sanding something. Look it up in Deuteronomy. When I'm on my deathbed, and you hear me say, "Hand me the sandpaper," it's time to pull the plug, lay the coins on my eye sockets, and get thee to a nunnery.

But all that is ancient history now. Poseidon was kind to us, where others were forced to lay prostrate against the lee rail, offering up their last dinner of Saltines and Velveeta. Our night-into-day crossing was an unearthly delight. A crescent moon aided our eyesight, while GPS glowed

On the Wind and a Prayer

corroboration as we eased out of Palm Beach into the middle of the night, a convoy of flickering running lights and flapping canvas. Four boats, trusting in a NOAA weather report, hit the ocean with raised sails and running engines, to get it over with, to make the crossing of "the Stream."

Deb and I, freshmen to this ritual, were wide awake to watch the night turn into dawn, then fully into day. The Gulf Stream's hue is always described as "indigo," and I have no better modifier for it. Luscious Indigo, maybe. Sounds like one of Deb's nail polishes. Our depth finder bobbed around at four to five hundred feet, as our compass argued with the GPS. "We are headed southeast," proclaimed the compass, while the GPS countered, "but we are traveling northeast." That was the Stream doing its thing, gently on this day, thank heavens. Without technology, I never would have known. Like children in the forest on a cloudy day, we were being taken for a ride by Mother Nature.

Our course described a lazy "S" as we entered and exited the current, and then, in a matter of moments, we watched in wonder as the depth finder started to climb. In the near distance, indigo was being displaced by gorgeous myriad hues of turquoise, and like a flaring airplane, we landed on the Little Bahama Bank. Set down! The bottom stabilized at twelve feet, a powder blue runway that stretched, along with our dreams, beyond the horizon.

What's Hot:
  A weather window!
  More stars than you've ever seen before
  Infinite shades of blue
  Sailors who've been there before
  An anchor that bites the first time
  Deep sleep

What's Not:
  Waiting waiting waiting waiting waiting waiting
  Sailors who know too much
  Fear of the unknown

Shout-Outs:

~ *Don and Linda, thanks for babysitting the "kids."*
~ *Joan and Rich, thank you once again. Your supplies kept us alive during the "Big Wait."*
~ *Too Too! What fun to visit with you and Rob. Hopefully we'll see you on the way back!*
~ *Hey, NFL: Hut one. Hut two. Big deal.*
~ *Bosco! Who do you figure is gonna win?*
~ *Kayface! Hugs and Kisses. Must take a transmission course soon.*
~ *Harley and Betty, how's Cuba?*

~~~

Too legit to quit: The requisite raising of the Bahamian courtesy flag

~~~

    This was the big one, not so much an overnighter as a through-the-night, into-the-night. The overall feeling was like that of being on a carefully dosed adrenaline drip feed. Others in the future would relate stories of horrible squalls, lost lunches, ripped sails, and rent egos. With the emotional cushion provided by the crew of *Epilogue*, along with mild weather, we had an easy go of it. Our only issue was caused by the extended length of our day. The group had decided to pass on by West End, which owns a spotty reputation for anchoring, to forge on all the way to Great Sale Cay. Weather information suggested we choose a more secure anchorage than Mangrove Cay, an intermediate stop that provided poor weather protection, it being little more than a pancake of land, not much to hide behind in a blow, particularly if you have to share the space.
    The sun gave out on us before we made Great Sale, and we found ourselves making our first night approach, into a harbor that was foreign to us in more ways than one. Then, due to our boat speed (I won't call Don a purest, but he owns a sailboat, and likes to use it as such) and a technical problem with one of the other boats, that had the third tending to them, we were the first of the fleet to approach the harbor. Here was a case where ignorance was bliss. We used our paper charts as reference, and our

eyes to spot the anchor lights of other boats, but I believed the chart-plotter imagery to a far greater degree than I was later to learn I should. In this case, everything correlated to an exceptional degree, or I would no doubt have grounded us again.

When Deb and I got our anchor to bite, it dawned on us we'd made it. We sat back and watched the lights of the other boats entering the harbor, sensing from the tense conversations on the VHF regarding hazards and holding that maybe we'd gotten away with, if not murder, at least petty larceny.

In the middle of the night came the weather that proved we'd made a fortuitous decision to ford on. The future would continue to reveal that, all too often for my taste, there would be tricky, multi-faceted decisions to make. One was never sure what the best choice would be until the aftermath. Often one had only to divine the lesser of evils. Complicating your decision would be folks contributing their own acquired information, as well as their own insecurities.

Clearly the more experience you have, the more you're able to at least settle comfortably with the consequences of your decisions. Even so, I think second-guessing other cruisers is probably one of the more popular hobbies practiced on the water.

Case in point: The next day was a blustery one. Folks were clearing out of Great Sale, but while most everyone was ultimately headed in the same direction, the question became which way do you round the island in order to get on your way? Heading counterclockwise and south seemed to make sense to me because it was a shorter route, and would put the wind essentially at one's back. Yet there were many who were uneasy about the constricted route through a series of shallows that, even to my squeamish estimation, seemed like a serviceable route.

In the end, we succumbed to mob psychology and followed a group of boaters who chose to endure a boisterous, clockwise, and upwind slog in the wrong direction (I never get over that aspect of sailing) that made me once again consider the structural integrity of my spine. We chose Charybdis over Scylla.

One of the side effects to traveling in the company of other boaters, whether mutually consensual or more or less de facto, is that you spend a lot of time wondering what the hell it is the other ones think they're doing. Why are they following that course, and not a course ten degrees to port? Why are they adjusting course now, and that way? Why are they fiddling with their sails now? It's almost soothing to see them screw up, so you can go, "Well that explains it. They're clueless. Okay then, why are we following them?"

It takes time to get comfortable with one's own skills, or at least recognize your own failings so you can spot the errors of others. People get sloppy, people make mistakes, and people may not care so much about sail trim, because they're on vacation. And people occasionally *do* know something you don't.

We were several weeks away from getting to meet Steve Dodge, the Abaco Guide guru. We were among the many devoted boaters using his widely distributed guidebook, but we were observing navigational behavior he'd later chuckle at while explaining. Having published handy waypoints (which happen to be precisely mapped coordinates) for use as general aids to navigation, he frequently hears of reported sightings of power boats racing to spots in the water, where they'll stop, adjust their heading, and continue racing off in a corrected direction. He has come to realize these are folks following precise paths to his various waypoints, as if absolute accuracy were crucial.

With GPS so compelling a technology, it's easy to find one's self pulling the same stunt, if only for the gamesmanship of it. We're almooooost there. There! We're at Steve's WHLSW waypoint. Turn now!

~~~

I've listened to wetted-down lamentations of old salts, as they bemoan the sullying of *Paradise* by GPS. I feel for the guys. I know they know their way around a sextant. I know I wouldn't be on this trip without those orbiting abacuses. I know the harbors are a lot more crowded as the result of all this modern technology. But I'm not sure how many of us have the right to claim exclusivity to a certain privilege, based on our chosen level of commitment. Did these guys make their sextants? Did they assemble their own chronometers? Did they chart the heavens after having determined we are not at the center of the universe?

I'm pretty sure I couldn't even make a hank of rope I could reliably hang myself with. I've never actually started a fire by whacking a couple of flints together. Hell, I can't tell the difference between flint and schist. So make room there, Queeg. I'm a natural rower, and it looks to me like somebody else manufactured that Yamaha you're yanking on.

~~~

Having finally made it to the Abacos, I began to fixate on the task of clearing into a new country. All the books play it close to the vest, insisting on a timely check-in. I think it would help those new to cruising, the one's buying the books, to keep in mind safety comes first, and finding a customs agent comes second. I was becoming anxious that we were going to get arrested for admitting we'd been in the country for days without making our way to a customs office. By the time we pulled it off, we'd passed islands harboring Bahamian customs agents, but not in harbors to my liking, given weather conditions and my inexperience with the local terrain.

We got legit in Green Turtle Cay, and in another weird kind of way, we decided we'd again finally made it, for now we were properly processed, and in the heart of the cruising grounds of the Abacos. We were anchored in the snug little harbor of an island visitors actually consider a vacation destination. Our cruising papers had cost us $150. Had our boat been a foot and a half longer, through the vagaries of the Bahamian bureaucratic process, it would have cost us double that, so my advice, if you own a thirty-six footer, is to saw off your bowsprit. Just a thought, if you have one, and are on a tight budget.

We'd lost our convoy, but met new folks on other boats in the harbor. We were invited on walks and get-togethers at the local watering holes. This again is simply how it works with cruisers. You spot each other, exchange a hello, and start comparing calendars.

While we enjoyed Green Turtle Cay, we knew we were within spitting distance of our Mecca, the spot which, from the beginning, served as the focal point of our trip. Whatever surprises we might discover along the way, whatever detours we might enjoy or suffer, the plan was to make Hope Town Harbour, in Elbow Cay. After a few pleasant days on Green Turtle, we took the next step.

Marsh Harbour is the central hub of the Abaco cruising grounds. Situated on Great Abaco Island, it is home to the Moorings fleet, the first company to encourage rent-a-boat vacations on a grand scale. People visiting the Abacos by air fly into Marsh Harbour. It is a bustling town, not terribly attractive, but strategically located, which means a lot to a sailor. The harbor is large and protected, with a fairly straightforward entry.

You know, I can't believe I caught myself using that phrase. You know what I really think? To anybody who knows a harbor well, its entry is straightforward. To a newcomer, every harbor entrance is a maze of dangerous obstacles and hidden treachery.

It still isn't too hard to find a place to anchor in Marsh Harbour, and it's awfully easy to schedule one's evenings around one of the ever-burgeoning institutions in the business of promoting human happiness. Oh, you know what I mean. This is the Bahamas, not Macao. If you're on a boat, you're going to visit Marsh Harbour on a regular basis while you're in the Abacos.

If we were within spitting distance of Hope Town before, we were in pinching range now. The issue now was, given its small harbor, which has for all practical purposes been filled to capacity with rental moorings, could we make it that last step?

We'd made attempts to contact the mooring tenders with no success while on Green Turtle Cay. Batelco, the nationalized phone company, don't even get me started on them. How do I put it succinctly? We are living in the twenty-first century, the Bahamas are closer to Miami than Key West is, yet an entrepreneur with a crate of empty bean tins and a ball of twine would pose a serious challenge to the government's communications monopoly, but for the strong arm of the law. Modernity may have arrived by the time you read this. In the mean time, there is Skype, the use of which, to procure a viable speaking connection, constitutes a Bahamian finable offense. So sue me.

We were having trouble with our VHF radio, getting significantly less coverage than one should expect. Something wasn't right, but I didn't know what. Probably something to do with the antenna, which was forty-five feet up in the air.

We should have been able to communicate with Hope Town directly, but got the next best thing. A guy at the Moorings heard us attempting to radio for a mooring in Hope Town, and he was the generous radio middleman who managed to reserve one for us. We were later to discover how fortuitous this was, for we ended up holding that mooring for two months while boaters late to the dance would be frequently disappointed. We had our reservation. We were set for the final push.

Chapter 12

Mecca

~~~

2/4/2006
Log of the Laura Lynn Update #14
Position: The poop deck
Hope Town Harbour, Elbow Cay

    There she was, after years of imagining, and months of living in a floating phone booth with a bad connection. Mecca.

Laura Lynn is moored virtually at the base of the lighthouse that has for years served as the focal point of our planned seabatical. We've stared wistfully at screen savers of Hope Town's beacon, taken over the course of two airborne trips, once with my siblings in 2000, and once just Deb and me in 2002. The lighthouse is one of three hand-cranked, kerosene-burning lighthouses left in the world. While all these optical wonders have a special effect on any human with an ounce of whimsy, this candy cane striped beauty brought me to tears as we headed down the harbor entrance. There she was, the icon that represented a shared dream to do something remarkable with our lives while we had it in us. We are now close enough to her at our mooring to see that she needs a paint job.

After enjoying a heady dose of euphoria, an odd feeling began to insinuate itself. You've heard us talk of the incessant moving, and the perpetual weighing of anchors to put more miles behind us. I was now faced with the fact that we had got to where we intended to get. It is beautiful, this island; the folks friendly, the cottages preciously pastel, the water crystal clear, blah blah blah. Curse me for thinking it, but I began to wonder what it was we were supposed to do next. I've heard of various forms of post-event depression, and thinking I might be suffering from a case, I started to panic.

So I got out the varnish and laid on another coat to all this wretched wood that bedecks our boat. Then I started to get a hold of myself. I relaxed, which induced a pleasant lethargy. Heck, I could sleep every day till noon and beyond if I wanted. I discovered island time. I took deep breaths. I began to glimpse nirvana. Then Deb entered us in a sailboat race.

The Hope Town Sailing Club is as nice a bunch of folks as you'd like to meet—a blend of humanity that includes lifers from the island, seasonal expats, roaming adventurers, and occasional lost souls like us. Well, we're not members, but you don't have to be to race; there is no fee to enter, and all they ask is that you play fair and try not to run into other boats.

There were ten boats racing on this day, and we managed to avoid contact with any of them. We sailed our hearts out, beating ourselves black-and-blue against the rigging in hefty winds, and came in last. We'd thought we'd had a chance against two boats not much larger than our dinghy, each sporting crews whose mean age appeared to be about eighty-six, but those geezers whupped us good. In fact, while I had my eye on one boat, I'm pretty sure members of the other crew snuck onboard and vandalized our cabin. That's sure what it looked like after the race was over.

Our last chance to avoid the "good sportsman" award was an attempt to nudge out a guy singlehanding a cutter rig. This fellow had three sails up and was tending to everything himself. Deb and I were working so hard, and he seemed almost bored, lightly skipping around his deck, making adjustments while his autohelm steered for him.

Anyway, he took us in the end, then beat us back to port, picked up his dink and was leaving again as we, licking our wounds, entered the harbor. We met Mike later at the awards banquet, after he'd taken his boat to another island for safekeeping and returned on a ferry while we were napping. He was headed off the next day to go skiing in Jackson Hole, the bastard. I was wondering if there were any cots available at the local infirmary.

We did sleep in the next morning, though we listened in to the Cruisers' Net at eight fifteen, on VHF Channel 68. This is a daily ritual for cruisers in the Hub of Abaco that one simply must not miss. Besides listening to the reliably spirited voice of Patty reading the weather report (vital), passage conditions (essential), local events (useful), and world news bites (what for?), you get such gems as this: an offer at "Buck-a-Book" to purchase, for one dollar, not only any book in stock, but on this day, a puppy with all shots administered and papers in order. Alternatively, if not into such a commitment, with any two-dollar purchase you could borrow the puppy for the day.

Are you roaring? Because we were. Also in the canine news, we were heartened to hear that a home had been found for the three-legged dog folks had been worrying over. That's what I like about this place: emphasis on happy news. The newly appointed American news anchors should give it a try.

One last thing. The observant among you will notice that much time has passed since I began this entry. Pretend you haven't noticed I'm already fifty. I'll catch up shortly, maybe. What can I say? We're on island time, mon!

What's Hot:

Island time, mon.

Anything with conch in it

Even more pet news on the Cruiser's Net: A man, having lost his pet turtle four years ago, and hearing of a recent sighting on a nearby island, was offering a $100 reward for finding him. He described his turtle as "secretive" in nature.

Manually operated lighthouses

No underwear.

What's Not:

Pardon our French, but a wet ass

Wet feet.

Saltwater spray on your glasses

A wet ass

Shout-Outs:

~ *Dave and Eileen, we celebrated our arrival in Hope Town with your Turning Leaf gift. Thank you so much! Give your young men our love.*
~ *Richard Cion, thank you for your gift of Steve Dodge's book. You've kept us off the reefs and in safe harbors since we've reached the Abacos.*
~ *Gloria, we love you more.*
~ *Jackie, thank you for all your shore-side help. We got the VHF radio and are now getting and receiving vital information.*
~ *Mary Epstein, we love you. Come visit. We have a boyfriend for you. He's only in his sixties, but seems mature.*
~ *Stacy, thanks for the s t u f f. You sure know how to make the most of island time. Gotta go, mon.*

~~~

Dinner and a concert

~~~

Two months, in a place that, if I had any sense, I would have insisted we stay two decades. With any luck, that's the time I have left on planet earth. This is an island I hope and pray never goes condo. Oh, the development is there. Money always finds *Paradise*, but money does different things in different places, and uglier versions, I think, will forgo Elbow Cay. There will be mostly tasteful applications of wealth there. I hope so.

A fairly benign rumor had sprung up back home that Deb and I were traveling around the world. I think it got to that stage via the adult version of that school game, "telephone," a learning tool used by teachers to show children how rumors are spread. A more reasonable mistaken assumption was that we'd headed to the Caribbean. We might have started that one ourselves, having retained little from long-past geography lessons.

The Abacos don't actually qualify for Caribbean status. They're practically a suburb of Miami, sitting offshore on a shallow shelf, separated in the mind by that stream we've mentioned. The islands are little more than stubborn patches of limestone crust that refuse to drown, at least for the time being.

As you walk the perimeter of Elbow Cay, if you have the stamina, you'll be halted at various points by some extremely daunting rock outcroppings, made so not by their height or steepness, but by their texture. As the limestone erodes in pockets, what is left is a dangerous pocked landscape that would slice open any human appendage sorry enough to meet it. I mean, you better be wearing serious footgear, and pick your steps carefully. Falling will most likely have serious medical consequences.

For this reason there is plenty of shoreline that is unsympathetic to casual strollers, and that may be playing a role in the island's development. People like the feel of sand between their toes, once they've paid their money to get away for a while.

~~~

It's amazing how much marketing goes into the pitching of a simple image: a mated pair of feet traversing a sandy beach. All manner of advertising competes on a global scale for our attention. We are besieged by print ads, TV, Internet, from travel agents and airlines, governments, and private clubs ranging the world over—each and every one trying to convince us to pack our fantasies and head to where we can take the blissful Walk the fashionable faux couple is taking.

Where are they? Hawaii? Thailand? Coney Island? There surely will be a photo of a lovely, limby woman, whose tasteful coiff suggests she isn't strolling the Jersey Shore. Which is not to knock the Garden State. Jersey has some perfectly good beaches for strolling, as we know. It has porpoises too. And now get this: we've heard that an enterprising Jersey watering hole is landscaping its premises each summer with shipped-in palm trees. Decisions, decisions.

If there's enough space in the ad, a few more photos will accompany the beach strollers, as assurance that no one will starve, and that there will be tennis and golf so one can fashionably sweat off the shrimp cocktails. Heaven help us if tennis and golf aren't available. The paintball lobby, though, is having a tough time making tropical inroads. After the strenuous activities have been completed, one can indulge in a massage and a Nickelodeon slime facial, before heading off for a heaping helping of ultra-sex.

That pretty much covers what you're supposed to do on an island getaway. Sleeping accommodations aboard the *Laura Lynn*, I again point out, are quite sumptuous, once properly rigged.

There is no golf course on Elbow Cay. I'm pretty sure I saw a tennis court or two, but so far, this is an island of less-regulated leisure. Hope Town is a lovely little place, with a museum that explains where it is you are, and who preceded you there. It is lovingly maintained by Tony and Elaine Bennett. We herein officially wish them all the very best.

An itinerant constable occasionally puts in some face time near the town dock, as a reminder that lawlessness will not be tolerated. There is a library, and a grade school. There are a few restaurants, a couple grocery stores, a couple liquor stores, and some knick-knack shops where one can purchase things that prove one has visited. There is a single bank branch that is open Tuesdays, from ten to two, weather permitting—meaning if the teller can't make it in on the ferry, business will have to be conducted with a handshake until pleasant skies again prevail.

I think that is just grand. It is rare these days that we can slip back to an age that was less formal and more familiar. The hub of Hope Town arcs around its pert little harbor, and pretty much everything happens in plain view. In the course of a few days, you get the impression you've met just about everyone living on the island. After an extended visit, you might think you've gotten to know most by name, if you've applied yourself.

The impression would be skewed, but it's fun to give it a try. Having honed our social skills along the Eastern Seaboard, it was no great stretch to introduce ourselves to anybody within earshot. Why, I wonder, are we generally less inclined to do that in our neighborhoods back home? What keeps us from welcoming new neighbors with an apple pie? Where are the block parties? We are surrounded by our fellow man, each with stories to tell, joys to share, and lessons to teach.

Step out on the porch. Look left. Look right. Extend a greeting to whoever appears.

~~~

I just had to go say hi to Sam on *Treasure*, after he appeared from his cabin, faced the setting sun, raised a conch shell to his lips, and made like a Viking. What a sound. What a tradition. What a bitch to saw off the end of that shell.

What I thought would be a simple lesson on how to amplify a Bronx cheer through a seashell, turned into a passion with me. The process of creating a conch horn begins, if you are a purist, with the harvesting of this remarkable creature.

The Queen Conch is a gastropod, essentially a huge escargot. It is generally found in shallow, grassy seabeds, crawling along at . . . now how *would* one describe that kind of leisurely pace?

When one considers how easy these things are to harvest, the marvelous ways they're prepared as food, and the attraction we have for the shells that announce from our mantles we've been to heaven and back, I wonder how much time it'll be before they too are gone.

For total immersion in Bahamian culture then, one must head out on the banks, snorkel for the conch, clean them, eat them, make a horn, and salute the day's demise. I say this because I pulled it off myself, with Deb's culinary aid, and feel somewhat smug about having fairly mastered the process, not unlike one of those snobs who can get around by shooting stars with a sextant.

~~~

Do not attempt this without supervision. The crew of Epilogue attempt to teach us a thing or two.

~~~

Subject: *Log of the Laura Lynn Update #15*
Date: 3/05/06
Position: Recumbent

Greetings to all, and sorry for the lengthy absence. Having reached the half-century mark, I'm now honing my talents as a shiftless old codger in order to avoid further responsibility. Deb will only listen to this nonsense for so long before she makes me be useful. Having just overhauled the engine, she's getting set to prepare a Nassau grouper she speared at dawn. Shortly, she'll be cleaning the boat bottom of sea growth so we can be more competitive during the cruiser races. Figuring I should share some of the load, I agreed to write you guys.

Here's what's happened since we last communicated, not necessarily in chronological order:

My siblings, John and Cathy, visited for ten days to celebrate my rapidly advancing decrepitude. They were welcomed by ten days of bad weather.

John taught us all how to race a sailboat, and we did rather well with him at the helm.

John and Cathy left, and I mourned their departure. The weather became splendid. I mourned further this untimely turn of events.

Deb and I utilized our newly acquired sailing skills at the next race to win the Good Sportsman's Trophy. For the uninformed, this award is earned by coming in dead last, in our case in spectacular fashion, by failing to actually finish. The wind died around the time that all competent sailors had finished, and the current commenced whisking us toward Newfoundland. The race committee then discovered a wrinkle in the space-time continuum, and declared us finished. We received a tumbler decorated with the Hope Town Harbour Sailor's Club burgee for our efforts. Splendid! We must come in last again soon.

Deb smashed her finger on a thing, and almost pitched her lunch. I hit myself for the seven millionth time on the same bulkhead passageway. We two share the dexterity of a newborn Irish setter on heroin. Also, our ability to graciously absorb pain matches a kitchen sponge's ability to absorb the water contained in a small harbor.

I wrote my own birthday ballad, which goes like this:

> Happy birthday to me
> I can't hardly see
> My spine's made of jello
> And it takes hours to pee.

We caught, cleaned, and ate several conch. Delicious.

We decided that people who catch and clean conch are not paid near enough for their efforts. I made a conch horn out of the shell of the aforementioned creature, and now salute sunsets in C flat.

Deb saw a shark near the boat, and will probably never enter the water again. She claims the fish was approximately thirty feet long, making it the largest nurse shark in recorded history. Somebody call a living Cousteau.

I speared a chub. Chub are not all that tasty. I then lost my spear on an ill-advised target. After a butchered attempt at filleting the chub, and given the cost of the spear, I estimate we spent approximately ninety-four dollars per pound for something one could get deep-fried at Red Lobster for $8.99.

We slept in a lot. We napped plenty too. You really have to try this if you're anywhere near my age. It's better than a free ride on Space Mountain.

I attended the local writers' circle meeting, and read one of my logs we'd written to you all. They applauded when I was done, or perhaps they applauded because I was done. No, they applaud everyone who reads anything. It is a very supportive group. If you have any ego problem whatsoever, forget therapy. Join a writer's club and read anything you've ever written.

Here's an example. I wrote this poem to my mom when I was maybe in third grade:

> Roses are red
> Violets are blue
> When it rains
> I think of you
> Drip, drip, drip.

I have the original in crayon. Do you suppose I could have been that cynical at seven? Mom saved it, perhaps to keep me humble when I reach maturity, a milestone I surely must be nearing shortly. I bet I'd get a standing ovation for it at the writers' circle.

We got another mystery leak. While it is still unsolved, it is much slower than the last one.

I learned to scull. This is essentially rowing with one oar, while standing up in a boat. I'm still not sure what to do with this new skill. I will say this: life occasionally offers you opportunities for dubious self-improvement. Always take them. For instance, I now know Morse code. Here's a dirty word:

… ….. .. _

Deb has been attending ladies luncheons on various topics. Deb, ladies luncheons, you say? Don't worry, she's not losing her edge. She's networking the tropics.

Since the first week of February, Deb has also been volunteering at the Wyannie Malone Historical Museum. Wyannie was one of the first loyalists who escaped the prevailing mood of the original colonies when things started to get ugly at the onset of the Revolutionary War.

Most of those living here year-round are direct descendants of those loyalists who got out while the getting was good. I feel strangely comfortable here. The curator and general manager of the museum do not want Deb to leave. Me, I'm expendable. There's also an Annual Artist Luncheon at the snazzy Abaco Inn, where Deb will be helping to set up a booth, and selling jewelry designed by a lovely new friend of ours. I'll most probably nap.

We've read lots of really good books. We haven't watched a lick of TV. At the gentle urging of Kurt Vonnegut, we conscientiously say out loud to each other, as the spirit moves us, "If this isn't nice, I don't know what is." We urge you to do the same.

What's Hot:
    Being called "the kids" at our ages
    Wahoo fillets in ginger/garlic sauce
    Buck-a-Book
    Skype
    Winning last place
    Not setting an alarm

Conch horns at sunset

Deb's sis Jackie is coming. Hooray! Oh my, we must start cleaning. This is going to cut into my nap time.

What's Not:

Watching your family leave you

Shout-Outs:

~ Bret Connors, thank you for introducing us to the Abacos. We are having the time of our lives.
~ Jan, still thinking of you.
~ Larry, thanks for the wild book. Fabtastic. I may never dive again, though. I gave the book (Shadow Divers) to the curator of the local museum. He's an ex-British Naval officer, with a penchant for history. He loves it too.
~ Em, Joe, and Tom, we wish you were here. We talk about you all the time. Are your ears ringing?
~ Too Too! Did you make the cut?
~ Dolli! Hooray!!! Keep chuggin, girl.
~ Boober, that makes you fifty too!
~ John Marietta, how come we didn't have your e-mail address? We'll get you caught up soon.
~ Bosssssssssssssssssssscooooooooooooooooooooooooooooooooooo

~~~

When in Rome . . . My side of the family

There is a universally-shared fantasy, I'm quite sure, about finding a deserted tropical island, upon which one could presumably do whatever one wished, without suffering any criticism, whatsoever. Implied in the fantasy would be the discovery, on said cay, of an abandoned (from the last and final war, let's wish) warehouse, stockpiled with all the canned ravioli, soda pop, and scooter pies one could possibly consume in one's remaining lifetime.

I'm all for scooter pies, although my personal choice would be Little Debbies. We each would obviously stock our *Paradise* differently. More importantly, though, I'd change one other aspect of the dream. I'd stock my deserted island with people. My kind of people. You see, I'm a people person. Most people are, which makes us a lot like . . . ants, I guess.

I've more than once attempted to cultivate one of those ant farms our parents helped us send in for when we were kids. I'm not going to say how old I was when I last tried, but as neither a child nor an adult could I get a civilization up and running. Still, I'm sure if it did, there would be little nooks and crannies where a solitary ant could have quiet time, if he or she so desired.

The point is, I stand by my ant-colony metaphor. People tend to congregate in groups, and much as we'd like to think ourselves unique, we're all pretty much doing the same thing: trying to keep the mound together, while a small band of the hyper-steroidals of the species try to dictate the rules. We're passing each other all day, humping produce, tending to the maggots, hoping to get our hands on a choice bit of greenery, if all goes well. All in all, we're a gregarious lot.

That's why, when I approach the lip of a dune with the promise of an ocean view at the crest, I don't necessarily want to see a deserted beach, like all those ads suggest. I kind of want to see some strollers; fellow humans enjoying the same thing, sharing the wonder.

It's like going to a movie. Have you ever gone to a movie, a comedy, say, and it's one o'clock in the afternoon, because you've called in sick (which I never, ever do), and there's only you and some other guy who feels guilty about calling in sick? Then something funny happens, and it's dead quiet, because each of you is waiting for the other guy to get the ball rolling. What if your sense of humor is off, and this is the serious part? This guy will think you're nuts, which always puts a damper on frivolity. So you both sit there, wondering if you're having a good time, and as a result, you're not. Not like if it was a packed house, and the most fearless of four hundred people passes Coke through his nose at the first funny thing, and the whole gang is off and running like intellectually-challenged politicians in a three-legged race. Joy is like that: a benignly contagious human condition.

So yeah, I like to see a few like-minded souls out there. When you pass each other, you can say stuff like, "Hi, isn't this just glorious? Don't you just want to build your own shack right here, and never leave? Isn't it a shame we have to head back to Michigan tomorrow? How long do you guys have left? Aw man, sorry. Hey, what's around the next bend? How far did you get? Have you been anywhere that beats this? Did you find that shell down that way? Do you suppose there are more like it? Where's a good place to eat in town?"

And so forth. That's how I like my beaches. Not with two hundred beet-red sunbathers you have to gingerly step over to find a quiet stretch, though. That's where the ant farm analogy breaks down for me.

What else goes into the making of a perfect beach? Much is written on the topic, and there are many published lists that purport to reveal the secrets of the world's finest beaches. These, I am sure, are about selling magazines and airplane tickets.

Because, essentially, the answer is a personal one. Nobody likes pollution, but does weatherworn flotsam qualify? Sometimes it's interesting to look at some piece of long-ago-jettisoned debris and wonder about its history. Does a freighter on the horizon spoil the view, or provide visual intrigue? When hitting the surf, do you like lengthy, shallow entries, or dramatic steep plunges? Do you prefer the facilities a seaside dive overlooking your beach towel provides, or are you capable of emptying your bowels in the sea?

I confess that each beach is a compromise for me. Isn't it just like life, again? A nice series of rollers spawned by an offshore storm is a dramatic sight, and might make for invigorating bodysurfing, but will most likely keep my honey pie out of the water; and what could be more sublime than a nice long aqua-embrace? Not hardly anything, I'll wager. In any event, Hope Town has some fine beaches to choose from.

Here is another thing to consider, when visiting a small island. Given precious few vacation days, would you prefer to spend it in a cottage facing the vast, unoccupied ocean, with nothing but the infinite blue staring back at you? Or would you choose the sheltered and occupied harbor side, so that when night falls, there is, rather than the sound of breakers rearranging the shoreline, instead the hum and glow of human habitation?

Deb is a harbor kind of gal, which certainly worked for us aboard the *Laura Lynn*. Each night we returned to our mobile home and the camaraderie of fellow boaters bobbing about us. Overhead, as soon as Jeffrey got the mantle lit, there was the soothing beam of the Elbow Reef Lighthouse—five white flashes, one per second, followed by a five second pause; the prescribed pattern repeated through each and every night until dawn, mostly without fail—arching across the horizon.

In the air were the various sounds of humanity reaching us from Captain Jack's, lulling me and my failing hearing to sleep, and occasionally inducing fits in Deb when musical selections were, in her estimation, substandard.

When I attempt sleep, there are certain things I require. Dark is one of them. I don't like nightlights of any kind. I once owned an LED clock that was just too bright. I had to replace it. I'm wondering if maybe, along with my bad back, I inherited overly thin eyelids.

I do like white noise, so the sound of wind, rain, and wave action, if it is continuous and nonthreatening, works wonders for me. It's an entirely different matter when it starts to howl, and pets start hitting the deck.

Distinctly singular noises are maddening also. A harbor full of tinkling rigging is music on the heels of a tropical breeze. A single halyard snapping against one's own mast is torture. I can't count the times I've stepped outside in my skivvies (more or less) in the middle of a chilly night breeze, to retension a line in an attempt to stop the cyclical slap that's been plotting to make me a serial killer by dawn.

I must also have legroom. I'm not tall, but I range through the night. I might just put in more miles on my mattress than I do on sidewalks during the day. I like to bring one leg up and leave one down. It doesn't matter which. It'll change in five minutes. And I like my wife by my side.

Deb, on the other hand, will sleep though a hurricane, though not a hot flash.

Sailboat designers have historically seemed intent only on providing sleeping quarters for corpses. Lay the rigor mortised body out straight, measure around the stiff, and presto: a berth. I've found this to be the case on modern designs to forty feet, though things may finally be changing, which means for a quarter mil or more you can trade up from a prison block mattress.

I'm a descendant of Goldilocks, so the mattress has to be just right. In an Elizabeth City Wal-Mart, we found a foam pad to place over our settee seats that provides a suitable level of comfort. Once I place my eye mask on so Deb can get her necessary reading in (one of our nightly requirements, she always outlasts me), apply a nasal strip so I wont snore, and possibly insert earplugs if the rain is coming down hard, I'm sitting pretty. Maybe not so pretty.

~~~

I read somewhere a compelling editorial that claimed we as citizens have our priorities backward. We all, which is to say nearly half of us, make sure we get to the polls when the presidency comes up for grabs, but are much less interested in local politics. This canny observer pointed out that our lives are far more impacted at the civic level. We all know the president's name, but few of us know who our own mayor is. New Yorkers of course do, but he resides over a constituency larger than many states, so what's-his-name doesn't count.

The essay repeatedly surfaced in my head, as Deb and I became involved in the local affairs of Hope Town. This wasn't our home, yet we volunteered, as we never had at home. Now obviously a good chunk of one's life is spent providing one's self with food, clothing and shelter, which can be a wearing proposition. Yet somewhere here is a lesson to be learned, and the nature of this community rendered a potent message. On this small island, insulated from the monster nation we'd temporarily eluded, we found ourselves making an impact. While significant consequences can result from the work of individuals on a global scale, the measure of a nation begins with the way we, as individuals, treat our own neighbors. Further, we cannot help but live on a personal scale. We seem incapable of fathoming the horror of Nagasaki, but will follow with keen interest the fate of a single individual on life support.

It's easy to see the attractions of a small community. An individual matters. We sense that our choices will have a noticeable, even lasting, effect. To care, or not to care, has civic ramifications. We forget, for a moment, that there are three hundred million Americans, each clamoring for a unique identity. I notice that *Time Magazine*, a revered source of civic information, recently indulged us all by making every single American *Person of the Year*. I feel honored and humbled.

The mere drop-off of garbage in Hope Town had a social aspect. With trash removal being a bit more complicated than shuffling out in one's slippers to the color-coded bins, boaters on their trip to the community dump would go out of their way to pick up their neighbors' garbage, to spare them the need to dinghy in at the appointed hours. Collecting your neighbors' garbage: weird, but cool. There were days I found myself disappointed that somebody had beaten me to the punch. Damn! I wanted to be the good neighbor today.

During the day, it was extremely easy to stay busy. We were volunteering locally, enjoying scheduled island events, taking day trips around the Abacos, getting together virtually every evening with fellow boaters. It isn't hard to imagine the horrible consequence of this kind of schedule. Time flew by.

Last call

Chapter 13

The Road to Return

Next stop?

It was a painful act, to head out of Hope Town Harbour for good. I'd proven something about myself that I'd pretty much known. I'm a homebody, and I'd made myself quite at home there. That was kind of the plan in the beginning, but I also knew it would take a minor miracle to keep us there, or a major force of will, which I do not own. So we followed the migratory herd that had proceeded us. Already, we'd seen cherished friends move on, and now it was our turn.

Not before, however, Deb and I had a sit-down to decide on our exit strategy, for which there were two competing plans. One was to head back the way we'd come, revisiting our favorite spots in the Abacos, and trying a few new places recommended to us. The thought was enticing. We'd still be in the Bahamas, but with the security of being familiar with the route. That kind of scenario happens to be right up my alley.

Which is why, in a fit of brazen contrariety, we convinced ourselves to go the other way, south, away from home, toward unknown waters. And as it turned out once again, without adequate charts.

Would this choice reap new rewards for your two maladventurers? Would it gladden our hearts in the end to choose the iffy path? Or would we pay the price of ignorance with yet more consternation and mayhem? Would we ultimately look back and say, "Well, that's what we get for going it this way,"? The answers, as is so often the case in life, were resounding yes's.

∾∾∾

Log of the Laura Lynn Update #16
Star Date 2006
Somewhere in the Abaco Galaxy

Here is our problem. We've made too many friends. As a farmer was once heard to lament, "I'm tireder than a one-legged man in an ass-kicking contest."

We continue to base our operations out of Hope Town Harbour on Elbow Cay in the Abacos. It's the bomb. Here's a lesson I learned long ago while hiking the Smoky Mountains with friends: If you happen to discover nirvana while on the winding road to heaven, heaven can wait.

Back then, we stuck to our plan and deserted a perfect little glen in order to trudge up a spirit-crushing set of switchbacks (invented by Disney for Space Mountain enthusiasts) for a view that turned up missing. Nothing at the top but biting wind, blinding fog, and for one of us a bout of diarrhea, with no refuge but the great outdoors and the sympathy of a few close friends. Wasn't worth the trip, was it, Boober?

Back in the here and now, meandering boats come and go, and we get reports of exotic ports of call to the South, but we've got responsibilities here! There are museums to maintain, sisters to entertain (Jackie, why did you leave so soon?), conch horn contests in which to participate, beaches to pick clean of debris, and our family of fellow boaters, whose invitations pull us joyously in mutually incompatible directions. We could use a secretary. We could use a vacation. We're starting to cave under the load of social pressure.

But I believe I've learned something about coping with pain. I think it's called transference. Let's say you have a chronic ailment that's always on your mind. In my case, it's my back. Certainly the raising and disassembly of the circus tents at Heritage Day didn't help the back, but popping my shoulder on the folding tables put the back pain on the back burner. The shoulder has been a real bother, so rubbing my elbows raw during the Abaco dinghy races was a nice diversion. When I pulled muscles in both hands (how do you do that?), I found that splitting my head open on our boat ladder was the perfect balm. The pain caused by that clobbering was insignificant next to the fear that I was chumming the water with my own aqua vitae. Dad always used to say that heads bleed all out of proportion to the size of the injury. I suspect it's different in the case of a limb that's been severed by a large ocean carnivore.

I forgot about the head wound recently when I got kicked in the face by a child I was teaching to sail. The jaw is no longer sore, but the lip wants to bifurcate. Don't make me laugh. Ouch. Hey, have you ever wondered why we continue to laugh while desperately trying to catch a breath to prevent passing out? Wouldn't you think whatever it was that set us to laughing in the first place would lose its comical allure next to the fear of never being able to inhale again? How can something be that funny? Here I am guffawing while in terror for my very existence. Design flaw!

I trust you've just taken a nice heady breath, skipped to this paragraph, and lo and behold we've skipped town. Amazing! We've severed the umbilical of Hope Town, scooted seventy or so miles south and east, to find ourselves in Spanish Wells. Anyone get a nosebleed?

Spanish Wells, named for freshwater wells the Spaniards discovered while setting about to enslave the indigenous populations they encountered in their New World before ultimately extinguishing them, are famous, we're told, for supplying ninety or so percent of all the lobster meat to the entire Red Lobster chain. No Spanish is spoken here. The majority of the population are again progeny of loyalists who escaped the tyranny of those revolutionary tea-trashers. Here I begin to dizzy myself with the ramifications of man's inhumanity to man. We keep running away from our uglier selves to set up shop on some new horizon, inevitably to perpetuate the iniquities we've run away from. Or maybe it's the mango rum talking. Yummy.

Burp. And now we're in the big city. Nassau, just like I pictured it, skyscrapers, snarling traffic, and Tinkerbell. Let's leave this experience for another log. We're outta here.

What's Hot:
   Being at the top of the food chain. Where is that, actually?
   Welcoming the sunset with a blow on the homemade conch horn
   Jalapeño olives. In fact, olives in general.
   Book exchanges
   Books. Turn off the TV, we beg you. Except if watching Food Network.
   Food
   Geocaching. More on that in future updates.
   Local knowledge

What's Not:
   Not having access to weather reports
   Humidity
   Dryness
   Oppressive heat

Bone-chilling cold
Oceans less than four feet deep
Small biting insects, which, we suspect, are at the top of the food chain
Grounding yet again. Will we never learn?

Shout-Outs:

~ *Jack and Carol, our condolences. Hope your boat gets better soon. Vince is taking great care of us!*
~ *Steve and Karen, cache on!*
~ *Bruce and Gail, sorry about UConn. How'd the women do?*
~ *Ludo and Hetty, I'm practicing breath control for the next conch test.*
~ *Gordon and Enid, BIG HUGS!*
~ *Em, if you wear your bracelet, I'll wear mine too.*

She sells seashells

Our first night out of Elbow Cay was spent at an old haunt from previous air-delivered trips. Little Harbour, near the southern tip of Great Abaco, is home to Pete's Pub. We had to go there because it's one of those you-have-to-go-there places, but also because it's a strategic hop-off point from the Abacos to points South.

Listen, about these have-to-go-there places: honestly, you really don't have to go there. I suspect when I die there'll be a whole bunch of those places I'll have never gotten to, despite having been gifted a book listing all of them so I wouldn't miss any. It won't weigh on my mind a bit, any more than the fact that I'll never have had sex with a professional dancer, which this guy I used to know told me I should do at least once. Deb's actually a pretty darn good hoofer, come to think of it, while I happen to own two left feet.

Anyway I try hard not to tell people they really must go someplace or do something. It sounds so smug. *I've been there, so now must you go. Take my authoritative word.* And really, there is no bagel like a Schlomo's Bagel. Porsche, accept no substitute. Oh, bite me. You really must.

By the way, when you finish this book, do go out and buy a boat and follow the path we took, precisely as we've laid it out. You really must. Before you die. Hurry.

∼∼∼

What I think one should strive for is to enjoy the places you do get to. I once had a really good time in the back of an old van loaded with film equipment and smelly furniture blankets. It happened in the middle of the night, and I'm not a night person. It was my first experience with a Sony Walkman. The album was Steely Dan's *Asia*. It rocked.

You really must stop watching TV and listen to more music. Music is the greatest. If I lose my hearing, I'll kill myself.

∼∼∼

Our next stop was to be Royal Island Harbour, at the recommendation of friends. From there we'd have a short jaunt to Spanish Wells, another small island adjacent to Eleuthera, itself yet another island on the path to still more islands.

Now let me tell you something. When you've never been to a place by boat before, say you're short on charts, and you're crossing a chunk of ocean to get there, you'll take the advice of a blind drunk with no appendages if he's got something to say about safe entry to where you're going. Give me what you've got, Cap'n Stumpy. Afterward it might not be a bad idea to question the bartender as to how the good captain came by his various impediments.

If you think I'm kidding about asking directions, ask Deb. I'm compelled, for fear of taking a single step in the wrong direction, to grill anyone I see. I hate going the wrong way for even a block. In New York City, that kind of mistake can set you back half a day. I once asked for directions from a guy in the city who was probably on crack, and very possibly comatose. Was it a muscle twitch, or had he indicated the necessity of a U-turn at our earliest convenience? Deb urged me to hasten on in the direction we'd been traveling.

Have I mentioned yet that Deb is no homing pigeon herself? Give her a map and she gets woozy, and that's if we're standing still on a dock. And though she'll kill me for passing it on, she's admitted to having failed high school geometry. If we didn't have GPS, we'd be Peruvian citizens by now.

We made it to Spanish Wells via a stop at Royal Island Harbour, thanks to Steve and Karen Grant of *Sea Echo* (they have all their appendages), and made a nice day trip to Harbour Island, thanks to the fast ferry. It's nice to let somebody else do the driving once in a while. While in the area, we enjoyed our first geocache find. Steve and Karen had taught us about that too, and you really must investigate this for yourselves as soon as you put the book down.

Here's what you have to know about Spanish Wells. Next time you go to Red Lobster and order up a namesake item, anywhere in the United States, odds are it came from this little island of resourceful lobster farmers. I did say farmers. Oh, and you really must visit the Ponderosa Shell Shop, the shopkeeper of which sells seashells and much more. She does remarkable preservation work on a range of sea life. Ask to see her shell mosaic work in her living room. Tell her we sent you. You really must.

It was upon leaving Spanish Wells that we ran ourselves solidly aground in a foreign port. After spending some time seeing if I might be able to induce one of my jugulars to spontaneously erupt, Deb took charge. She called the folks who were tending the local moorings, and they advised us to hail one of the government ferries that constantly moves commuters about. Deb did so, and in short order we were hauled off the shelf we'd perched ourselves on. Our thanks to that kind captain, since we were out of TowBoat US territory. In any event, you really must get towing insurance, for as they say, it isn't a question of if. I'm not messing with you now. You must, or you're just, just, going nowhere fast.

What I remember about the grounding the most is that I really hate groundings, even if it's a soft, cushy one. Deb actually fears for my life at times like these, as I get so bent out of shape. There I am, mere feet from a deep channel that taunts me, telling me I might as well forget my plans for the day.

I start running around like a madman, launching the dinghy, getting the outboard mounted, running a kedge out to somewhere, then winching it in, running the engine, attempting to heel the boat, and swearing at every failed, futile attempt. I imagine that with every passing second the tide is running out on us, to leave us stuck there till the next day, when we'll awaken to find our hubcaps have been stolen.

I wish the Cousteau team had been there to record my underwater struggle with our kedge, which had to be uprooted from the seafloor before we could be safely hauled to deep water. Unable to free it from the dinghy, I had to snorkel to it and carry it across the sea bottom while Deb hauled the rode in. I might've had a shot at the Bahamas funniest underwater video.

Free at last, yet what was again supposed to be a pleasant sail to a place reasonably close by became a sprint to that place, there to navigate the intimidating intricacies of a new harbor, and get safely settled before nightfall.

~~~

Location: The Belly of the Beast
            Bimini

Ahoy, and batten down the hatches, maties. We sit here on the snarling wet lip of the precipice, the Geronimo of the homeward bound, the scimitar of the Great Bahama Bank. The wind is blowing like a superstitious sumo wrestler at his birthday party, like the Bronx Bombers at the 2004 ALC Series, like an overbooked . . . I think you get the picture. Anchored perilously here in Bimini, I've got plenty of time to read Tom Robbins. His similes roll off the tongue like a sack of Teflon marbles, like a busted egg off the hood of an overindulged Vette, like . . . I'll stop now. This is what can happen to you when you want to sail home, but the ocean will make chum out of you if you try.

Perfect time for a recap. We left you, I think, in Eleuthera, an island shaped like it sounds, some kind of internal organ, the function of which you really don't want to know. Maybe it's the foul weather talking, but here's my general take on the Bahamian chain. They offer very little topographical relief, appearing to the eye like so many cow pies dropped by a heard of floating steers on their little wet doggie trail.

What sounds like a dig is not intended as such. We have had a marvelous time. The people are irreplaceable. Nature is what it is. If in a few years we melt down enough of the ice cap (highly likely), these islands will become submerged humps on the Great Bahama Bank, something for boaters to steer clear of on their way to the Virgin Islands. Until that day arrives, I encourage Bahamians to plant more palm trees. They need more palm trees, and pelicans, and porpoises. The Big Three Ps of my heart's desire.

I'm sorry. It's the wind talking. It's howling like the low hyena on the totem pole, like an undergassed dental patient, like Yankee fans in 2004. And we're in the harbor of this wind-spanked island waiting to get off the boat for a walk, but our dink, as you all know, does not inspire confidence in such a joyride. What then to talk about?

Oh yes, geocaching. You've got to look this one up at www.geocaching.com. We were turned on to this by fellow boaters Steve and Karen, and we had a great time turning an otherwise aimless day of tourist-stomping (let's go see what's on the next island) into a purposeful treasure hunt. Armed with a handheld GPS unit (what, you don't have one?), some coordinates, and a clue or two, you set off to find a cache hidden by some impish soul. These caches have been planted all over the world, there for you to discover, autograph, perhaps take something therefrom (a shell), and leave something therein (a post card), high-five over, replace as found, and thereafter go off to have a victory Kalik. Beats chatchka-shopping at the local tiki hut.

We celebrated by running aground the next day on our way to Nassau. It took a couple hours and a government ferry to haul us off, just in time to make NeverNever Land before sundown. We crashed Atlantis on Paradise Island the next day. Hey, Toto, I don't think we're in Kansas anymore. It's an aquatic Chuck E. Cheese on hallucinogens. It's Soylent Blue. We were drawn to it like moths to a furnace stoked on phosphorescent pheromones.

You know what's so great about it? No concessions to knowledge. No signs indicating the genus or species of any living creature. An occasional tour guide may point out the difference between a sturgeon and the diver vacuuming its living room, but in general this is the playground of the id. You are there to burn your flesh and bankroll, pack up, and leave before the next tour bus vomits its new load of patsies. It's way cool, man. Pack a dozen bathing suits, and don't forget the MasterCard.

After soaking our senses on this aquatic OZ, we set off to pay the price Poseidon metes out to the unwary. On our boat journey west, we were forced by our boat's top end (7 mph) to anchor in the middle of the Great Bahama Bank. Eighteen feet of water in every direction, and no Tom Bodett to leave the light on. We dropped anchor to rest for the night.

Then the wind started to hobbyhorse us the way it was really fun for two minutes when we were kids. Then the anchor light failed to light. Then we spent the night fearing a ship would run us over. A few boats did pass by, and we had brief congenial chats with captains who assumed we were underway (moving), seeing that we had our tri-color light (indicating a sailboat is on the move) on (since it worked) to avoid a collision at sea (since at least they'd see us). No, Cap, we're not moving, except for up and down, up and down.

The dawn finally began to insinuate itself, something we rarely encourage, and we got one of our earlier starts to our next intended port, Bimini. But we didn't quite make it. Time and weather provided Bimini's defense, and we ended up off the east coast of Cat Cay, kind of nearby, having nearly died trying to negotiate its western, ocean side. Lesson relearned: discretion is indeed the better part of valor. It took us one more day of wind and chop to get to the fairly unprotected harbor here, given the present wind direction, and we are once again in the midst of waiting for the weather window that will put us back at Deb's mom's place in the States. Which means, you guessed it, high-speed Internet access.

What's Hot:
    Tom Robbins
    Tomato sandwiches
    Skipping winter
    The distant scent of Dunkin' Donuts

What's Not:
    Laying out two anchors in a blow
    Getting rocked to sleep by over-exuberant sea gods
    The local scent of the holding tank
    Waaaaiiitttiiinnnnnnnnngggggg

Shout-Out:

Father Bob, William Dentzman Jr., Grand Tickler. Thank you for watching out for us. Rest in peace.

What treasures await us?

~~~

    We'd sampled both the bitter and sweet associated with foreign waters. When I say foreign, I mean completely new to our experience, as I'm convinced that a single harrowing entry into a new port of call will serve any sailor a lifetime. You may not be assured a perfect landing next visit, but the single memory will serve you well for decades to come, changes to navigation notwithstanding.
    Before making Bimini, we'd made strange radio contact with what might have been aliens from another dimension. As we approached Cat and Gun Cays, neighboring islands to the south of Bimini, with the intent to cut between them and make our way northward on the Atlantic side, we contemplated the sea state we might encounter there. For a few days the wind had been blowing from the west, and if we'd learned anything in all this time, we'd certainly retained a healthy respect for the roles of fetch and water depth in relation to wave action.
    We were working our way across the Great Bahama Bank, with the wind on our nose, and so once again were working the engine to get to where we were headed in as short a time frame as possible. It occurred to us that the Bank itself, as well as the islands to windward, were keeping the seas down. But we'd have to approach Bimini from the Atlantic side, as far as we could tell from what charts we had. Don't even ask.

Okay, Deb had bought the 1980 cruising guide for a buck at a fair on Man-O-War Cay. It included some nicely interpreted pencil drawings.

It stood to reason that the wind, coming hard off the Florida shore for the previous couple of days, might be delivering something impressive in the way of wave action by the time they reached the shallows off those cays. With little else to go on but our newly honed instincts, we radioed ahead to ask anyone for a report. The only response we got was an unidentified voice of a woman, who calmly assured us she was anchored happily on the Western side of Cat Cay. The cut between Cat and Gun, she further purred, was passable.

To this day I wonder if I'd entered some time warp and spoken to a ghost from a different period. While the report seemed counterintuitive to local conditions, we trusted the voice and ventured through the cut, even as we found ourselves entering a churning maelstrom.

I was truly frightened. As we started to motor north past the cut, I hoped something would change real soon, that this was a temporary issue caused by something, uh, temporary. But as we adjusted course to head for Bimini, we started to take waves more on the beam, and were rolling excessively. There was all manner of noise down below, as we were in no way prepared for the violent motion. I was steering constantly to take waves more safely, yet still make way toward our destination, which in the best conditions would be an hour away. Perhaps, I thought, we should make our way out into deeper water, but at some point we'd have to head north, and what if it never got better?

I had no thought as to the right course of action, when I heard Deb say, "Should we turn around?" It was as if her voice were attached to my hands on the wheel. I spun it, and while our retreat wasn't pretty, it was the quickest way back to safe water. Minutes seemed like millennia as I pointed for the cut that got us into this mess. When we finally rounded the southern point on Gun Cay, I felt the overwhelming relief that comes with the reaching of calm waters. Tonight this would be the safe place to be. Tomorrow would be another story, but we'd deal with it when the time came.

There never was a boat on that other side of the island. For the life of me, I'll never know quite what that radio contact was about. Could I have misspoken West for East? Was this some sick practical joke? Hard to fathom, a prank that could cause a boat to founder. It was unlike everything we'd experienced from fellow boaters on the trip.

By the time morning came, the wind had clocked, and what had been our temporary safe haven was now a place it was best to leave, as soon as possible. That day we made a safe pass on the Atlantic side and entered the harbor at Bimini.

Out of the frying pan, into the fire. As our log indicates, our experience on Bimini, or more accurately, on our boat at Bimini, became another waiting game. After a day or so of bobbing about in heavy winds, we finally said screw it, let's get our foul weather gear on and get off this tub.

Not to belabor the dinghy issue, but again much consideration should be given to the source of transportation that will ferry you around at the many stops you'll make on your trip. Were we to do it over, we would travel with a more weatherly tender. Be that as it may, we survived with *Em*.

Having made it safely to shore, my observation was *vive la difference*. There is a remarkable dissimilarity between getting thrashed around at anchor, the wind's power amplified by the sounds of discontent in the rigging, and strolling a palm-lined sidewalk in womblike protection from the elements. It's easy to wonder if the whole boat thing might be a mistake. Out on the water, we felt besieged. Sitting at Sofie's, having a civilized lunch of whatever Sophie chose to serve that day, was downright decadent. Aside from my incessant, privately maintained concerns for our boat's welfare, we were carefree vacationers.

Bimini seems to be at a crossroads, and I hardly know what that means. There is a vaguely disquieting vibe there, fueled in part by the distinct signs of abject poverty. I'd felt that weird Caribe-influenced nexus once before, on a business trip to Jamaica, where it's kind of hard to have a good time thoughtlessly blowing a Jamaican's annual salary on a night of debauchery, if you own half a conscience.

Development is gestating in Bimini, overlaying what appear to be the ruins of a previous heyday. I am no historian, nor do I understand the economics of development. We met some lovely people there, and maybe it was the ill wind wreaking its effect, but the place gave me the creeps. I began to see it mostly as our jumping-off place, and we attempted to make the best of the situation until we'd found agreeable weather, and perhaps amenable travel companions.

I'm sure Einstein got it right with his equation, although I might not have used the same letters to describe the experience. The assertion that time is relative is most certainly proven in a dentist's chair. Waiting out this damnable wind in Bimini made me consider the upside of plaque removal.

We were supposed to be enjoying ourselves, after all. Instead, what we were doing was imagining what it must be like to experience this place as a native, which is to say with the patience of an angel, confident the good times would eventually roll. This is the Purgatory theory of salvation: this sucks, but we're paying our dues, but this sucks.

We discovered yet another pleasant Canadian couple (is there any other kind?), Peter and Claudette de Koning, of *Sinfonia*, and after sharing a few meals on land and aboard, we together snuck out one morning around 3:00 AM, for the States.

This time my confused brain doubted the veracity of our GPS's stored memory, the course saved from our approach several days earlier. GPS doesn't always know where things really are, but it does know where it has been. In the tense predawn hours, my doubts threatened us and our tail escort with yet another grounding, when I chose to follow my muddled mind's interpretation of the bobbing channel beacons in the dark. Deb's night vision proved more acute; we narrowly averted disaster, and were finally headed in the direction of home.

The night was generous, the light breeze the temperature of one's cheek. On this crossing, the Gulf Stream would aid us with its northern set. Our biggest concern was the monitoring of the sea lanes. I call them sea lanes, but there are no painted stripes out there, no fluorescent road signs, no speed bumps or soft shoulders. One might consult a chart for likely traffic, but out there, particularly at night, to an eye with only three previous night's worth of experience, lights presumably attached to boats were heading in no predictable direction. Their speed was also difficult to discern. More than once, I confused a bow with a stern. Still, we managed not to become an appendage to the ground tackle of a much larger vessel that night.

Traffic of a different nature greeted us upon our triumphal, though completely ignored by the press, reentry into the U.S. We were back, having found the place we'd left several months before in the middle of the night. We tracked our reintroduction to American civilization by watching the growth of the signal bars on our long-dormant cell phone. Can you hear me now?

This time it was a sunny day, on the brilliant start to a holiday weekend, and therein lay the problem. Lake Worth Inlet was a madhouse of pleasure boaters. Every Floridian and his mother were packed onto something that could marginally float. All were in a frenzy to get to someplace other than where they presently were. Peanut Island looked like Normandy on D-Day, had Normandy been serviced by a floating pizza parlor.

It was a shocking reentry to American civilization, one that gave us pause once we were finally secured far from the madding crowd, at the anchorage where we'd bitten our nails off waiting for our chance to leave America in January.

A globe-trotting sea journalist that goes by the name of Fatty Goodlander took a lot of flack when he once editorialized on the stateside state of affairs, as experienced by one who'd spent a good deal of time circling the globe with his wife, Carolyn. He'd been predictably pounced upon by the love-it-or-leave-it faction—always an attractive group—when he dared detail some of our cultural foibles. I remember that article, and thinking he was going to catch it from the patriot brigade.

You know what? It took us a couple of months living a stone's throw from Miami to see what he was talking about. I'm all for hot showers, but you could forgive a saucer-load of Martians who, having stumbled upon our peculiar culture, had pulled back the ladder and continued on to Venus, in search of a more congenial habitat.

These boaters, well you could have convinced yourself they'd just picked up the keys to the Carver this morning. They had little sense of nautical decorum, but were certainly in high spirits. Their boats, had they been living organisms, would have had more than one activist group working to set them free. They were loaded to the gunwales with stuff, animate and otherwise; kids, pets, megacoolers, and inflatable thing-a-ma-jigs. They looked like floating Toys "R" Us stores. The people themselves, they had some meat on them, boy. Freeboard was one precious commodity.

We were, nonetheless, home. And the homebody in me was happy. I knew the path ahead, because I'd been there before. Plus I'd learned a few things along the way, which was one of the reasons I could now get so huffy about all these cretins out here raining on my personal parade.

The worst, in terms of traffic, would be over. We'd seen the mad Easter dash to the center of wild abandon, made all the more wild by the fact that these folks had been sitting out their own bad weather. Listen, cabin fever I get. Maybe this was the proper way to return from an idyllic trip to the Bahamas, to the American version of Carnivàle.

I was happy this time to take the inside route back to Stuart. There was none of that *we're seasoned sailors, let's go outside* stuff. The seasoned sailor now knew it would have taken longer to backtrack, putting in extra mileage to head out an inlet a few miles behind us. Then, out a ways into safe water, before heading in the direction we wished to travel, and then reverse the procedure at whatever inlet was convenient to our destination. Which happened to be our infamous St. Lucie Inlet. Cue bout of uncontrollable chills.

One or more of the guidebooks does a good job of pointing out the strategic challenge of going outside. Comparing actual mileage, one can see that not all outside paths are the shortcuts one might imagine after meandering along the ICW for a couple days. Much weight of one's decision should include one's social proclivities. Are you a "just me and the sea" kind of person, or a "back-road searcher of honky-tonks" kind of person. I found myself to be of the latter persuasion, but from time to time Deb and I decided to shake loose a bit. Variety is, as they say, the spice of life.

At Stuart, we tied up in a donated slip so we could enjoy more face time with Deb's family. Official thanks go out to John, Peg, and Bill, the crew of *La Vie Dansante*. Hope to see you all again soon, you guys.

Chapter 14

Lubbers Redux

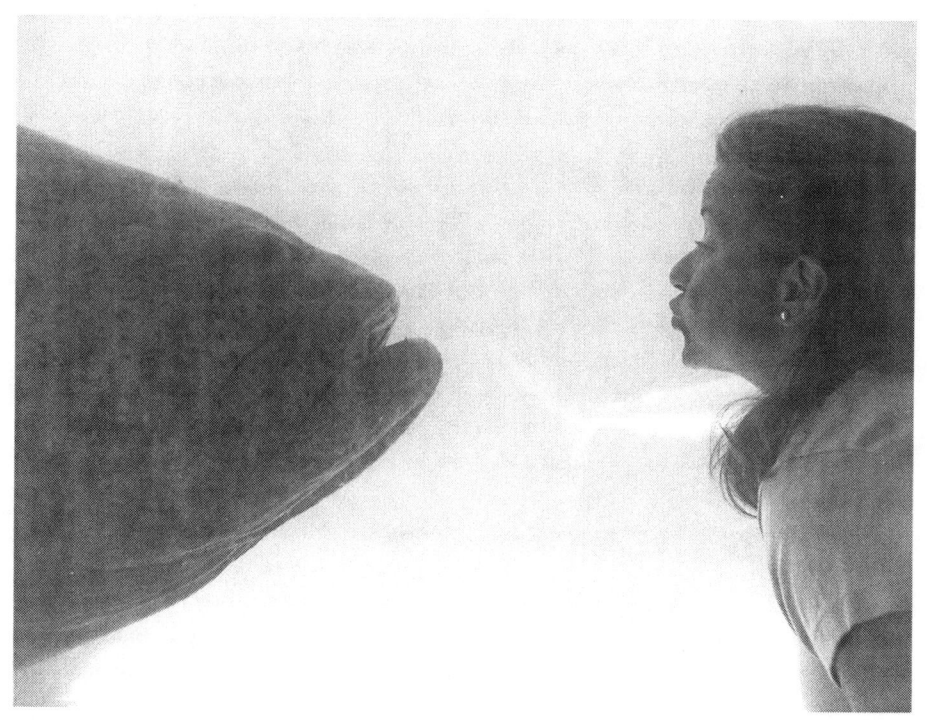

Farewell, sweet island denizens

Log of the Laura Lynn Update #18

We're baaaaaaaaaaack. Snuck out of Bimini before daybreak (almost grounded a-freaking-gain), crossed the Gulf Stream (no sweat; piece of cake), ran the Easter Gauntlet of lunatic boaters at the inlet near West Palm Beach (nearly turned around in fear and loathing), and finally parked the Laura Lynn in a borrowed slip near Deb's mom's home in Jensen Beach. Once again, we've turned in our sailor badges in order to infiltrate the world of land dwellers.

Time for a homecoming celebration, and effect some repairs. Affect some repairs? Fix stuff. So I got Rich, Deb's mom's hubby, that is to say my step-father-in-law . . . listen, the women already get it, and the guys don't give a rat's backside. I enlisted Rich to hoist me up the mast to fix that infernal anchor light, with Deb's sister's guy (simple enough) Brian backing Rich up with the spinnaker halyard.

Bad choice. Brian should've been the bull (what a hunk Jenn scored. You go girl!) Rich was scheduled for a stress test the next day. Bad news, as he stepped off the treadmill. Warning, Will Robinson! Alien plaque attacking! Off to the hospital for an angiogram. Bad news. Time for more stents (look it up, as you'll probably be sporting a few of these one day, baby boomer).

Rich rushed by ambulance to different hospital, with femoral artery doing Vegas imitation of Dante's Fountain. Bad news. The four new stents didn't hack it. Too much Edy's Triple Chocolate Fudge Chunk Supreme, with help from Hershey's Condiment Dept. (Author's note: Hershey's syrup was reportedly used in the era of black-and-white films as the most authentic substitute for blood onscreen. Really. Watch the bathtub scene in Psycho. That's chocolate syrup spewing out of Janet Leigh).

Specialists confer. Bad news. They recommend open-heart surgery. Tough decision. Rich "You The Man" Shea makes it. Quadruple bypass. That's where they kidnap arteries and veins from other parts of your body and say, "We need you guys someplace else. Move out." Do not pass GO. Do not collect cheeseburger. Next up, Rich doing his Crocodile Dundee impression: "You call that a scar? That's not a scar. Now this . . . is a scar."

Good news so far: I didn't kill Rich to fix a light bulb. Bad news. Hospital gown fits poorly around Rich's backside. Please keep Rich in your thoughts and prayers. Regarding the gown's fit, I'll be fine after some recuperative therapy. Final bad news: Rich will be setting off metal detectors for the rest of his life, meaning he'll have to endure the crotch wand every time he flies Jet Blue. I pity the security agents who get that assignment. Maybe they'll let him keep his shoes on.

So we're hanging around a little longer, to prepare for Rich's homecoming. Life is what happens to you . . .

This wrinkle in our itinerary has placed some time in our hands. Deb has responded with new boat curtains and a flock of throw pillows of various sizes, the spawn of an ancient Singer work station. What's with women and pillows? You'd think they could drink them at a football game. Perhaps these things can double as flotation devices.

What, on the other hand, have I accomplished? Well, Father Time has given me the opportunity to search my soul and contemplate the genius of country and western music, which is all that plays in this neck of the woods, Bubba, except for that other crap. And may I say that no other art form plumbs the depths of human emotion with such forthright honesty, such soul-searching ennui, such, I don't know, je ne sais quoi, like Country.

Masters of the lyric hook, country crooners (croon, I guess that's what that chicken-choked yodel is called) are fearless when it comes to wearing their achy-breaky hearts on their chaps, kuhunh. Seeing as I've got time on my hands, I thought I'd dabble in another 10 list.

Here then follows the life cycle of a relationship, the ten-step process we've all stumbled through once or twelve times, as illustrated in the themes of popular country songs:

Step 1: I'm the luckiest guy in the world, cuz I got a girl who can drink all my drinking buddies under the table.
Step 2: Somethin' must be wrong, cuz I just caught my girl keying the side panel of my Dodge pickup.
Step 3: Girl, the magic's gone, so I'm goin' fishin' with my drinkin' buddies, and versey vicey.
Step 4: Just got back from fishin', and I can't believe my girl left me, and took my bird dog with her.
Step 5: Life was lots simpler back in the seventies, when I had fourteen girlfriends.
Step 6: I wish my girl would come back, at least to return my backup tackle box.
Step 7: She'll come back just as soon as she remembers how great it was, livin' on love and stolen junk food from 7-Eleven.
Step 8: I'm so lonesome I'm gonna shoot myself, just as soon as the Talladega 500 gets over with.
Step 9: I don't need nobody long as I got NASCAR and the Bass Channel on my dish.
Step 10: I'm the luckiest guy in the world, cuz I got a new girlfriend, and she can drink my old girlfriend under the table.

What's Hot:
   Straight-tail lizards (Florida's own)
   Incisions longer than the Florida coastline
   Red Necks. To illustrate, we note the following encounter: we recently followed a liquid container truck sporting the image of Yosemite Sam, both guns drawn. His warning: "Back off. We ain't haulin' milk." The company: Danny's Septic Service.
   Jenn's new squeeze, Brian
   Daytime leatherback nesting sightings

What's Not:
   Curly-tail lizards (left 'em in the Bahamas)
   Five in a canoe
   Fire ants

Shout Outs:

~ Tina and Pierrick! Magnifique! See you in France!!!
~ Weetha, thu thukeenie breth ith juth fabuluth, ebm mithouth buthuh.
~ Dr. Wigley, our teeth thank you, our gums thank you. And the tori, they're behaving themselves.
~ Louie, you're one guy we'll turn on the TV for. All the best with the new show.
~ Brian, we'll go fishing next time.
~ Ben, congrats on your new brother!

~ Vincent Symonette of TPA Marina, thank you so much for taking care of us in Nassau. We are eternally grateful.
~ Art, we'd crew for you anywhere. Except St. Augustine.

Fair winds,
Paul and Deb
S/V Laura Lynn

∼∼∼

Vincent and Tanya, of TPA Marina, babysitting the clueless

Chapter 15

Enter the Dragons

You think you're in trouble now . . .

We were on our own, again, retracing our path for home. It comforted me to have some idea as to what was ahead. There'd be surprises, since we were in essence hovering in space, but we now had an intimate feel for the boat, and I knew most of the trip would have a familiar ring. There were places we expected to revisit, and places we planned to avoid.

When we speak to recidivist snowbirds now, those who do this year in and year out, or when we read from the logs of those who do this sort of thing regularly, we sense the comfort level that comes from familiarity. As with everything we do in life, from learning to talk to dealing with our physical impediments as we age, shorthand smoothes the wrinkles.

Deb and I fell back into routines we'd taken months to develop. Ooh, I feel a smile sneaking onto my face. I remember the early days of the trip, when each chore seemed formidable. That insurmountable task, approached of necessity, becomes a mere challenge. Over time, the challenge recedes to novelty. A few anchorages along, novelty acquires a patina of ritual. This is the heyday of the trip, when you are one with each other and the boat. If you lose the fervor, ritual becomes routine. When the Oreos run out, you flirt with the slippery slope toward the rut.

This evolution is, I think, a natural one. Key in keeping the ritual aspect alive is in changing things up and taking breaks from the mundane. While boaters like to think they left that all behind, the ordinary is very much in evidence at sea as well. Whether you are pushing yourself physically on the outside, taking on the weather and fighting the fatigue of constant movement, or choosing the challenges of the inside and the hours-on-end concern for obstacles, you will reacquaint yourself with the hypnotizing effect of mindless repetition. Monotony, it turns out, was not boxed up with the office supplies back home.

Deb and I decided again to go outside for a stretch, this time forgoing the chunk of Florida from Cape Canaveral to the same inlet that had been the terminus of our first overnighter at Fernandina Beach, Saint Mary's. There we planned to give the town another shot at charming us. After that, we'd give Georgia the chance we'd previously denied her.

~~~

Subject: Log of the Laura Lynn Update #19

Ahoy all,

Veterans of these updates may recall this crew's rather cavalier detour around the great state of Georgia on our way South. Goaded on by peach purveyors, Vidalia venders, and other favorite sons, we decided to see what Georgia had to offer. We discovered along with her many wonders a few good reasons to take the business loop around the state. The repercussions of our meander were, in a word, biblical.

They began at sea, on another overnighter, to get us the heck out of Florida. We were trying to make some time after having hung around Chez Shea to see what Rich's scar would look like. Very impressive. I wonder if something like that could keep you out of a bar fight (You want some of this, pal? Bring it!).

At daybreak, away from any sight of land, they started to come. Swarms of them, two by two, locked at the abdomens in desperate copulative embraces.

In what seemed an attempt to repopulate the world in a single day with beetles, the creatures overwhelmed us. They clung to the canvas, the rigging, our clothing. A mournful minority toiled on without soul mates, swept joylessly toward the open sea. Where on earth did they come from? Where did they think they were going? How the hell do we get them off the boat?

These, we've been told, are what Georgians call "love bugs." The good news is they don't bite. The bad news is the next plague to arrive did. For days, hordes of voracious horse flies dogged us, and when given an opening, they made us wish we were flying Delta. The transit through

Georgia gave us experience with at least three subspecies, which I shall call, for want of a resident entomologist, the brown-eyed, green-eyed, and orange-eyed horseflies. Do they interbreed? A mating attempt was never observed. This was a feeding frenzy, and we were the floating smorgasbord.

Our sole defense, besides flailing like epileptics on disco night, evolved into something of a sporting event. We have on board a device we call "The Flyminator," an electric swatter that looks a bit like a badminton racket rigged by a utility company. It'd been generously donated to us by our pals, Canadian cruisers Peter and Claudette, of Sinfonia. Man, Canadians have all the fun.

There is a distinctly subversive pleasure one takes in fry-swatting a bug that had been out to do you harm. You can actually see the sparks shoot off them as you volley them overboard.

As the name suggests, The Flyminator fared well against horseflies, but was useless against the plague of reptiles. They showed up in the form of an eight-foot alligator drifting past our boat while I was fishing for something a little more tender for dinner. For the record, from our perspective, one alligator constitutes a plague. All shore-leave activities were cancelled that evening.

The next day we summoned enough courage to command our bite-sized dinghy to shore on Jekyl Island, where a nature preserve student from U of G filled us in on gator info. They generally avoid humans, but there seems to have been a recent rash of attacks that have taken lives in Florida. To paraphrase Roy Scheider in Jaws, "We gotta get a bigger dinghy."

I am not a religious man, but I confess to having made a silent plea that nothing might happen to the Laura Lynn that would require me to inspect her below the waterline till we made significant progress northward. It must have been on a Sunday while the Lord was resting. Satan, however, had an ear tuned.

At our next anchorage, about thirty miles up the river, we managed to foul the trip line (a buoyed line designed to extricate the anchor if it gets caught on some underwater obstruction) on our prop, killing the engine and requiring a snorkel trip to undo the mess. Visibility was about three inches in a murky current. All that was missing was the mood-enhancing soundtrack from the aforementioned thriller as I set about hacking away at line wrapped repeatedly around the drive shaft. It was then that I was visited by the final scourge, that of the iniquitous barnacles.

A growth of Beelzebub's minions filleted my hands and forearms like so many nervous med students at the anatomy table. It didn't hurt so much, but made me consider whether or not, as with sharks, alligators were drawn to the scent of blood in the water. Whatever the case, it turned out not to be feeding time. Job done, and we're now in South Carolina.

Any regrets about the Georgia leg? HECK NO! We had a grand time in Savannah with Lynn and David Flannery, who treated us like royalty. Dinner, great conversation, a tour of their fair city, and get this: hand-delivered Krispy Kremes the next morning at the boat as a send-off. So if you ask us, Georgia is second to none when it comes to down-home hospitality. Almost worth losing an extremity for. Thanks you guys. Y'all are the best.

One last Georgia chore: pick up a copy of "Midnight in the Garden of Good and Evil."

What's Hot
  Krispy Kremes, delivered right to your boat
  "Moon River" by Johnny Mercer
  Dordogne, France

What's Not
    All manner of natural plagues and pestilence

Shout Outs:

~ *Rich, thank you for the sports updates.*
~ *Joe, you the man! Thanks for schlepping our luggage back to NY!*
~ *Lynne and David, thank you for showing us your Savannah.*
~ *Captain Art, we're almost there!*
~ *Brian, thanks for the tune-up.*
~ *Lew, we're thinking of you. (Barbara, let him know, okay?)*

Fair winds
Paul and Deb
S/V Laura Lynn

Time for an appendage inventory

It is an unsettling revelation to a modern man such as myself that there are creatures out there (and I'm not talking microbes, which are plenty scary in their own right) that will stalk and eat us, given the opportunity. When that ancient reptile surfaced and idled past like a Post-Cambrian nightmare, I felt a sudden sea change, a kind of 9/11 moment. Not to seem disrespectful, but I wondered if Steve Irwin's last thoughts might have been something on the order of, "Jeez, we were only making a movie here!"

One of the annoying habits Americans have, is their whiney incredulity in the face of perfectly normal disasters. Bad things happen to little children and puppy dogs. Horrors of epic proportions befall hordes of the tragically innocent. Hell visits earth with disheartening regularity, which is all fine and dandy to an American, as long as his own lab test comes back negative. We live in such an insular environment that our misfortunes, often delivered at the hands of our own stupidity, are seen as grounds for class-action lawsuits. Someone else has got to pay a king's ransom for the fact that I chipped a tooth gawking at a Calvin Klein billboard.

Had I actually bought the farm, courtesy of an overgrown lizard, that would truly have sucked for me, and maybe Deb. Could she have somehow sued the State of Georgia? These days, I imagine it would be possible, even with Mr. Cochran now decommissioned. As it is, it'll probably be the little monsters that get me, if I don't succumb to a condition my parents passed down through the invisible agency of DNA. Can you believe it? My very own parents, thinking only of themselves and the full moon. I tell you, they'd be hearing from my lawyer right now if they weren't already dead and gone.

~~~

Chapter 16

Onward and Upward

Floor, please.

We were again in the heart of the ICW, those Southern Atlantic states with a view, small towns with character, and a waterway that is interesting without being terribly taxing.

Georgia and Florida form the colon of the ICW. The worst of the shallow meanderings were behind us, where back ranges had us staring the wrong way, off the stern, for a good part of the day to keep from grounding. It was an interesting visual acuity test, for a while. Imagine heading down I-95 in reverse, using the rear view mirror to stay on the road. That's an unfair analogy, but imagine it anyway, just for fun.

We cheerily anticipated the livelier scenery, familiar towns, and intricacies of navigation made easier from experience. It continued to amaze me that, where we had previously traveled, virtually every step of the way was like viewing a movie in reverse. There were the distinct bridges, and even a few remembered voices of the tenders. There were bends we'd hugged, stumps we'd avoided, fuel docks we scraped our gelcoat on. There was that stand of trees I wished I'd taken a picture of on the way down, now making me wonder what I'd seen in them the last time. The human mind is a spooky thing.

Those are a lot of miles to remember, memories fed by senses tuned to a livable pace. For most of my life, those sensory gifts went unheeded thirty thousand feet below me while I concentrated on the backrest that stared me in the face. What's this? In the event of a water landing, plant face firmly in crotch and cry like a baby.

We gave Beaufort, Carolina a second visit, and were promptly kidnapped. We really had no special reason to go ashore until it was supplied us by a single-hander flying an MIA flag. Jim was a human anachronism, a gregarious, hard-lived vet who seemed to have finally hacked his way out of the Indonesian jungle to join our time zone. His smallish sloop was in need of mechanical assistance. All he needed to make her happy was a wire coat hanger, with which he intended to use to ream out his heat exchanger so his engine could keep itself cool.

Much like geocaching, a simple, goal-oriented task often gives purpose to an otherwise aimless stroll. Rather than simply check out a town we'd already visited and found just peachy thanks, we now had a mission.

Just try tracking down an old-fashioned wire coat hanger these days. Failing the presence of a dry cleaner, and Beaufort did fail, one must travel back into time. We did so via the time-warp portal that is Lipsitz Department Store, where the shop owners, Joe and Lucille, genially held us hostage for our time, and so we came to know their life history.

The Lipsitz family has been in the retail business in Beaufort since 1902, and it appears they are still attempting to sell off some of the original inventory. Modernization of the store's interior, if it is being considered at all, languishes on the back burner.

I really don't know how long we were in the store, and I forget much of the specifics of this couple's life, but is life really about specifics? We all stockpile the joys and sorrows, victories and failures, close calls and resultant life-lessons through this veil of giggles. All travelers passing through Beaufort should be so merrily detained. It's an experience you can't get flying at thirty thousand feet, unless you're seated next to Richard Reid.

Okay, I'll give you one specific. There is a story Joe shared that is impossible to forgive my not retelling. It seems a while back, a woman came into the store looking to buy a bra for the first time. She was a largish woman, apparently a late bloomer, and untrained in the rules of social decorum. Against his better judgment, Joe offered his assistance, as Lucille might have been restocking some far recess of the store.

Joe asked what cup size the woman required, at which point she lifted her blouse and replied, "I don't know, you tell me."

This, I trust, is an accurate rendering of the story. I heard it from Joe, so obviously he'd managed to restart his heart. If you get to Beaufort, I'm sure he'd be glad to retell it. It's clearly gotten good mileage over the years.

Continuing our time travels, we beamingly delivered the needed coat hanger, chosen from among Lipsitz's generous selection, to Jim. It's heartening to know how sometimes a small act can cause such an inordinate amount of joy.

There was something about Jim that caused the heart to ache. He seemed all at once fearsome and cuddly, with deeply leathered skin drawn over boney ribs, stringy hair, a bushy mustache, arms bathed in grime, yet overall a general sense of congeniality. A smile lit up his face when he took the hanger, and he gingerly asked, "Do you guys burn?"

Deb and I exchanged not-so-subtle glances before the shared epiphany landed. Ah! Do we *burn*? Well, no we didn't, burn. We occasionally, uh, doused.

I suppose it dawned on us all that but for a slight cultural mismatch we'd come delectably close to having a very interesting evening. As Deb and I headed back to our boat, we wished Jim well. We still do.

∼∼∼

I prefer small towns to big cities, the way I prefer a Wendy's menu to a Greek Diner's. I hate being overwhelmed by options. So do, I think, most folks who happen to inhabit large cities. There are too many possible friendships to forge, so we clam up and say hello to no one. There is nothing wrong with a city-dweller, as I see it, except his dwelling. Inside each urban inhabitant is a decent soul yearning to be sociable.

A lot of visitors are put off by the gruffness of New Yorkers. I try to explain that you'd be this way too if you had to face the complicated calculus required to navigate your daily commute, which includes wait time for elevators, and jitney-to-train-to-subway downtime. The chip on our shoulders over how great our city is, well it's just what we learn to parade around after watching the news. Nobody actually visits any of the stuff that makes New York the cultural pit stop it proclaims itself, except out-of-towners and aesthetes.

It takes a certain kind of animal to survive in a city. I like to imagine Donald Trump trying to make it in a rural community on his own without his dad's seed stash. Mess with people in a small community and you'll be standing on your lawn at two in the morning watching a bonfire in your skivvies.

Big cities don't crop up to awe visitors. They evolve to securely contain the locals, and give them a forum for commerce, which is to say a place to buy overpriced groceries, and sell things that babies choke on.

Occasionally a museum dedicated to a local fetish goes up, let's say warfare. In Charleston, you can learn a bunch about the Civil War, which as I understand it, is winding down now in the South's favor. Charleston was an anchorage this time on our way north. It's just too big and busy for this New York City boy. All I wanted was some motor oil fit for a diesel engine.

~~~

My kind of town would have been Georgetown, if the local ATM hadn't eaten our money.

Georgetown is the kind of place you try your hand at making a postcard of. It has that look that says, *We got 'em at the five and dime, but feel free to give it a go with that snazzy new digital.*

Georgetown has a vibrant waterfront, with a new boardwalk made exotic by its posted "Do Not Feed the Alligators" signs. Christ, here we go again. You can attend the annual jazz festival if you aren't eaten alive trying to make it to shore.

In this quaint town, a modern-day glitch sucked the charm right out of the day, as we spent hours trying to decide who now owned several hundred of our dollars we'd planned to extract from that modern marvel, the Automated Teller. We swiped, it prompted, we input, it whirred, we waited as it counted and then spat out our receipt. No money, however, was regurgitated through the magic maw.

We spend much of our lives practicing for when things go right. When they go wrong, we're like those ants whose mound has just been kicked in by the neighborhood menace. The bank folks were as pleasant as could be, but their records indicated we had received our money. They didn't have it, and our New York bank didn't have it. Charming community. You must pay a visit, and use your credit card.

With the staff's sincere promise we'd recoup our losses one day, we knocked on wood and made another withdrawal, this time successful, then surveyed the threatening sky and swift-boated back to HQ, where we hunkered down and plotted our next foray north. Sometimes you seize the day, and sometimes the day seizes you. I think you know where.

~~~

North of Georgetown is some of the prettiest scenery to be had on the waterway, miles of winding Waccamaw River that could convince you you're blazing a new trail into the unknown, were it not for the reliable osprey-encrusted mile markers and the patrols of bass boats whizzing by. I don't much mind the presence of either.

I grew up in the suburbs of the twentieth century. I'd be dead now without modern civilization. I can't find my way out of a building without glowing exit signs to light the way. I'm allergic to most forms of nature, and I'm reassured by the presence of other humans, which convinces me I'm not in the process of walking off the edge of the earth. Guardrails keep me from plunging into ravines. Put me on a rickety Ferris wheel operated by a one-armed, glass-eyed carny, and I'm cozy as a clam. Climbing a tree on my own, I shake worse than the leaves.

We each discover our own level of adventure. I read recently of a report that claims the presence of certain chemicals in my brain play a strong role in my willingness to head up the mast, or out to sea. I can't measure those levels, other than to recognize the relative state of my unease when I venture such things. I think it's good to monitor one's feelings and then revel in the self-awareness, whether you're a lion or a mouse. If a mouse, then be the best mouse you can be. Embrace your vermin nature. To ignore it is to place yourself, if not in peril, then in serious discomfort, and who needs that? The future, it seems, will belong to those of us who exhibit those qualities that most closely mimic those of the cockroach. For some reason, Donald Trump again comes to mind.

∼∼∼

At a certain stage of a trip, one becomes cozy enough to start recognizing details of boating life, and then draw parallels to existence in general. One notices, for instance, the distinctive life cycle of a square sheet of paper towel.

If it is lucky enough to live a long, fulfilling life, and you're doing your job to economize to the point of neurosis, a sheet of paper towel will first serve in the kitchen area, sopping up fairly hygienic fluids. It will then be set aside to dry, to be used repeatedly until it can no longer be trusted in that arena, at which point it moves on to grayer tasks. Slimier substances become its *raison d'être*. It will sop questionable stains. It will work the floor. It is still suitable as a hanky.

Soon the towel is experienced enough for the really awful tasks: head duty, bilge assignments, engine work. At some point, its fibrous structure may break down, but it can still be depended on to come to the aid of fresh sheets as backup. Finally, it gets dumped in the waste. Still, its job is not over.

In an emergency I've gone to the well. There I was, near the garbage receptacle, in need of an absorptive ally. I looked up at the paper towel dispenser, looked at the job in hand, and failing the resolve to do in a perfectly good slice of Mr. Brawny, went diving for what I could find in the midst of egg shell fragments and mystery muck. There, more often than not, was a gummed and tattered yet willing remnant to see me through. To every thing there is a season.

There are times when a paper towel will meet an untimely end, when in the heat of the moment one grabs a pristine piece and tosses it into the fray without careful deliberation, in what can only be described as arboreal homicide. How could such a thing happen in this day and age? I'll tell you how, you simpering calf. Life's earthy fan must be fed.

∼∼∼

Be careful what you wish for. On our return trip to the scenically petite harbor at Southport, where even the desert menu features shrimp, we managed to snag the only free dock space mentioned in the guidebooks.

I was still stinging from the trip south, where after a full day of travel we'd watched a sailing couple beat us to the score by maybe three minutes. Three gonad-grinding minutes. My general love affair with fellow boaters tends to sour when it comes time to park. In a harbor the size of a large bathtub, we were forced to be the sole anchored vessel, having to launch the dinghy, mount the engine, and otherwise tax our recently scoured and perfumed bodies before heading ashore for any kind of sanctioned fun.

On our way north, we found ourselves sitting pretty at the free dock while a cruising family became the sole anchorers. We watched them resort to the admittedly clever strategy of temporarily letting out enough anchor rode to allow the kids to hop off their boat onto a downwind dock. Quite creative, but we preferred our position. A calm night was forecast. *What could go wrong?*

In the middle of the night, a *thunk* and a lurch announced what it was that could. At the cusp of low tide, our starboard deck had become pinned under the dock. The wake of a passing shrimp boat had provided the necessary wagging motion to wedge us underneath.

Rushing to get us unpinned before the tide rose to make us a physics experiment on floating levers, I put my foot through a portlight while seeking a stable platform from which to throw out my back. Glass fragments showered our bed. We lost hours of sleep cleaning up the bloodied shards and setting an anchor to keep us off the dock for the rest of the bungled night. Deb expended additional psychic energy trying to convince me to employ a more measured response when crises surfaced in the future. I believe I said I'd try.

We've been staring out our portlight through a packing-tape patch job ever since. Bring lots of tape. All kinds.

~~~

When plans were hatched for this book, I was faced with a conundrum. Having consumed many of the books from authors who'd preceded us, I feared that a string of horrible events would need to befall us in order for me to spin the proper yarns. I certainly didn't want any part of that scenario. Still, I wanted to fill the pages with something besides smug reveries and formulas for colorful mixed drinks. I will say this, though: I do believe alcohol is one of God's ways of saying, "I'm sorry."

It turns out that no amount of wishing for the best will keep you safe and sound forever. You might as well hope you never have to vomit again, and there are few things in life that, however literally brief, seem to last an eternity, as when one feels compelled to upchuck.

I can summon from memory a few of the times I've been forced to reverse the normal process that provides bodily sustenance. Every time the feeling comes around I dread the act. I beseech the powers that be to let this torch pass, right up to the moment it becomes a sure thing, and then I embrace the act with the fervor of a born-again. All fear is quashed, replaced by the urgent need to find solid handholds and keep one's aim true.

∼∼∼

You saw *Jaws* right? You bet, because you're an American. What was the scariest thing that happened in that movie? There is no question, is there? One hundred four percent of all viewers say it was the opening skinny-dip scene. There is no blood, there are no disembodied parts (that all comes later), and you don't even see the shark. Therein lies the power of the imagination, when gripped tightly in the embrace of darkness.

Here is the report I filed after a day of much disturbed weather, when we found ourselves revisiting Mile Hammock Bay, an anchorage just south of Camp LeJune where Deb and I had experienced our first fretful grounding on the way south:

It was my worst nightmare. My worst nightmare. Now the skeptical among you are suspecting that little more than dramatic hyperbole is on display here, and it is true that I have a dangerously active imagination, one that seems to loiter on the dark side. I'm also a light sleeper prone to some pretty strange phantasms. Let's put it this way then, though it sounds a bit like an SUV commercial: it was the likeliest horrible boating scenario I most commonly and frequently obsess over. I was now in the middle of it, most definitely wide awake, and buck naked to boot.

Deb is the mover-shaker of this crew. I come along for the ride. Left to my own devices I'd have been content to prepare for a trip the length of the Long Island Sound till the day I was deposited in an assisted living facility. Deb sees the big picture. I see the demons lying in wait for those who follow their dreams. Deb suggested as an alternative to my proposed Block Island odyssey (a trip, mind you, of over a hundred miles, and some of it in open water, for gosh sakes) that we instead head to the Bahamas.

Did I mention that Deb is an excellent salesperson? Which is why, I pondered only for an instant, I was now standing in my birthday suit in the middle of the night with a howling, wind-driven rain pelting my privates. I was presently attempting to start a recalcitrant engine as our Laura Lynn dragged toward the military base near which we'd anchored at the end of our day's run. We appeared to be commencing our assault on a civilian boat immediately downwind. After that strike, I assumed we'd proceed to somewhere along the shore at Camp Lejune in North Carolina. Were I to have daydreamed further, I might have imagined the local military opening up with a defensive barrage, thus putting to an end the nude terrorist menace attempting to infiltrate their encampment, and putting me out of my wretched misery once and for all.

I do not mesh well with stress. Occasionally I catch health professionals referring to beneficial forms of the affliction. What a bunch of hokum. Stress is always bad. I don't need the character it is purported to build. If you ask me, all it builds is plaque on my artery walls. Ironic then to find myself in such a predicament, on such a trip, in what had been a campaign to purge all the seething bile formed by a quarter century of big-city angst harbored in a small-town boy. Here on this ancient, leaking tub, stripped like a Perdue chicken waiting for his trip through the rotisserie.

When stressful events occur, I become agitated and, worse still, tongue-tied. Every part of the boat becomes a thingamajig. Deb is left to wondering if I want her to rig a spring line or put on her life vest and jump overboard.

So there I was, screaming at her over the din for my eye things, and she's thinking my glasses, which isn't at all a bad guess. What I meant, though, was ski goggles, which I still consider one of my clever ideas for the trip, because my corneas were feeling like a couple of over-easy eggs getting a Tabasco basting.

Next I wanted something to put on, because rather remarkably, in the few moments it'd taken me to get relative control of the boat, I'd taken to shuddering from a pervasive chill. I have no idea what I might have said by way of clothing request, as Deb arrived at the companionway offering a pair of gym shorts. I must have been an embarrassing sight for her, in consideration of our fellow boaters, who I assumed were all comparably underdressed while in the midst of saving their own boats and skins. What a sight for the heavens to behold, this navy of scampering bodies, caught under the illumination of nature's monumental strobe lights. It was as if soon-to-be-fallen angels were taking photos of the apocalypse they'd incited.

Having finally worked out the wardrobe issue, with each of us in our foul weather gear, I prepared myself to babble incoherently about the present need to somehow retrieve our anchor and then reset it, with the various crew duties and logistical considerations to follow forthwith. I hoped I might be given the momentary gift of tongues, and that all would be clear to Deb. Instead, she disappeared toward the foredeck, into the night. All was lost.

Now why would that be? Well here's why I was convinced. This old boat of ours has no windlass. We've always raised anchor by hand, which has never been a problem with the lightweight "lunch hook" used on our regular day trips. When, however, we upgraded to a heavy primary anchor and added, through ignorance, oversized chain to the equation, the resulting loads proved too much for Deb's physique. While my dime store back, an ancestral bequest, makes it no more pleasurable for me, the task of weighing anchor had since fallen exclusively to me. Look forward to my next article, "Things Our Next Boat Must Have," hopefully in the near future.

So you see, all was now lost. We were dragging anchor, I was stuck at the wheel playing dodge-boat, with Deb at the bow attempting who-knew-what-all somewhere in the bowels of the tempest. All I could do was carry on with the task I would have assigned her, that of getting the boat positioned for as easy an anchor retrieval as possible, making sure the rode wouldn't foul the prop in the process. Then hope for a miracle.

While contemplating the inscription for my gravestone (Here Lies the Ship's Fool: He Who Never Had a Prayer), I began to hear, mingled with the wind, rain, and incessant peals of thunder, the sound of chain rattling down the hawsehole. Interesting. This was a task Deb couldn't do on a still bay, on a calm summer day. Yet from a pitch black heaving deck (after a time no man in turmoil has ever accurately gauged), and over the roar of the heavens, I heard her scream, "It's up!"

She hadn't broken a nail. I become watery now at the memory of Deb staring at her hands, wondering how she'd done it. They were sore, as was her own back now, but so much worse could have happened to her, to us that night. I delineated each and every calamity I could imagine in the ensuing days. Instead, we'd reset the anchor, and it had held the rest of the night, through a lightning storm of startling beauty that was wasted on us.

I'm not a religious man, but frequently when pangs of doubt gnaw at me, I've pleaded with unknown deities to spare me certain contests of human will. To boaters so inclined, I'd suggest you save yourself the trouble of such entreaties. Pray instead, when the inevitable visits, for fortitude, clarity of mind, and perhaps a little luck.

∼∼∼

*Red sky at night (take our word for it) . . .
Mile Hammock Bay under more congenial conditions.*

∼∼∼

You might have thought I'd rather spend more time fearing a terrible storm overnight at sea, and I definitely put in my time entertaining that daydream. But there were just a couple of those days to concern myself with, and a real sailor will tell you a lee shore is the thing to worry about. When you're doing the ICW, there is no escaping the lee shore. It's staring at you from both rails every day, all day long.

Fear is the occasional companion through this journey. It is experience, however, that teaches us when fear is warranted. This is no boastful claim of superior knowledge on my part. After all the trip taught us, I still consider myself a fledgling sailor with a powerful lot left to learn. I will however admit to recognizing the qualitative difference between exclamations like, "Holy Jeez, what in hell have we gotten ourselves into?" and "Aw nuts, here we go with this shit again!" Neither is a pleasant exhortation, but most of us will acknowledge that the devil we know is preferable to the devil we don't. Unless, of course the recognizable devil that shows up for the umpteenth time just seems too much to bear once more. When that happens, bitch all you want, but don't let it affect your bailing efficiency.

~~~

I promised to let you in on what happened in Beaufort, *North* Carolina on the way back too. Remember the orgy down in Lake Worth? Same mess in Beaufort. It was Woodstock without the mud, which somehow failed to make the scene seem more palatable. I don't much like live events bristling with the nervous energy of a public execution. We took a loop to reconnoiter this anchorage clogged with desperate revelers, found no place to fit in, and so continued on to Oriental, the place where we'd been given the gift of hot water, and where we'd stockpiled other pleasant memories in a more intimate setting.

~~~

We'd reached a familiar fork in the road, with no scarecrow to help with the decision. What we had, though, were some wonderful memories of Elizabeth City and the North Carolina Visitor's Center. We decided to take our old route north, foregoing a look at the Virginia Cut. This is more akin to my typical thinking pattern, but there was something else at work here as well.

There was a bittersweet element to the path taken. Deb and I knew it would be a long shot to think we'd do this trip ever again. We wanted another chance to socialize with Fred, an institution on this waterway, and while he now has in place a more than able team of Rose Buddies, there was a lingering sense of the finality of all things in the air. One has only to remember that Elizabeth City is a welcome waystation at the end of the Great Dismal Swamp Canal route of the ICW, a route perennially threatened with extinction by a blinkered federal administration far more adept at all manner of destruction. Were the canal to be terminated, Elizabeth City would become for cruisers not a welcome stop along the path, but the inconvenient terminus of an out-of-the-way dead end.

At Elizabeth City, we were again met by able bodies poised to take our lines, and coax us into a complimentary slip. From there, we freshened up to prepare ourselves for the nightly get-together under the big tent provided gratis by a local restaurant. Great food there, I feel compelled to point out.

This trip though, after some cheese, wine, and sailor yucks, we tried a new and intriguing dinner motif. The local cinema has revamped its seating to include dinner tables housing self-dimming lighting and courtesy phones. We ordered up some great eats, provided by the adjoining restaurant, while we watched a movie. You really must . . .

Next stop, the North Carolina Visitor Center, where Penny Leary and her staff continue to do what they can to keep the place afloat, despite funding cuts by a government with more exciting things to spend its money on. Even I have come to "hate our freedom."

The raft-up this time was even bigger—four deep now—and the accompanying smorgasbord outstanding. We invited Penny's gang to take a peek inside our boats, to show them how we lived. We thanked her for her efforts to keep this remarkable place running, the only federal center in the nation that welcomes both autos and boats as a respite for journeys into the heart of America. Continue fighting the good fight, Penny.

Another chance to ride the liquid elevators at the Dismal Swamp locks, most notably the Deep Creek lock on the northern end, where entertainment is provided by Mr. Robert Peek. This time I was his unwitting accomplice, being drawn into a conch-blowing contest. I have myself to blame, as I offered up a note when we'd failed to provide any hard offering from the islands.

It turns out none of the group who shared the lock on this trip was aware of Mr. Peek's playful request for a proper tithe, something I'm sure was instigated by cruisers past. His post is decorated with shells, all gifts proffered by the constant flow of northbound travelers.

I wasn't about to give up my horn, but I'd *pflonk* a note or two for him. At that suggestion, he challenged me to a duel: winner take the loser's horn. I was game. I should have known better. After I gave it my best shot, Robert pulled out an iridescent shell of his own making, and I knew my number was up. I don't know if it was a piece from Bach or Sousa, but Mr. Peek's performance received a suitable ovation.

To his credit, he allowed me to keep my shell, though I'd clearly been outclassed. I now consider myself the proud caretaker of a conch horn on permanent loan from Robert Peek, locktender of the Deep Creek Lock on the Great Dismal Swamp Canal. When you head through on your way north from *Paradise*, if the route is still open, make sure you save a shell for Robert.

The frivolity over with, the doors to the Deep Creek Lock were opened, and we were expelled into the watery runway to Norfolk at Mile Zero.

~~~

Well hello again, Chesapeake! We'd split off from a casual fleet of northbounders we'd shared the Deep Creek Lock with a few hours earlier. As the waterway widened from the two-track of Mile One, so our intentions diverged. Deb and I found ourselves singularly driven to leave the hubbub of Norfolk behind us. Been there and done that on the way down.

We'd all been listening to the weather (duh), and heat and humidity were conspiring to commit random acts of violence in the area. There were three voices in use by NOAA during our trip. One was a proto-voice, whom we referred to as Herb, after Herb Hilgenberg, the renowned volunteer weather router. It was, I think, the first electronic voice to deliver actual humans from the drudgery of repeating weather over and over and over. Then there was the new couple, a male and a female voice, who spelled each other over the course of a day. Is it possible that even computers can be moved to boredom?

I haven't figured out why NOAA requires three voices to do the weather, particularly in its seemingly fickle desire to keep Herb around, given his monotone lisp and otherwise peculiar diction. He, for instance, insists on referring to buoys as "booties," which prompts in me some peculiar nautical imagery. His voice is a little off-putting, given the relatively perky and well-enunciated pronouncements from the new co-anchors. Maybe it's a union thing. Or maybe there are those among the living at NOAA who are actually friends of Herb, not wishing to see him retired. A few more reports, and maybe he can afford to have his speech impediment debugged.

~~~

It's unsettling enough, listening to the hum of silicone-chipped indifference telling you you're in for an ass-whupping if you're within radio range. It's another thing altogether to look up and see it stalking you with crowbar in hand. As the airwaves began to crackle with the sound of real emergencies developing, we saw, rising over the horizon, a presence black and massive. There are times in life when words simply . . . sorry, lost my train of thought.

Once the shock and awe had been registered, we set about getting our sails down, our foulies on, anything that might get sucked off the boat stowed, and our emotions prepared. We finished with most of the chores.

Ironically, with all that blackness overhead, what I most remember was getting baptized by a wall of white, in a spume-filled sucker punch to the face. We were maybe half a mile from shore or so, the direction of the front's approach, but what fetch there was more than sufficed for this beast. We hobby-horsed in the madness for maybe twenty minutes, which I suspect means ten. It still felt like suitable time had elapsed for the universe to begin collapsing again. I was looking forward to that trophy lobster dinner we'd have all over again with Pete and Runi aboard *Dancer*.

With the diesel churning, I simply did what I could to keep our nose to the wind. Piece of cake. I say this not because I wasn't scared silly (we heard on the radio of a lost crewman on a capsized boat) but because, in the scheme of things, this was child's play. The squall was short-lived, the seas relatively manageable, and our requirements basic. We had no serious gear failure to test our mettle. We simply had to hold on, keep our wits about us, and not do anything stupid for a very short while. I've heard firsthand tales from folks who had to hold out for days on the ocean, on boats that regularly tried to become airplanes. And then books have been written. Curse those books.

That day, it had looked like the legions of angels had stayed out late and pissed off the boss. It wasn't the last time we'd see this kind of vengeful behavior. Occasionally, we'd have enough time to see systems attempting to head us off at the pass, and more than once we would turn around (have I mentioned I just hate going the wrong way?) to try to avoid a confrontation. Occasionally it would work.

With this new chance to view the Chesapeake, we rediscovered that when the waters widen, friends tend to disperse. It's one of those things, like family members heading off to school, getting hitched and starting families of their own. If two or more boats wish to stay together, they can do it, but the variety the Chesapeake offers can tow folks in mutually incompatible directions. You take the high road; we'll take the low road. You want to make that little cove again off the Little Wicomico, where you first saw dolphins; we can't miss Hilda Crockett's all-you-can-eat feeding frenzy on Tangier Island.

Tangier Island is one of those places that show Darwinism at work. Take a population, isolate it, and watch it develop into its own little world. There are other communities along the Eastern Seaboard that, set apart by water and force of will, illustrate the reality of evolution. Islands can be viewed as large-scale petri dishes, which isn't the fun way to view them, I'll admit, unless you're partial to vinyl pocket protectors.

On our way back. we only once revisited an anchorage on the Chesapeake, Solomons, for convenience sake, and even that place had changed in the short while we'd been gone. There was now a flock of commercial moorings where only months earlier boats could anchor for free. The future was knocking on our hull the following morning. We'd managed to drop a hook despite the limited parking space, though as it turned out, a bit too close to one of those mooring balls. No harm, no foul.

Annapolis, that sailing destination everyone insists one must visit by boat, lived up to the hype. It manages to be modern and charming, urban and villagelike, all at once. We'd been amiably informed by the constable charged with extracting our mooring fee in Spa Creek that we'd fortuitously arrived on race night, and were well situated for a view.

I'll never forget the sight of hordes of racers screaming through the packed harbor. The wind was right for a majestic display of spinnakers, as these single-minded racers dodged moored boats on their way toward the dramatic dead end at Spa Creek Bridge. The hooligans knew precisely what they were doing, and did in tight quarters that at which I'm inept, though given an entire ocean. They dowsed all sails in about a boat length's run, turned on dimes, and prepared for the awards ceremony while hurling friendly insults at fellow contenders. You really must show up on Race Day in Spa Creek and take a mooring.

~~~

About Mid-Chesapeake, our land-based existence began to reinsinuate itself. Deb was back in communication with old business associates who'd been awaiting her return. We also had a France trip to look forward to, the result of a wedding invitation. I was beginning to feel like an emotional single-hander, sensing that Deb's mind was traveling with increasing frequency to other locales. At one point, there had been the suggestion by a potential employer that I drop Deb off "somewhere" so that she'd be able to fly to meetings in New York for your basic high-level negotiations. Feeling a bit forlorn, I was looking at Baltimore as a potential dump-off site, when word came to us that a summit could wait. I'd get to keep my mate for the duration of the trip.

Had we intended to continue on for another year of cruising, or even decided to sail through the summer, as many others were doing by exploring Maine, I'm sure we'd have adopted another mindset. There was, though, the distinct sense that we were on the last leg of the journey, and sprinting at that, back to a life we'd previously abandoned. True to form, I must have been thinking the boat only had so much more left in her, that she was ready to pop a stave, if there were such a thing onboard. Or perhaps the engine would throw a what's-it, of which I knew it to have many, and every one crucial. It was the rearing again of the ugly mug of my own insecurities.

We were running increasingly into squally weather. Where otherwise would our May flowers come from? And already there was a report of the first tropical storm forming off Africa, in what was predicted to be another banner year for hurricanes. Say it ain't so, Herb!

We were having trouble with our starter, which was becoming progressively more finicky, despite several recommended remedies. I was beginning to feel like what soldiers call a "short-timer," expecting, with rising tension, a mine to get me the closer we got to home. On a memorable occasion north of Annapolis, with the expanse of the Chesapeake egging me on, I turned the wheel over to Arty the Autohelm while Deb was below, and then took my eyes off the road for a bit. When the gong sounded right next to the boat I just about jumped ship. A big channel marker ghosted past, spitting distance from the boat. Once I got the heart started, it was back to manual steering.

There was the aroma of self-imposed urgency in the air as we leapfrogged along. But who says you can't have fun in a hurry? Come to think of it, it may be that most fun is had on the run. Does there not always seem to be a clock ticking around a good time? Whether it's lunchtime, or the weekend, or a yearlong boat trip, as Andrew Marvel pined to his coy mistress, "Always at my back I hear time's winged chariot hurrying near."

Lest one forgets, a professional is usually there to remind you such things as, sir, you're fifty now, and it's time to take a gander at the canal up which no canoe has ever paddled.

Chapter 17

The Final Push

The author, having what is referred to as "the time of one's life"

We bid adieu to the Chesapeake, thankful that the crab pots that drove us crazy on the way down were in dry dock on the way back. Was there a moratorium on crustacean-hauling? Yes, it turns out man's ability to extract every last living thing from its hiding place is occasionally curbed, and the crabs had been given a government-subsidized breather. I was thrilled we didn't have to keep a constant lookout for those miserable buoys.

We were back at another old haunt, Chesapeake City, where, while contemplating dinner options, we found ourselves curiously cornered in the street by a local maître d'. Recognizing us by description, he informed us that a Captain Art Ross had reserved a table and a bottle of wine for us. That guy.

We had a scrumptious last meal in preparation for our last look at another infamous body of water, Delaware Bay. This time it lived up to its reputation.

We got an early start on our transit of the C&D Canal, timed the current well, and hit the bay with a favorable current and wind. Sometimes, though, you can have too much of a good thing. The wind was barking, and the Delaware gave a lesson on the role depth has to play in the formation of wave patterns. We were shooting along between eight and ten knots for much of the day, not quite keeping up with the rollers that would raise us up, rock us around, and drop us back down, each threatening to break over the stern but never quite pulling it off. I spent far too much time looking back at the threat, until I realized the *Laura Lynn* always seemed to know just when to lift her rear up to let them pass. I started then to concentrate on the somewhat less intimidating view ahead.

Halfway down the bay, we considered our only option to pull over, into the Cohansey River, but the thought of putting us broadside to the waves, and my desire to get this stretch of nasty water over with kept us going. I wasn't comfortable until we'd safely made it into the Cape May Canal.

Cape May hadn't seemed to change since we'd left. It was still overcast, windy, rainy, and inhospitable. We decided to dinghy to shore out of spite. It was the longest, wettest, nastiest dinghy ride of the trip. Had this happened on the way down I would most assuredly have purchased a larger tender.

While we were miserable, we made it to the floating restaurant in the harbor with a sense of accomplishment not dissimilar to the one of crossing the Gulf Stream. We also figured the trip back would be less troublesome, given the wind direction, so while everything but our back sides dried off, we dug into some piles of seafood with a measured abandon. You never quite know what the future has in store for you.

~~~

We could almost smell home now. We had the Jersey Coast again, and would soon be in our backyard. We knew the stops, and we pretty much thought we knew where the anchor would drop, and how many more times the engine would have to start. Weather reports sounded favorable.

Have I driven home the importance of weather yet? Can you imagine where you'd be right now if it weren't for your utility company and what was once thought to be an infinite trove of moldering dinosaur muck? You'd be poking embers, rubbing stinging eyes, and longing for the invention of the chainsaw, that's where.

In Atlantic City, we decided to change things up a little (don't deny yourself the luxury, but question the desire sternly when it surfaces) and so headed to an anchorage tucked around a bend, up a narrow stream, at the cautious suggestion of our infamous Skipper Bob. All went well, I'm pleased to say. There'll be none of that *Boy what a mistake that was* kind of talk this time. In fact, this odd patch of water had a limbolike quality to it, with the gambling edifices of Atlantic City to the South, suburban sprawl to the West and North, and us seemingly mired in a marsh that awaited the final push of human expansion. One other boat shared the momentary lull in development.

To accentuate the surreal nature of our position, our phone rang, and when Deb picked it up, a vaguely familiar voice asked if we were planning on doing any gambling. Well howdy, neighbor. That other boat we'd only glanced at to keep our distance was an old friend from the Abacos. Bob and Gail, aboard *Star*, were on their first northward push, after having chosen early retirements in order to cruise full-time. We'd enjoyed some fine times with them in Hope Town, and assumed we'd never catch up with them again. They'd made a quick exit of the Bahamas, and were aggressive sailors, enjoying the performance provided by their able Bristol 38.8. They preferred offshore work, so it surprised me that we'd caught up with them.

Annapolis had been their home town, and they'd decided to stop and spend some quality time there. Now it was possible to enjoy our last days on the road with them, swapping hosting duties, and sharing stories made in each other's absence.

From Atlantic City, we made our anticipated return to Glimmer Glass Cove, escorting *Star* through that tricky labyrinth. Man, that's a tight fit under Glimmer Glass Bridge. As we left the next day, a new bridge tender chastised the previous tender's generosity in letting a couple of sailboats through, vowing that the future might never see another masted vessel pass. We heard he'd been rammed more than once. What a shame. Try to pass at high slack tide, if you get the chance to pass at all.

There was one more anchorage to make before we'd be pulling up to our dock. Bob and Gail convinced us that, rather than run back in behind Sandy Hook, where we'd made our very first night's stop, instead to carry on a bit farther and tuck in behind the Statue of Liberty at Liberty Landing.

Great idea. There is a nicely protected anchorage there, and it put us in easy striking distance of home. I'll not forget the feeling of seeing the Verrazano Narrows Bridge appear out of the mist as we approached New York Harbor. Nor will I forget Deb's animated face as she began to call anybody and everybody willing to hear that we were knocking at the front door.

There were still challenges, as there always will be till you sign the title over to the next inspired owner, but there are also admittedly symbolic moments we choose to indicate a chapter's end. We'd chosen this tableau for the card announcing our intention to set off on our adventure. My sister had drawn us at the bow of the *Laura Lynn* with New York's skyline, noticeably bereft of twin towers, receding astern. It was here that I'd discovered the mystery leak that had flooded the bilge on day one. I'd bailed like hell, and Deb had kept sailing south, away from home. There was more to do, and Hell Gate to come, but sailing under the Verrazano seemed like we were brushing our feet on the welcome mat.

There is something about familiarity. It's like hot cocoa and a pair of flannel PJs with the footsies built in on a chilly winter's night, the radio having announced that school is cancelled for the next day. New York Harbor may seem like an intimidating body of water to some. I don't have a lot of experience negotiating it, but I've been on those waters a lot. I've ridden the Staten Island Ferry many times for work and play. I've ridden the ferries to Liberty and Ellis Islands. I've gone over and under about every bridge. I was married to Deb in New York Harbor in 1995 aboard the Schooner Pioneer, operated by the South Street Seaport Museum. I've viewed the harbor from about every conceivable angle, including one that no longer exists, the observation deck of Tower One. Deb's thirty-fifth birthday was celebrated at *Windows on the World*. We still have the menu, signed by chef Michael Lomonico, who'd been delayed by some sort of appointment on his way to work the morning of September 11. I heard the first plane fly over our apartment a few days short of Deb's and my seventh anniversary, thinking it was a truck driver putting too many rpm's on his hard-running diesel.

~~~

The engine started one more time. We headed out on the morning of June 10 with a favorable current running up the East River. Did I say favorable? On our last day, the *Laura Lynn* made her quickest time of the trip, hitting a scorching 13 knots. I don't know how that's possible. When I add the top published speed of the current near Hell Gate with our theoretical hull speed I still come up short, but I took a picture of our speed on the GPS readout. It's a guy thing.

The kind of speed that impresses a sailor, in the world we landlubbers inhabit, is like limping up the down escalator. I secretly suspected it wouldn't be long before I was once again behind the wheel of a car, cursing traffic that crept at a rate of, say, 20 mph. I wouldn't be wrong.

As we approached our home harbor, the scenery became more and more familiar. In the past, we'd been fair-weather sailors who'd kept sheepishly close to home. It had in recent months begun to strike us as hilarious how a trip to a neighboring harbor had once seemed such a momentous task, requiring the consultation of confusing maps, and the activation of confounding equipment. We'd made it this far in the past maybe six times. A little while later, as we passed under the Throgs Neck Bridge, we were back in our bathtub.

~~~

Homebound travelers all seem to lament how the last few miles pass too quickly. At the Olympics, track-and-field winners are given victory laps with their national flags. I'm guessing those athletes, at that moment of self-accomplishment, have enough adrenaline left in them for another marathon. We'd had a short run home and made great time. We had no appointments on our calendar. Our summer was open.

Calls to family and friends the previous night had resulted in a planned rendezvous at the dock in the late afternoon. But like so many other days along the ICW, our timing was off. We'd been done in by the Jello Effect. Well, we could circle the harbor for a few hours in anticipation of the riotous fanfare that would most certainly have greeted us. A bobbing Mylar Popeye balloon, at the very least.

We decided instead to finish the trip. Paying a farewell to Bob and Gail, who would be continuing on with their watery retirement, we headed for the dock.

There, at the spot where it had begun the previous year, we were met by a committee of one—good old Lew Petta. I tell you what. Lew is all the fanfare a homesick boater could wish for. He took our lines, and we cleated off to the dock as if we'd just returned from a spin around the harbor.

~~~

Log of the Laura Lynn Update #20
Date: Today
Location: Home

One more time for emphasis: home

What's Hot:
    Municipal plumbing
    Criminally luxurious showers
    Alternating current up the wazoo
    Home Depot
    Staples
    Wendy's
    Pizza parlors
    Ice cream parlors
    Nail salons
    Cable Internet
    Head room
    Refrigerator/Freezers
    Watching a thunderstorm from the living room window
    A dedicated bed
    A house that doesn't drag in heavy wind
    65mph speed limits
    Family and friends
    Back yard barbecues
    Room to dance
    Skipping the weather report
    Dry clothes
    Fresh underwear
    Standing straight, tall and unwavering, mostly
    Fading bruises

What's Not:
  Traffic
  Vehicle insuring/registering/inspection
  Allergies
  Bills that escaped initial detection
  Figuring out how to fit two homes into one
  Worrying we'll lose our edge
  What still passes for news
  Missing our boating friends

Shout-Outs:

To all you guys out there who faithfully shared our adventure, thanks for coming along. We appreciated the company. We received much encouragement along the way, not the least of it concerning my desire to try to make some sort of living with words. I'll let you know if a book comes out of all this.

Fair winds,
Paul and Deb
S/V Laura Lynn

~~~

I can't think of a better reason to leave Paradise for home (the author with his niece, Emily)

Epilogue

The Journey is the Thing

The smile that lights my life

Deb is back at work with a new job that keeps her challenged, while I'm sitting here doing this.

I did succumb somewhat to past vices, and have slithered back to some of the work I'd sworn off at the commencement of the trip. Failing to reinvent myself along the way far surpasses any shame I might feel for my nautical ineptitude. If the book gets published and my sister reads of this she'll kill me. I gave her strict instructions to do so, and she's a devoted sibling.

I find myself working on yet another "reality show" for television, this one pitting canines against one another in competition to be the chosen pet of a family from New Jersey. We've humiliated every human on the planet; now we're going after the dogs. A year ago yesterday, Deb and I were in Florida, preparing for the Gulf Stream crossing. Yesterday, I was getting leg-humped by a Cockapoo from an animal shelter. A sea cruise is no panacea, let me tell you.

I myself have been the subject of a documentary. Back in the land of reality, and having turned fifty, I've undergone a battery of tests designed to remind me once again of my own mortality. The colonoscopy was a pleasure to experience, once the fasting/purging phase was completed and the laughing gas subsequently administered. There's some footage you probably won't see on the Discovery Channel.

The most recent insult was one of my own making. I got into a car accident. After all those worrisome miles on the ICW fearing a catastrophe at seven miles per hour, I casually pulled into the path of a car that was doing forty-five. How's that for irony? If there's a lesson there, it's keep all your insurance policies current. The body was spared, the car fixable, the ego totaled.

∼∼∼

The summer following the trip found us staying close to home, only once venturing to another harbor for an overnight stay, partly to rekindle the feeling, partly, I suspect, to prove to ourselves we'd somehow changed and become seasoned sailors. It was just like riding a bike, in the rain.

We'd picked a new harbor, which turned out not all that convenient to cruisers. We dinghied to shore, walked into town, looked around, saw how we'd have been disappointed had there been chores to tend to, got some ice cream, got wet, and headed back to the boat. I wasn't quite thrilled with where I'd anchored, a little too close to a busy channel.

∼∼∼

We vowed that anytime we headed out on our boat, we'd keep an eye out for the telltale signs of cruisers passing through. To the discerning eye, a cruiser's boat looks different. It looks lived in. It looks *ready*. That in and of itself was a fun game to play, but we made it a point to welcome these travelers to our fair harbor, and ask if they needed assistance of any sort.

I was out shopping one day when I had a special sighting. A couple a little too old to be backpacking in the suburbs were redistributing their groceries as I drove through the parking lot of the store they'd just plundered.

"You guys cruisers?" I asked, perhaps a bit too enthusiastically.

"Uh huh," came a less playful reply. They were busy, you see.

"May I offer you a lift anywhere?"

"No, that's okay. We need the exercise."

They had to be kidding me. They were loaded to the gills, and had a serious slog ahead of them. Man, I'd been there. I'm all for staying fit, but I'd have been riding shotgun in a heartbeat, with that load. They must have thought I was going to kill them both, dump their bodies, and take their canned goods.

I was emotionally crushed.

Later in the season I had opportunities to redeem myself when two separate boatloads of old friends came through, on their way south after summering in Maine. Bob and Gail were back for another go-round on *Star*, and Jim and Debbie, another great couple on their homemade Bruce Roberts-designed *Someday*, made a pit stop.

It was a pleasure to take our friends to breakfast, provide laundry facilities, and take each couple on a shopping foray. I know they were all thankful, but I'll bet they weren't as thankful as we were for their company. We reveled in the stories they'd picked up in recent months, and felt the buzz of our adventure returning. We took a look at the keel damage Jim and Debbie had sustained at the hands of Maine's harder underparts. Yikes. They built their boat well. Had ours taken a hit like that, we'd have become part of Maine's scenic coastline. They'd used lots of fiberglass laying up their hull. Can you believe it? They'd made their own boat *from scratch*.

Each time we waved goodbye to our old friends, our reacclimation to an earthbound existence betrayed us. Standing firmly on the dock, as they maneuvered dinghies piled high with bags of supplies, I found myself juggling two thoughts: Those poor devils. Those lucky devils.

From time to time, Deb and I play a new game. When either finds the other caught in a silent, pensive moment, the question is popped, "Where are you right now?"

"That spot where we saw our first manatee." It's as good an answer as countless others that come to mind.

I visit our girl from time to time, sitting there on her jack stands, flanked by considerably larger and more modern boats. I only have eyes for her. As I circle her to make sure all is well, I recognize the dents and dings accumulated along the way. I remember that one gouge we got in McClellanville at the old fuel dock. The sound that raised nailhead made as it keyed our hull still causes me to shudder.

The armor of long-deceased barnacles clings to parts of the hull, despite a power wash. I hate those little buggers. I remember bleeding into water I feared was stocked with famished alligators, while I tried to cut the fouled trip line away from the drive shaft.

I see the chores awaiting fairer weather. That drive shaft needs a new zinc, and the prop is in a box somewhere, full of barnacles, along with the raw water strainer. There's a piece of tarp over the broken portlight, the spreaders need to be repainted, and let's not even talk about the rest of the woodwork. The list will end the day Deb pours my ashes over the stern.

～～～

My brother-in-law Geoff was the first to ask if we'd experienced an epiphany of any sort during the trip. I had my answer at the ready.

There really was no earth-shaking discovery out there. We'd only proven what we'd already suspected: if you want something badly enough, it is attainable. So often, the greatest impediment in our lives is self-doubt, followed closely, if not led by, a disquieting sense of directionlessness.

I don't mean to dismiss the debilitating sense of not knowing where one's path should lead, since it dogs me to this day, but I do think fear often causes us to mislabel the cause of our inaction. If you can come to accept that all paths in life will have challenges that must of necessity be overcome, the wheels start turning, and the world becomes your oyster. Take a gander, if you have the stomach for it (I myself choose to look the other way), at the covers of magazines that command our horizons, trumpeting the rise of mediocrity to dazzling heights of bling-adorned celebrity. That ought to be inspiration enough for all of us.

There are rare exceptions to the rule of acquiring your heart's desire. While I can flap my arms till doomsday, I still find myself firmly attached to the earth (though I've happily fulfilled a certain dream, to float effortlessly, with a scuba certification). Our mothers, too, hasten to point out that there are things we perhaps shouldn't wish for. By now, I think we know the difference.

By and large we sink our own dream-laden vessels before we've given ourselves the chance to push off, by simply failing to believe in ourselves. Dreams can be daunting, but where there is a will, there is usually a way.

It is much easier for Deb and me to believe now. In a few years, it will be her opportunity to turn fifty, and she has a hankering to experience a broader expanse of the planet. The plan then is to pick some places we'd like to visit, for the culture, for the education, to contribute something, however miniscule, to the betterment of our fellow travelers. There will be no plaque attached when we leave.

We'll leave our *Laura Lynn* behind, because that's not what we want to do this time around. We're confident she'll be fine. She knows what she's doing.

I'm letting you in on this now, as a way to start the ball rolling. At some point I'll have to begin a book, if for no other reason than to leave a paper trail that keeps me from very possibly chickening out.

Because you know, it all seems like a dream to us now.

Remember?

Section III
Appendices

Are you one of those folks who must write down every detail of an experience? One of our favorite cruising authors is Beth Leonard, who, along with her sailing companion, Evan Starzinger (the name alone compels one to read of their exploits), raises the level of detail-taking to a noble perversion. They've traveled the globe, they know their stuff, and they seem to have written every bit of it down.

I began with honorable aspirations, but faced with the repeated choice between working out fuel consumption algorithms and watching the sun set, with one arm wrapped around a glass of Merlot and the other around my girl, my resolve evaporated like an Oreo dunked in Parmalot. I say, whatever feeds your fetish. I just think it's nice the way authors fill out their books with lists of stuff at the end. It's like the prize inside a packet of Jack in the Box, a product which has gone dreadfully downhill in peripheral excitement since I was a kid.

What follows then are lists of things to make you feel like you got your money's worth, and more:

Appendix I

Our Ports of Call

(Feel free to pick your own)

SOUTHBOUND, beginning from our home harbor of Manhasset Bay, in New York
New Jersey
Horseshoe Cove, Sandy Hook
Glimmer Glass Cove, Manasquan Inlet
Atlantic City, east of the bridge by Harrah's (nice light show!)
Cape May

Delaware
Reedy Point

Maryland
Chesapeake City south anchorage basin
Georgetown, Dyer Creek off the Sassafrass River
Rock Hall, Swan Creek
St. Michael's
Little Wicomico
Solomons (Back Creek)

Virginia
Hampton Roads, Mill Creek
Norfolk, Hospital Point

North Carolina
North Carolina Tourist Center
Elizabeth City courtesy slips
Alligator River, near the entrance to the Pungo Canal
Belhaven
Oriental
Beaufort
Mile Hammock Bay

Wrightsville Beach
Southport

South Carolina

Barefoot Landing (raft-up)
South Santee River
Charleston
South Edisto River @ Alligator Creek
Beaufort

OVERNIGHTER *(out Port Royal Sound, in St. Mary's Inlet)*

Florida
Fernandina Beach
Jacksonville
St. Augustine (slipped one night after anchor fiasco)
Daytona Beach
Titusville
Melbourne
Vero Beach
Stuart, Southpoint Marina (extended mooring stop)
Lake Worth
Peanut Island

Bahamas
Great Sale Cay
Black Sound, Green Turtle Cay
Marsh Harbour, Great Abaco
Hope Town Harbour, Elbow Cay (extended mooring stop)
Little Harbor, Great Abaco
Royal Island Harbor
Spanish Wells (mooring)

HOMEWARD BOUND
Bahamas
Nassau, at ATA Marina, capably manned by Victor
Great Bahama Banks (somewhere in 18' of water)
Gun Cay
Bimini

Florida
Lake Worth
Stuart (slip courtesy of Bill, John, and Peg, crew of *La Vie Dansante*)
Vero Beach (mooring)
Cocoa Beach

OVERNIGHTER (out at Port Canaveral, in at St. Mary's Inlet)
Fernandina Beach (Amelia Island)

Georgia
Jeckyl Island (watch for gators)
Back River (buoy incident)
Moon River (named after the song, not visa versa)
Thunderbolt (docked)

South Carolina
Beaufort
Charleston (repeat)
Georgetown (do not feed the ATMs)
Waccamaw River

North Carolina
Southport (free dock fiasco)
Wrightsville Beach
Mile Hammock Bay (the Big Drag)
Oriental
Little Alligator River
Elizabeth City courtesy slip (repeat)
North Carolina Visitor Center raft-up (repeat)

Virginia
Poquoson
Deltaville, Jackson Creek

Maryland
Solomons (repeat)
Tangier Island (slip)
Spa Creek, Annapolis (municipal mooring)
Chesapeake City (repeat stop, but anchored this time)

New Jersey
Cape May (repeat)
Atlantic City
Manasquan—Glimmer Glass Cove (repeat)

New York
Liberty Island
Manhasset Bay (home!)

Appendix II

Boat Cards and Birthday Shirts

We learned late in the game we should have been carrying the boater's version of a business card. This is our collected stack, plus the signatures I acquired on my birthday shirt. While we met many other boaters along the way, it is to a large extent a "Who's Who" of our adopted community. If your see any of these folks on your trip, please say hello for us.

Abundantly Blessed, Gordon and Murf
Alesto, Lee and Sherry Haefele
Amadon Light, Jean and Tom Goldson
American Dream, Ken and Teresa McDaniel
Aquilegia, Phyllis and Peter Prideaux
Aurora, Paul and Nancy Jacobs
Avocet, Klaas and Bettie van Esselstyn
Bahama Banks, Pegge and Mike McLaughlin
Caesar's Ghost, the indomitable Di
Current Mistress, John and Theresa
Chautauqua, John and Fran Morrison
Dancer, Pete and Runi Arnold
Dolphin, Jack and Carol Snyder, and Cindy
Eagle Light, George and Sue
Epilogue, Don and Linda Weiner
Evening Star, Robert Engel
Flyer, Mike and Bonnie
Grace B., Jack and Dee Denman
High Stepper, Doug and Connie
Ishmael, Carl and Pat
Island Girl, Alan and Joyce Bartlett
Kokopelli, Stan and Annie Connally
La Vie Dansante, John and Peggy Patterson, and of course, Bill
Last Dance, R.J. (Bob) Ragan

Linda G II, Fred and Lind Gassmann
Muskrat, Pete and Anne Thomson
My Bonnie, Earl and Sue Lamar
Mystic, Gordon, and is it Lorie?
Naiad, Bob, the singlehander
Nancy Dawson, Randy Sherman, Susan Brown and Tom Eidt
New Horizon, Dave and Carol Pohl
Omega, Dick Turner and Sue Langford
Option, Jerry and Carolyn Hoyt
Orient Express, Bruce and Gail Barton
Pendragon IV, Ian and Sharon Joyce
R.J. Greenstone, Dave and Laurie Burt, and their dogs
Reach, Jack and Carol Neades
S.V. Trader, Steve and Jean Purdy
Sabrena, Bob and Jackie Whitaker
Salltaire (and *Sunbeam*), Wink and Cindy Merrill
Sandpiper, Bob and Win
Sapphire, Dick and Janet King
Sarah Wilmot, the entire crew
Sarracenia. Harlie and Betty Johnson
Sea Echo, Steve and Karen Grant
Sea Holly, Ray and Heather Lockhart (with guests Peter and Chris)
Seastar, Paul and Pat Myre
Second Wind, Ken and Donna Erb
Sinfonia, Peter and Claudette de Koning
Slancha (or some such Gaelic-flavored name), Ted, Catherine and Hannah
Someday, Jim and Debbie Sherwood
Spirit, Kim Rody (www.fishartista.com)
Star, Bob and Gail Phillips
Summer Spirit, Rick and Wendy Hardy
Surf Song, Betsy and Doug Moody
Sweetwater II, Ludo and Hetty Beerman
Trader, Stever and Jean Perry
Treasure, Sam and Anne Hummel
Vagamundo, Natalia Moyano and Luis Martinez
Voyageur C, Bill and Loena Roberts
Yampah, Sarah, Ben and Terese

... *and Whim of Arne*, Enid and Gordon Harrington-Tapsell

Fair winds, Enid. We miss you.

And be sure to keep a lookout for Captain Art Ross, aboard *Coaster*, somewhere near Oxford, Maryland.

With The Man

Appendix III

Books we read before we set off

I'm certainly hoping our book will have helped to provide for you what these below have for us: information, inspiration, and a bit of courage to take on a challenge we might not have otherwise felt up to. These folks show you how to go. We say, "Go, go, go."

Aiken, Zora and David, *Good Boatkeeping* (McGraw-Hill, 1995).
Bode, Richard, *First You Have to Row a Little Boat* (Warner Books, 1993).
Callahan, Steve, *Adrift* (Houghton Mifflin, 1986). *This is one you might want to save till after you've returned.*
Casey, Don, *Inspecting the Aging Sailboat* (McGraw-Hill, 2005).
Chapman Piloting, Seamanship and Small Boat Handling (Presently in its 64th Edition). One might consider taking this one along were it not for its sheer bulk, equivalent in mass to a three-year stack of porn.
Cole, John, *Away All Boats, A Personal Guide for the Small-Boat Owner* (Henry Holt and Company, 1994).
Coomer, Joe, *Sailing in a Spoonful of Water* (St. Martin's Press, 1997).
Cooper, Bill and Laurel, *Sell Up and Sail* (Sheriden House, Inc., 2000).
Copeland, Liza, *Cruising for Cowards* (4th *Printing*) (Romany Publishing, 2003).
Junger, Sebastian, *The Perfect Storm* (HarperCollins, 1997) Just because.
Kroenle, David, *Know Your Boat* (McGraw-Hill, 2002).
Michener, James, *Chesapeake* (Random House, 1978).
Munns, Harry, *Cruising Fundamentals* (McGraw-Hill, 1991).
Pardy, Lin and Larry, *Cruising in Seraffyn* (Sheridan House, 1992).
Seidman, Don, *The Complete Sailor* (McGraw-Hill, 1994-95).
Sobel, Dava, *Longitude, The True Story of a Lone Genius Who Solved the Greatest Scientific Problem of His Time* (Penguin Books, 1995).
Vanderhoof, Ann, *An Embarrassment of Mangoes* (Broadway Books, 2006).
Watterson, Steven Wright, *A Year in Paradise: How We Lived Our Dream* (Eagle Cliff Press, 2001).
Wing, Charles, *The Liveaboard Report* (McGraw-Hill, 1993).

And one infamous book that shall go unnamed, but serves to show that inspiration can be extracted from the least likely of sources.

Appendix IV

Books we carried onboard

*These were our primary reference materials. The important thing to note here is that one should acquire **up-to-date** charts and guides for your entire projected trip. Redundancy is highly recommended. We failed to practice what we now preach (we once found ourselves navigating the Great Bahamas Bank with a guide from 1983 that we got for a buck. Some deal, huh?) and paid for it in lost sleep and well-deserved verbal abuse from Captain Art. Make sure you have the cash and room available for the literature that will get you there and back safely.*

The Audubon Society's Field Guide to North American Seashore Creatures (Alfred A. Knopf, Inc., 1981).

Calder, Nigel, *Nigel Calder's Cruising Handbook, A Compendium for Coastal and Offshore Sailors* (McGraw-Hill, 2001).

Calder, Nigel, *Boatowner's Mechanical and Electrical Manual (2nd Edition)* (McGraw-Hill, 1996).

Calder, Nigel, *Marine Diesel Engines, Maintainance, Troubleshootingg, and Repair (2nd Edition)* (McGraw-Hill, 1992).

Chart #1 Nautical Chart Symbols Abbreviations and Terms, prepared jointly by the U.S. Department of Commerce, NOAA, and the Dept. of Defense.

Chesapeake Bay Magazine's Guide to Cruising the Chesapeake Bay (Chesapeake Bay Communications, Inc. 2005)

Dodge, Steve, *The Cruising Guide to Abaco Bahamas 2005*, (White Sound Press, 2004)

Embassy Guides Long Island Sound to Cape May, New Jersey (Maptech Inc., 2004).

Kettlewell, John and Leslie (editors), *The Intracoastal Waterway Chartbook* (4th Edition), (McGraw-Hill, 20020). *If you're "doing the Ditch", this one is it. It's a flip chart showing a couple miles each page. We followed our progress with a little boat with "stickum" on the back.*

Moeller, Jan and Bill, *The Intracoastal Waterway: Norfolk to Miami, A Cockpit Cruising Handbook* (McGraw-Hill, 1997).

Pardy, Lynn and Larry, *Storm Tactics Handbook* (Pardy Books, 1996). I say this with all due respect: *These two are nut jobs. I expect them to one day publish "Scaling Mt. Everest in a Hand-Carved Canoe."*

Pavlidis, Stephen J., *On and Off the Beaten Path, The Central and Southern Bahamas Guide* (Seaworthy Publications, 1997-2002). *We forgot to put it onboard. Shit! Thus the ridiculously outdated, though eminently affordable 1983 guide.*

Peterson, Roger Tory, *A Field Guide to the Birds East of the Rockies* (Houghton Mifflin, 1980).

Reeds Nautical Almanac: East Coast 2005, Carl Herzog, Editor.

Rombauer, Irma S., *The Joy of Cooking* (Simon & Schuster, 1997). *Deb needed no help whatsoever.*

Skipper Bob, *Anchorages Along the Intracoastal Waterway (Ninth Edition)* (Copyright 2003 by Skipper Bob). *Occasionally you will curse its inaccuracies, but only because Skipper Bob has the cojones to attempt a comprehensive dissection of a continually evolving waterway. One might just as advisedly attempt to publish an inventory of Beyonce's clothes closet.*

Skipper Bob, *Marinas Along the Intracoastal Waterway* (7th Edition published by Skipper Bob, 2003). *Ditto.*

Wheeler, Elizabeth and the Editors of Chapman Piloting, *Cooking and Entertaining on Your Boat* (Hearst Communications, Inc., 2003). *Like I said before.*

Young, Claiborne S., *Cruising guide to Coastal North Carolina* (John F. Blair, 2001). *A loner from Art.*

Young, Claiborne S., *Cruising guide to South Carolina and Georgia* (John F. Blair, 2002). *Ditto.*

1980 Yachtsman's Guide to the Bahamas, (Tropic Isle Publishers, Harry Kline, Editor-Illustrator). *The islands are still pretty much where they were a quarter century ago, but we now recommend spending a wad on the current literature.*

In addition we carried the service manual for our engine, as well as the owner's manual for that engine, and what passed for the one for our boat. We had a first aid manual published by the Red Cross, to augment Deb's training she received prior to the trip. My advice to her for anything more serious than a splinter would have been to roll me overboard, and take the helm.

Finally, we carried a binder full of articles pulled from several years of *Cruising World* and *Sail* magazine subscriptions, as well as printed material gleaned from the World Wide Web. Oh, what a web it is.

Appendix V

On the Web

With the understanding that websites are as ethereal as the weather, here still are sites we found helpful at the time. With all sites, I keep an eye out for a links button.

http://www.cruisingworld.com
http://www.sailmag.com
http://www.boatus.com
http://www.go2marine.com
http://www.westmarine.com
http://www.rigrite.com
http://www.ndbc.noaa.gov
http://www.sailboatowners.com
http://www.docksidereports.com
http://www.uscgboating.org
http://www.setsail.com
http://www.briontoss.com
http://www.goodoldboat.com
http://www.ndbc.noaa
http://www.latsandatts.net
http://www.cruiseguides.com/triptic/start.html

Postscript

Us, sinking and not knowing it.

How many of you forgot about the nasty leak we experienced early on in the trip? Easy to do, when you're sitting at home, snug as a bug in a Trump comb-over. Well, rather than bog you down in technical mumbo-jumbo (Sebastian Junger was berated for that with *The Perfect Storm*, by readers who just wanted him to *keep the terror coming, dude!*), I tossed it here in the back for the techno-flakes. There are so many engineers riding around in boats, it makes a liberal arts grad want go hop on a horse, if he weren't allergic.

As alluded to earlier, the true culprit was suggested by Harley Johnson (a fellow literary man!), of *Sarracenia*, back at the North Carolina Visitor's Center. There in the swamp it became evident that this was water coming from outside the boat, below the water line, as evidenced by the distinctive coffee-colored stuff found in the bilge at this stop.

The Great Dismal Swamp is a tannin-tinged freshwater system, whose characteristic tint gave us a big clue. Ruling out a leak from our freshwater system and water coming over the deck during a rambunctious sail, we looked at the possible points of ingress we knew were designed into the *Laura Lynn*.

It is a sobering list, the one that shows you how many holes have been bored into your boat below the waterline, any one of them capable of sinking her in short order. Here is ours:

Laura Lynn's Through-Hulls

(*P* refers to port side; *S* to starboard; *C* to the centerline)

Below the Waterline

1. Head Intake, and Deck Wash In (P): *This is how we flush our toilet. The entire ocean is your toilet tank supply side. Sharing this hole is a pump that sucks ocean water up to a deck fitting so you can wash crap, in the more general sense, off the deck of your boat, without wasting freshwater. Good for cleaning muck off the anchor.*
2. Head Sink Out (P): *Water from your bathroom sink shoots right out the hole in the side of your boat. Or back into it if you're sailing hard on a starboard tack with the seacock open.*
3. Macerator Out (P): *Mash it up and flush it over the side. Icky-poo, but legal three miles out from the coast. Hey, fish do it in the ocean too.*
4. Centerboard (C): *There will be no test, but you should remember the earlier lesson.*
5. Transducer (P): *This is our depth-finder's sonar sending/receiving gizmo.*
6. Speedo (S) *This tells us how fast we're traveling "through the water" as opposed to "over ground." Think about the effect of current, and mull it over for a while. Ours doesn't work, but it's there—a little waterwheel trying to send information to a gauge, designed in the early seventies, and probably nonfunctional by the midseventies.*
7. Galley Sink (S): *Kitchen sink, the same deal as the head. You better damn well know what the head is by now.*
8. Raw Water Seacock (S) *The ocean is, among many other things, the boat's radiator. It is pumped up and circulated through part of the engine, to keep her temperature cool. As a side note, the term "seacock," after all these years, still makes me giggle.*
9. Rudder Stock (C) *You turn the wheel up top. The rudder moves down below. The boat changes course. How would you do it, Einstein?*
10 and 11. Grounding Plates (P and S) *Don't ask me. I'm told they reduce the odds of our being struck by lightning, despite the fact that our mast, a metal rod thrust forty-five feet into thin air, is the only thing we can see for miles around that isn't at sea level. Or is it, they reduce the odds of our being damaged when a lightning strike occurs? Just slightly off-topic, what the hell is electricity anyway?*
12. Old Transducer (S) *See "Transducer" above.*
13. Drive Shaft (C) *Without which you would never go anywhere ever again, at all.*

Above the Waterline

14. and 15. Cockpit drains (P and S) *You have a brain.*
16. Engine exhaust (C) *See above. Cue Jeopardy final question tag song.*
17. Fuel Tank Vent
18. Holding Tank Vent
19. Manual Bilge Pump (S) *There to give your electric bilge pump emotional support.*
20. Electric Bilge pump **(P!)**

Twenty holes, intentionally drilled through the hull of a boat, most of them below the waterline. Good grief! It's a wonder boats float at all, given the peppering they've taken from the manufacturer and subsequent owners. Yet an inspection of each and every one of the below-the-waterline areas came up negative. How could an above-the-waterline hole cause a killer leak?

Within that last sentence lies the insidious and possibly fatal danger of the flawed assumption. Take a look at the last through-hull on the list, the electric bilge pump exhaust port. Water that necessarily makes its way into the bilge of the boat (okay why? Come on, why?) is pumped back out through a hole just above the waterline. Just above the waterline, here's a clue, *most of the time.*

Ironically, what made this problem a bitch to diagnose was that it showed up only now and then. It happened maybe twice before the trip, during some hard sailing (remember, we were fair-weather sailors) that led me to believe it had either found its way into the boat via water coming over the deck, or through our sink. It seemed to happen mostly when we were sailing upwind, particularly when heeled to port (the sink is on the port side), but the water could be found on the starboard side too.

It happened only now and then, but when it did happen, it was dramatic. Water was found so far forward, it was easy to think the water was entering from near the bow. I'd actually used a small submersible video camera I'd purchased for fun, to try to scope the bilge. It was a diagnostic attempt not unlike the procedure performed on yours truly months later, when specialists plumbed me for intestinal polyps.

On the trip, I also discovered a leak at the fresh water deck fill, which made me think maybe we were half filling our tank and half filling our bilge. But the tannin-tinged water said no, this is water our boat is sitting in.

~~~

Let's cut to the chase. We were victims of a back-siphon effect, caused by reverse flow from our electric bilge pump. How was water entering the boat through a hole that was above the waterline? The answer was, it wasn't. It was coming through the bilge exhaust when that port was below the waterline. When did that happen? Most frequently when we were sailing hard on a starboard tack.

But that happens a lot, right? Well, more often than the leak surfaced, but it depends on your sailing habits, and it turns out the leak required another element. We had to start the siphoning effect by running the bilge pump while we were on a starboard tack, and we needed some starter water to get the process going.

Here's an example of what was going on. Put on your thinking cap. You have sitting before you a tall glass of juicy Tang. Don't ask me why. It was good enough for the astronauts, and we're talking science here. Now insert one of those bendy straws, because they're fun. Then start drinking through the straw.

The glass is your hull, full of orange bilge water, your cheeks working in conjunction with your oral cavity form a nice pump mechanism, and your stomach is the ocean. Suck and swallow, suck and swallow, suck and swallow.

Pardon me, I just took an emotional break. Now take your mouth away from the straw to belch, and everything should just be dandy with the world.

Now start sucking again, but this time take a break with your mouth full of Tang. Relax your jowls. What does the Tang do? It heads right back into the glass. Imagine if that straw extended all the way back into your stomach, which also happens to be higher than your glass on the table. What would happen now? Your glass would overflow with the entire contents of your stomach, which is *the ocean*. Gross doesn't even begin to describe the result. Your glass is a goner, sweet cheeks.

But what about the Dismal Swamp? We weren't sailing hard on a starboard tack. We were putt-putting around in fresh water, which happens to be less dense than salt water. Which means things that float in it don't float quite the same. They sink just a teensy bit. Then when you start to motor along, and your quarter wave begins to grow (we'll save the quarter wave seminar for the next book) and your sweet little counter transom buries herself a little, that above-the-waterline through-hull becomes a below-the-waterline menace. And then, because I'm concerned we might be sinking, I turn on the bilge pump and set in motion the chain of events that have the capacity to sink the boat. Somewhat ironic, wouldn't you say?

The solution, of course, is to install an inline siphon break, a simple, inexpensive device that breaks the siphon effect. But you knew that all along, didn't you, Sherlock?

Chapter the Last

I swear

Island Time

What is this? I suppose it would have been the epilogue, had I not already written one. Those of you who've traversed this far most assuredly are wondering if I'll ever shut my tiresome yap. But then it's a book, so you can pretty much see where you are. Not like the show *24*, whose horror-mongers never seem to know when to pack in the senseless slaughter and call it a day. To those alarmists, I'd suggest Ambien. They should ask their doctor if it's right for them.

Anyway, Deb and I have taken a needed vacation from the grindstone we've reapplied our noses to, in the late winter of 2006, which is to say early 2007. I'll give you one guess as to where we headed.

We cheated this time, and flew via an undisclosed domestic "air carrier." Key words for the day: slave ship.

Let me tell you something: I almost wish we took the boat. I'd safely stowed my Swiss army knife in the checked baggage. There was no sharp obstacle on my person, no anarchic asthma inhaler, no arched, cynical attitude. I was in too good a mood to let anything get to me, I thought. The only threat I packed was foot odor.

I'll give you one guess what they confiscated at security. They took our yogurt. Our effing yogurt.

Give me some credit. I got this far into the book before finally succumbing to the f-word. I must win something for that. A Hummer, perhaps? How more troop-supportive could I possibly get?

You must suspect where this is all going. Sooner or later Stephen Jobs's R&D department will make it possible for explosive eyeliner to take down a jumbo jet. I then predict Hooters Air will rule the sky with its monopolistic, all-nude, hairless flights to everywhere. You heard it here first. Call your broker now, and schedule a Brazilian bikini wax.

Coach fare air travel now makes two months on a small boat seem like a Royal Caribbean Bacchanal Cruise. I was almost sucked into the stratosphere when I took a leak at thirty thousand feet in a defecation capsule that made Laura Lynn's head look like the penthouse suite at the Riyadh Four Seasons.

Somehow we'd scored nonreclining seats. I must have been wearing my "Kick Me" shirt. I'm an average human male, and I was forced to French-kiss the guy in the row ahead of me for three hours when his seat reclined into my lap and buckled me forward. Friendly skies, indeed.

Fresh water is now cheaper to obtain on Bahamian Out-Islands than on American . . . I mean, undisclosed domestic air carriers. What were formerly complimentary snacks now carry price tags reminiscent of the cargo waiting to pauper hotel guests in their fridge-bar. When flying, you are no longer allowed to carry your own water aboard to stave off dehydration, but flight attendants are licensed to sell you derivative shares in an artesian well scheduled to be sunk on Vanuatu in 2010.

When we stepped on to the ferry in Marsh Harbour for the twenty-minute ride to Hope Town, everything got incredibly better, really fast. In short order, I was staring through salt-encrusted lenses at a giant candy cane.

By the time we'd stowed our gear in our rented house on the harbor (I believe we brought more for the week than we'd had on the boat), traded out winter attire for shorts and flip-flops, and walked to Vernons to buy staples, we were hearing ourselves being hailed on the VHF. While salivating over the freshly baked bread in aisle three (aisle four will put you knee deep in the harbor) we heard the *Laura Lynn* being summoned by old friends, Bruce and Gail of *Orient Express*, on Channel 68. Vernon let us pick up. We were being invited to the Special Eclipse Edition of the Full Moon Party.

What sights for sore eyes were in attendance. We hit the beach feeling like a couple of hopeful pledges at a college for traveling gypsies. Time-tested boating couples were arranging their various plates of appetizers on the rocks, while a bride and groom exchanged vows on the soft sand.

The gang had reassembled. Steve and Karen from *Sea Echo* had planted a travel bug in the only geocache on the island. We took it, and replaced it with a shell saved from a meal at the River Cafe in Brooklyn, in honor of the wedding of our great friends, Tinna and Pierrick.

Ludo and Hetty sported the same bright smiles, and Ludo once again outlasted me on the conch horn.

Bruce and Gail were teaching us all to obsess over long-ago broken beer bottles, in the aim of creating distinctive jewelry.

Di was back, looking for stalwart crew to aid in her quest for dinghy glory.

Dave and Carol were smiling their way around the island.

Wink and Cindy were busy as always, with their many social duties. I can only guess how they'd behave in an urban setting.

John and Bill made it back, with Peg once again missing out on the fun during the tax season.

And there were our Gulf Stream babysitters, Don and Linda.

Minding the shore were Tony and Elaine, Pim and Eleanor, Phillip and Janet, George and Sue (who this year had gone to seed, as in land based), Audrey Malone, and Vernon and his near biblical loaves of bread. Buddy was off captaining for someone, but Harold was minding the moorings.

Shelly, Sylvia and Natasha were still turning heads at Harbour's Edge Restaurant, while Teresa, Lambert and Francis were wetting them at Froggies, with daily excursions to the reefs.

There were some notable no-shows, but then we'd almost bagged the trip ourselves as too logistically challenging to pull off. For each face we missed, there was a new one to meet and memorize.

Seven days after we'd arrived, after conch-horn contests, boat races, beachcombing, geocaching, novel reading, boat hopping, cruisers' net-listening, chatting with the locals, and catching up with people who'd adopted us as family a year ago, we found ourselves deserting this outpost of colonial expats in tears.

But not before we spotted yet another boatload of friends entering the harbor. Those lovely souls, Harley and Betty, onboard *Sarracenia*, had seen fit to check out Hope Town minutes after we'd cleared Eagle Rock at the harbor's entrance, on the ride to Marsh Harbour. I almost leapt off the ferry and started swimming for them.

I believe I've earlier recited Mr. Wolfe's adage that you can never go home again, but technically Hope Town isn't home, and it seemed just the way we left it in April of 2006. There were our friends again. There were those places we'd frequented. How many special places, I wonder, does a soul need in the course of a lifetime, if those places guarantee such fond memories each visit?

~~~

Paradise Found

I could go on and on, like the drunken toaster at a wedding reception, unwilling to relinquish the mike till he's expelled his every last confession (hey, I'm self-published; I paid for the privilege), but this is your journey now. As Matt from *On Da Beach* would say, float on . . .

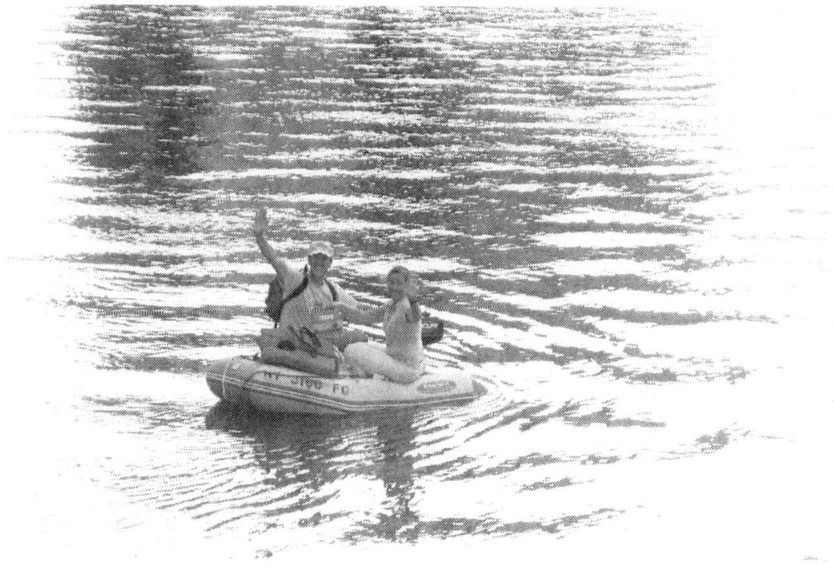